Raymond Williams and Education

Also available from Bloomsbury

A History of Education for the Many: From Colonization and Slavery to the Decline of US Imperialism, Curry Malott
Critical Human Rights, Citizenship, and Democracy Education: Entanglements and Regenerations edited by Michalinos Zembylas and André Keet
Education, Individualization and Neoliberalism: Youth in Southern Europe, Valerie Visanich
Education, Society, and the Philosophy of Louis Althusser, David I. Backer
Friedrich Froebel: A Critical Introduction to Key Themes and Debates, Tina Bruce
Lacan and Education Policy: The Other Side of Education, Matthew Clarke
Norbert Elias and the Sociology of Education, Eric Lybeck

Raymond Williams and Education

History, Culture, Democracy

Ian Menter

BLOOMSBURY ACADEMIC
LONDON • NEW YORK • OXFORD • NEW DELHI • SYDNEY

BLOOMSBURY ACADEMIC
Bloomsbury Publishing Plc
50 Bedford Square, London, WC1B 3DP, UK
1385 Broadway, New York, NY 10018, USA
29 Earlsfort Terrace, Dublin 2, Ireland

BLOOMSBURY, BLOOMSBURY ACADEMIC and the Diana logo
are trademarks of Bloomsbury Publishing Plc

First published in Great Britain, 2022
This paperback edition published 2023

Copyright © Ian Menter, 2022

Ian Menter has asserted his right under the Copyright, Designs and
Patents Act, 1988, to be identified as Author of this work.

Cover image: Prof. Raymond Williams, 1985
© Mark Gerson Photography/Bridgeman Images

All rights reserved. No part of this publication may be reproduced or
transmitted in any form or by any means, electronic or mechanical, including
photocopying, recording, or any information storage or retrieval system,
without prior permission in writing from the publishers.

Bloomsbury Publishing Plc does not have any control over, or responsibility for,
any third-party websites referred to or in this book. All internet addresses given
in this book were correct at the time of going to press. The author and publisher
regret any inconvenience caused if addresses have changed or sites have ceased
to exist, but can accept no responsibility for any such changes.

A catalogue record for this book is available from the British Library.

Library of Congress Cataloging-in-Publication Data

Names: Menter, Ian, 1949- author. | Apple, Michael W., writer of foreword.
Title: Raymond Williams and education: history, culture, democracy / Ian Menter;
with a foreword by Michael Apple.
Description: London; New York: Bloomsbury Academic, 2022. |
Includes bibliographical references and index. |
Identifiers: LCCN 2021028703 (print) | LCCN 2021028704 (ebook) |
ISBN 9781350185395 (hardback) | ISBN 9781350185401 (pdf) | ISBN 9781350185418 (epub)
Subjects: LCSH: Williams, Raymond–Criticism and interpretation. | Authors,
Welsh–20th century–Biography. | Education–Great Britain–History. |
Culture–Study and teaching–Great Britain. | Education in literature. |
Social classes in literature. | Educational sociology–Great Britain. |
Educational equalization–Great Britain. | Education–Philosophy.
Classification: LCC PR6073.I4329 Z835 2022 (print) |
LCC PR6073.I4329 (ebook) | DDC 828/.91409–dc23/eng/20211101
LC record available at https://lccn.loc.gov/2021028703
LC ebook record available at https://lccn.loc.gov/2021028704

ISBN: HB: 978-1-3501-8539-5
PB: 978-1-3502-2682-1
ePDF: 978-1-3501-8540-1
eBook: 978-1-3501-8541-8

Typeset by Integra Software Services Pvt. Ltd.

To find out more about our authors and books visit
www.bloomsbury.com and sign up for our newsletters.

This book is dedicated to Maggie Walker and to the memory of my parents, Jean and Jim Menter.

Contents

Preface		viii
Foreword *Michael W. Apple*		xi
Introduction: To the Life and Work		1
1	Biography and Education – Raymond Williams's Educational Experiences	9
2	Education in Fiction and Fiction in Education – Raymond Williams's Novels and His Analyses of English Literature	27
3	The History of Schooling in England – Education in *The Long Revolution*	55
4	The Significance of Adult Education	79
5	Culture, the Academy and the Role of the Public Intellectual	97
6	Cultural Studies and the Educational Role of the Arts and Media	123
7	The Theoretical Legacy – Structures of Feeling; Cultural Materialism; Base and Superstructure	147
8	Conclusion – Language and Culture; Tradition and Revolution	173
Notes		183
References		188
Index		199

Preface

When I set out to write this book in early 2020, it was planned to be my main 'retirement project'. Little did I anticipate it becoming a 'retirement *and* lockdown project'. We have all had to find ways to keep ourselves sane over these trying times and working on this book has certainly helped me.

My fascination with Raymond Williams began many years ago and has continued throughout my life. The reasons for this are personal as well as intellectual. Williams, born in 1921, was the son of a railway signalman and grew up in the border country of rural eastern Wales. He went to the University of Cambridge in 1939 to study English. The Second World War intervened but not before he had met Joy Dalling, a student at the London School of Economics who had been evacuated to Cambridge. She was to become his wife and they would have three children, a daughter and two sons. When the war was over, Williams returned for his final year at Cambridge, before taking his first full-time working post as a tutor in adult education, based in Sussex. In 1961 he returned to Cambridge, as a lecturer in English.

My own father, James (known as Jim) Menter, was born in the same year as Williams, 1921, also the son of a signalman, in the coastal town of Deal in Kent. He too went to Cambridge in 1939, but to study physics. During the war he worked as a scientist for the Admiralty, largely based on the west coast of Scotland (close to where I later worked and lived for a few years), where he was involved in developing underwater sonar equipment to be used in detecting submarines. He returned to Cambridge to complete his degree and there met my mother Jean Whyte-Smith, who had arrived as an undergraduate towards the end of the war. They married in 1947 and had two sons and a daughter. In those early years of their married life they were – like the Williamses – very much leftward leaning. I remember *The Morning Star* being one of the daily papers they read. Unlike the Williams family however, they stayed on in Cambridge while my father carried out doctoral research at the Cavendish laboratory and then he got his first full-time post as a research scientist working for an industrial company.

The similarities in these two biographies were one of the stimuli for the development of my fascination with Raymond Williams and his work. While my father developed his career in the field of science and technology with a profound belief that developments here would significantly enhance human life, Williams followed the path of politics and letters, with much the same aspirations. The women whom each of them married played crucial parts in their lives, in both the personal and the professional dimensions.

*

The amount of scholarly writing on Williams is enormous and reflects the esteem in which he is held. In writing this book I am deeply indebted to all these scholars. Although not all of their writing is uncritical and there is a strand of commentary which suggests that Williams's own writing could be dense and sometimes convoluted. There is more than a grain of truth in this; however, there is in the end no alternative to reading Williams in the original version. In writing these words, I am reminded of the first time I read the trilogy *A Scots Quair* by Lewis Grassic Gibbon (a book well liked by Williams – see Chapter 6). It took me a long time to 'tune in' to the language he uses, but eventually I did and it has been the same with reading Williams. The more I read, the easier it became. Another issue with Williams's writing is its unconsciously gendered nature. Pronouns are almost invariably masculine and although he wrote extensively about novels by women writers, the politics and critical scholarship he drew on is dominated by men. No doubt this reflects the culture of the day – indeed, the contemporary structure of feeling – but it can make for some discomfort when reading his work in the early twenty-first century.

My aim in writing this text has been to offer what I believe to be the first book-length exploration of the significance of Williams's work in the study of education. One doctoral thesis from the late 1980s tends to support this view (Stevens, n.d.). Williams has been far from ignored by educational scholars and I have cited many of them in the chapters that follow. However, it does seem to me that the contribution he made, the way in which he saw education as a key element in achieving social progress, is today more vital than ever. Certainly, the technologies and forms of communication now available are very different from those in the second half of the twentieth century. At the same time ways in which neoliberal ideologies and the rise of populist politics have prevailed in many societies around the world have demonstrated the deep salience of the type of critical educational activity espoused by Williams.

For those wanting a more general introduction to Williams's life and work, beyond its educational significance, I would recommend reading the two full biographies (Inglis, 1995, and Smith, 2008 – but not necessarily in that order) and also the excellent volume by Eldridge and Eldridge (1994), sub-titled *Making Connections*.

*

My deepest thanks go to Maggie Walker, my wife. To introduce a second personal note into this preface, discussions of Raymond Williams's work, especially *The English Novel from Dickens to Lawrence*, was one of the things that brought us together all those years ago. Since then we have maintained our enthusiasm for his work, and Maggie has been a huge supporter of this book project, reviewing, commenting on and editing every chapter as it emerged.

Back in the early days of my own interest in Williams, I remember walking Somerset paths with my brother Will, discussing especially *The Long Revolution*, so many thanks to him as well. The rest of the family have also been enormously supportive while this project has been under way, with our children, their partners and our grandchildren frequently asking me, 'How's the writing going Dad/Ian/Granpa?'

Thanks also to Raymond Williams's daughter, Merryn Williams, for her encouragement. Colleagues at Kellogg College, Oxford (where I am now an Emeritus Fellow), David Grylls and Jonathan Michie, read and advised on Chapter 4, which discusses Williams's engagement in adult education. To make a third personal link to the project, I would point out that Kellogg College is closely associated with Oxford's Department for Continuing Education, the descendant of the Oxford Delegacy, which was Williams's first full-time employer.

Maggie and I are both members of the Raymond Williams Society, which keeps us in touch with relevant events and publications (including the journal *Keywords*). Thanks to their officers, especially the Secretary Phil O'Brien, for all their voluntary efforts (see: https://raymondwilliams.co.uk/.)

Finally, I warmly thank Michael Apple for so kindly agreeing to contribute a foreword for the book. Among US scholars working on education policy, he, more than any others, has consistently recognized the distinctive contribution Raymond Williams has offered to our field.

Ian Menter

Foreword

There are a number of compelling reasons for immersing oneself in Raymond Williams's work. He spent a good deal of his life trying to answer questions about the relations between culture and economy, about the lives of 'ordinary people' and what counts as high-status culture, about how the distinctions between 'worthy' people and 'worthy' knowledge solidified class relations, and how cultural distinctions that (some) people accept as common-sense mask the tense and antagonistic struggles that organize and disorganize a society. Yet he was guided by a powerful recognition that all of this was a site of contestation and agency, that it embodied the possibility that it could be different. With his powerful claim that 'culture is ordinary', he set the stage for a radical and insightful interrogation of the form and content of the cultural assemblages of unequal societies like our own. He was compelling as a writer in doing this in ways that influenced entire generations of critical work in education, literature, cultural theory and many other areas.

Let me say something personal here. As I began my initial work on the complex relationship between power and knowledge in education during the late 1960 and early 1970s, one particular author provided insights that had lasting effects on me and so many other people. That person was Raymond Williams.[1]

It was not only his powerful talents and insights as a writer that drew me to him. Something else made a difference. This was our similar biographies. I was what was called in the United States a 'red diaper baby', someone who came from a deeply political working-class (and often poor) family. One fact about this stands out here and helps to also explain one of the reasons why Williams excited me. I was from a family of printers, an occupation that itself was often very political and that prized working-class literacy and the critical role those forms of literacy could play in social transformation.

There were other similarities as well. As he had, I too had spent time in the armed forces. After doing most of my undergraduate work as a part-time student at night while teaching in poor and usually minoritized communities, I too ultimately was awarded a postgraduate scholarship to attend one of the most highly rated universities in the nation. The realities of class experience associated with this, of 'belonging, but not belonging', of always being both inside and outside of dominant cultures and institutions, made me appreciate Williams even more. I am certain that I am not alone here.

In books such as *Culture and Society* (1958), *The Long Revolution* (1961), *The Country and the City* (1973), *Keywords* (1976), *Marxism and Literature* (1977) and, later on, *The Year 2000*[2] (1983) and *Resources of Hope* (1989), and many more, Williams provided a powerful rereading of the historical and contemporary politics of what he called 'the selective tradition' and its tensions, functions and contradictions – and as a site for social transformation. In the process, he gave critical work in and on cultural institutions, including schools and the media, essential tools to engage in the uncovering of some of the most complex interconnections among cultural form and content, differential power and access, and the class realities of our societies. While Williams's focus was consistently on class relations, his work had a major impact on issues surrounding race and gender as well. Indeed, a good deal of what we now call cultural studies in general can be partly traced to his initial efforts. He did all this while authoring insightful and timely novels that illuminated the complex lives, structures, cultures and identities within largely working-class communities.

To anyone who has read some of my own work, especially the earlier efforts in, say, *Ideology and Curriculum* and *Education and Power*, the influence of Williams is clear. When I first read his work, it was transformative. *The Long Revolution* in particular had a profound impact on me and many others. Its analysis of the struggles of 'ordinary people' to win schooling that was respectful of their lives, to democratize the media, to redefine literacy and to challenge hegemonic apparatuses in general provided a subtle and positive picture of the nature and power of agency and of cultural and social movements. It also gave many of us involved in education reasons for at least partial optimism in a time when a good deal of critical analyses told us that cultural struggles inside and outside of schools and universities were basically epiphenomenal and had little lasting power and effects. One can trace the more nuanced understandings of social movements, of 'ordinary actors', of the importance of the ideological and the cultural in the formation of movements and identities to work by Williams and others during that period of time. In essence, Williams played a truly major role in critically analysing and in justifying what Antonio Gramsci, the noted political theorist and activist who influenced Williams, called a 'war of position'. This embodied a counter-hegemonic politics that insightfully maintained that action on and in *every* sphere of social and cultural life is important for lasting social transformation, not only the struggles over the economy.[3] The impact of this in many fields was profound.

Closer to home in education, it would not be possible to fully understand the critical sociology of education, and especially the sociology of curriculum, without centring the voice of Williams. Nor would it be possible to grasp the conceptual and political debates in education and in the area of cultural studies in general over base and superstructure, the significance of cultural struggles, 'relative autonomy', and so much more without seriously dealing with books such as *The Long Revolution, Marxism and Literature, The Country and the City* and others. They were, and continue to be, foundational texts, as they should be. This sense of the debt we owe to Williams as a path-breaking scholar, as a political actor and as an educator in the larger sense of that word is made clear in Stuart Hall's reflections on Williams's influence and on his crucial role in the formation of critical cultural studies. As Hall said, Raymond Williams was one of 'my fathers'.[4]

In this Preface, I have purposely directed our attention not only to Williams's importance in education but also to a broader range of elements of Williams's work. Understanding the relationship of Raymond Williams in and to education requires that we also situate our focus in a more extensive series of discussions and debates. This requires us to think of education itself well beyond the walls of formal institutions of schooling, to critically examine the larger arena of cultural politics and the possibilities of creating a more robust democracy. This is where the book that you are about to read enters.

In *Raymond Williams and Education: History, Culture, Democracy*, Ian Menter has set himself an ambitious task. He engages with Raymond Williams's work and influence on education writ large. By itself, that is a very real accomplishment. But Menter does not stop there. He places this within Williams's larger corpus of work, by examining his novels and essays, his corpus of extraordinary interventions in social and cultural theory, literary analyses, political efforts and pedagogic work. All of this is connected to important moments of Williams's biography. When these elements are put together, not only is the breadth of Menter's analysis clear, but the result leads to a valuable picture of the connections between Williams's influential educational work and that extensive body of critical cultural analysis, political interventions and fiction. In the process, Menter makes these relationships even more visible. In doing this, the book allows us to better understand many of the reasons that Williams had such hope in the agency of people to act back, to create a culture and an education that was responsive and democratic.

The book itself, thus, is a reminder of why Williams refused to be disillusioned. As Williams himself put it, 'We must speak for hope, as long as it doesn't mean suppressing the danger.'[5] His commitment is clear in the following:

It is only in a shared belief and insistence that there are practical alternatives that the balance of forces and chances begins to alter. Once the inevitabilities are challenged, we can begin gathering our resources for a journey of hope. If there are no easy answers there are still available discoverable hard answers, and it is these that we can learn to make and share. This has been, from the beginning, the sense and impulse of the long revolution.[6]

Raymond Williams and Education: History, Culture, Democracy provides us with a picture of what the 'long revolution' meant in the life and work of Raymond Williams, and what it means to those of us who continue some of the most important struggles to build a place for a truly democratic education in that revolution.

Michael W. Apple
John Bascom Professor Emeritus of
Curriculum and Instruction
and Educational Policy Studies
University of Wisconsin, Madison, USA

Introduction: To the Life and Work

In a period of great tension and necessary conflict it is especially important to be sure about names. In our own quite exceptional difficulties, it is especially important to be sure what Welshmen mean by 'English'. I grew up in border country, where the names learned at school were of general and rather vague geographical areas: England to the East, Wales to the West, and where we were, too small for the maps, a village in Monmouthshire, coloured this way or that or dubiously hatched, by what seemed the mapmaker's fancy.
(Williams, 1983, reprinted in *What I Came to Say* (1989:64))

Raymond Williams was born on 31 August 1921 in the Welsh village of Pandy, close to the border with England. He died at the age of 66, on 26 January 1988 in Saffron Walden, Essex. During his lifetime he became one of the leading intellectuals of the British left, leaving an extraordinary collection of writings, including fiction, political analyses and literary criticism. Today he is most often remembered as a leading socialist and as a founder of the field of cultural studies. He has been the subject of two book-length biographies as well as numerous other works that have discussed the many contributions he made to political, cultural and intellectual life.

Although in his academic work he is best known for his literary criticism and cultural theory, there is a great deal in his writing, as well as in his political life, that shines a brilliant and original light on many aspects of education, and this is the distinctive focus of this book. A relatively small number of education scholars have recognized his significance in the field of education studies, but hitherto there has not been a concerted attempt to pull together the insights that can be drawn from his life and from his published work that help us to understand the nature of education in contemporary society. That is the ambition of this book and in adding three terms to its title – history, culture, democracy – I seek to draw attention to three particular dimensions that are crucial to our understanding of how Williams developed his own understanding of education.

Williams was totally committed to the importance of an historical lens in making sense of contemporary phenomena. It is only through following trajectories of development that it is possible to appreciate why social relations, institutions and life experiences are as they are. As for culture, Williams famously asserted that 'culture is ordinary' (Williams, 1958/1989[1]), which was a way of reminding us that our 'ways of life' shape all of our experience. Indeed, this is no longer seen as a radical idea, and is now often taken for granted in public discourse, but this was far from the case in the 1950s and 1960s. As for democracy, Williams was committed to a strongly community-based form of politics with self-organization at its centre. Although being firmly 'of the left', indeed of 'the New Left', as it became known, and although he was the lead editor of *The May Day Manifesto* (Williams, 1968b), his own political persuasion argued for what he memorably called a 'long revolution' (Williams, 1961/2011), a steady move towards full participation and greater equality in society. A key element of this long revolution lay in education – education as a set of institutions and as a process of learning and development.

There are several elements to supporting the case that Williams's contribution to education is highly significant. First, the simple point that he was a teacher through and through. His whole life was about engaging intellectually with others, seeing knowledge and understanding as key elements in the realization of humanity. Always challenging inequality and oppression, he recognized that knowledge was powerful and in all his engagements, whether in politics or in letters, he strove to deepen his own and others' understanding, always with a deep degree of integrity and respect. Vitriolic though academia and politics can be, and whilst not afraid to engage in sometimes quite heated debates, Williams always sought to apply reason and provide evidence for the case he was making at the time. This rationality was combined with enormous creativity, deeply inspiring to those who heard him or read his work. These are some of the qualities of teaching, of the teacher, that are deep within the spirit of education for democracy.

Second, he directly addressed questions of educational provision. His analysis of the development of schooling in England exposed the deep contradictions in the provision of a 'universal' education that was deeply divided, not least along lines of social class. His own biography, particularly as one of the few working-class grammar school boys to 'make it' to Cambridge, one of the most elite universities in the world, only served to reinforce this analysis. But as well as arguing the case for inclusive, common or 'comprehensive' schooling, he also argued forcefully for the protection and promotion of the humanities and social sciences within higher education, at a time when policymakers were emphasizing the importance of science and technology (and Williams did not demur from agreeing these areas of study were also crucial). His passionate commitment to adult education also derived from his experience and values. He saw such provision as essential in supporting intellectual development within the wider community, especially for those who had not had decent educational opportunities earlier in their lives.

Third, through the development of methods of what became known as cultural materialism, Williams provided a range of analytical tools and critical concepts that can be deployed in the analysis of educational structures, policies and processes. His careful development of a nuanced view of the relation between economy and society and the placing of education as a key element of this relation continues to be valuable. Although deeply influenced by Marxist ideas, he was one of the most original, thoughtful and particular users of these theories in insisting that cultural matters, including education, were as much a matter for concern in challenging inequalities in society, as were questions about the ownership of capital or the means of production.

Fourth, in his analyses of literature, drama, film and television he was a key founder of what is now referred to as cultural studies or media studies. He brought some of the insights from anthropology, sociology and literary criticism into a combination that showed new connections between cultural activity and social life. The realization that these creative forms have social and political power has perhaps been present in our understanding for many years, but the distinctive way of bringing these disciplines to bear and to connect them was at that time radical, and indeed met much initial opposition from conservative forces both within the academy and within the political establishment.

As we shall see in Chapter 1, Williams's values and critical perspectives were fundamentally shaped by his childhood in Pandy, in the Welsh borders. His father worked on the railway line that followed the border from South Wales up to Hereford, Shropshire and the Midlands. It was a rural childhood but one which had connections with the urban centres of industrial Wales and England, where the labour and trade union movements were so central to the lives and communities of miners, steelworkers and industrial workers. At the age of 11 he started to travel to the nearby market town of Abergavenny to attend the grammar school where he encountered a curriculum which included many elements of the cultural traditions of the British – indeed English – establishment.

In a series of interviews with some of his New Left colleagues (Williams, 1979/2015), Williams himself provides fascinating accounts of his subsequent entry to and experience of the University of Cambridge, in 1939. While experiencing real uneasiness with many of the social aspects of this experience, he began to combine his deep commitment to the working class with a growing involvement in political activity. But he also started to develop original and distinctive insights into the deeply conservative traditions of the study of English literature. His time at Cambridge was interrupted by the Second World War. He joined the army and became commander of an anti-tank unit, fighting in the D-Day landings of 1945 and in the northern European campaign thereafter. On returning to Cambridge and after completing his degree, he gained employment in adult education, working for the University of Oxford extramural delegacy, in collaboration with the Workers' Educational Association (WEA). He remained deeply committed to the provision of high-quality adult education throughout his life.

Williams developed two parallel writing careers which stayed with him throughout his life. The one for which he is best known is his work on literary criticism and cultural theory. Over his lifetime he published important and original works on film, on drama, on fiction and perhaps most distinctively on the relations between English literature and society. His books *Culture and Society* (Williams, 1958/2013) and some years later, *The Country and the City* (Williams, 1973/2011), opened up new ways of understanding these relations. But there was also a strand of work which sought to analyse the wider relations between cultural institutions and democracy. So, in 1961, *The Long Revolution* (Williams, 1961) and then again, many years later, *Towards 2000* (Williams, 1983) offered startlingly fresh insights into these matters. He came to describe his analytical methods as 'cultural materialism', and he also wrote a number of works which outline this approach, including *Marxism and Literature* (Williams, 1977). Throughout this journey of discovery he was led by a deep fascination with words, their origins and their power to shape human life and experience. This was how *Culture and Society* originated and what led a few years later to one of his most popular works, *Keywords* (Williams, 1976), effectively an extended glossary of English words that he judged to have had significance in the development of contemporary society.

However, in Williams's deep commitment to the power of fiction to provide insight to human life and social relations, he himself was also a novelist. In many ways he saw this second strand as his most important writing. His 'Welsh trilogy' started with *Border Country* first published in 1960 (Williams, 1960/1988), and continued with *Second Generation* (1964/1988) and *The Fight for Manod* (1988). Between them, they provide a fascinating account of his analysis of the changing personal and societal relations which he experienced. His final novel, *People of the Black Mountains*, was completed by his wife, Joy Williams, after his death, and is an epic two-volume[2] fictional account of the history from primordial times through to the twentieth century of the Welsh borderland land which provided his strong roots (Williams, 1989, 1990).

In Chapter 2, the importance of fiction in Williams's work is explored in much greater detail. We look at his own novels to explore what they reveal about his understandings of education, again both as a process and as a set of institutions. This includes a consideration of how he understood teachers and teaching, leading to a discussion of his great interest in the work of D. H. Lawrence. But we also consider the wider ramifications of his analysis of fiction and identify one of his most important and original concepts, 'structure of feeling', which can be used to analyse a wide range of fiction, including other novelists' accounts of schools and schooling.

In his political and sociological analysis of education as a public institution, to which we turn in Chapter 3, Williams provided a seminal account of the development of education in Britain – but especially England – in *The Long Revolution*. Education is seen as one of the key planks of the steady move towards an egalitarian and democratic society, which Williams believed was emerging in Britain. He placed education alongside other cultural institutions, such as the press and public libraries, as providing one of the mechanisms for ensuring that all citizens could become politically empowered to play a part in the development of a democratic society. Tracing the history of English education from the seventeenth through the twentieth centuries, he shows how competing forces have shaped the nature of the school curriculum – or curricula – as we should say when schooling is itself divided into different types of institution. Williams's commitment to non-selective comprehensive education was a key platform in his politics. In this chapter we also give some consideration to the radical changes in English education that have occurred since Williams wrote these accounts. Indeed some would say quite directly that 'the long revolution' was put into reverse in the 1980s as Margaret Thatcher and her New Right governments sought to bring market forces into educational provision and to bring much more differentiation (and selection) into play. We also consider the ways in which the 'fracturing' of the UK – remembering Williams's deep interest in the relations between Wales and England – has led to a significant degree of divergence in educational provision across the four nations of the 'United' Kingdom.

I have already mentioned Williams's involvement in and commitment to adult education and this is the focus of Chapter 4. Williams's name is still much talked of in today's adult education circles and is frequently invoked when such provision is under threat. The Workers' Educational Association continues to this day but also continues to encounter great funding difficulties. Universities' provision of adult education has declined considerably since Williams's time, with only a small number still having an extramural (or equivalent) department. The chapter also considers the links and parallels between Williams's view of the significance of adult education with those of another great socialist educator, Paulo Freire. Although the two never met, there are interesting similarities in their thinking about the power of education. Williams also held great store by The Open University in the UK. The idea of open learning, which could lead to degrees and other qualifications, was a radical one in the 1970s, when the OU was established. The extent to which this institution has maintained its radical edge might be questioned today, but it has certainly played a significant part in opening up higher education to a much wider range of people.

Williams was very much a public intellectual, taking part in many campaigns and movements and using various media to enter into debates on a range of matters from educational provision, workers' rights, the environment, to nuclear disarmament. However, as an academic he did not reside easily in university life, encountering a number of barriers at different times in his working life. In Chapter 5 we consider the question of cultural capital (not a term Williams used much himself) as a way of understanding the often tense relationships Williams had with a number of institutions and organizations, including universities. Gramsci's concept of the organic intellectual is invoked to consider how Williams became an influential leader in British and European leftist groups. His roles, for example in the development of *The May Day Manifesto* and in the development of the journal *New Left Review*, are considered as well as his associations with other leading left wingers such as E. P. Thompson, Stuart Hall and Perry Anderson. The chapter concludes with a discussion of how the role of the university has changed since Williams's death and how managerialism and performativity of a kind he would have detested and critiqued have come to prevail in the cultures of higher education.

Chapter 6 turns to consider the educational role of the arts and a range of media. Williams fervently believed that the press, television, radio and film, as well as the more mainstream established forms of novels and theatre, were potentially powerful in supporting the long revolution. They could all act as forces for democracy. However, he was also well aware that these same means of communication could be shaped and controlled by conservative forces which might seek to exploit them for personal financial gain and also as bastions for defending market capitalism. His interest in George Orwell and his early association with Richard Hoggart and other kindred spirits stem from these concerns. Indeed, it was these kinds of concerns that led him to examine culture in such depth. He effectively rejected simple distinctions between 'high' and 'popular' culture and insisted that culture is ordinary and everywhere. This comes through strongly in his fiction but also in many of his theoretical writings. The concept of structure of feeling is revisited here, to show its power as a concept for examining these relationships. The chapter concludes by asking what has happened to the idea of creativity within educational provision today, as well as discussing the place of media studies and cultural studies in the curricula of schools and universities.

Williams's theoretical legacy and its relevance to the study of education are reviewed in Chapter 7. As well as structures of feeling, we draw together what is understood today by 'cultural materialism' and consider its contemporary relevance and usefulness. Drawing on an influential paper which he wrote for *New Left Review*, called 'Base and superstructure in Marxist cultural theory', we consider how his ideas connect with those of social and educational theorists and sociologists such as Basil Bernstein and Pierre Bourdieu. I suggest that Williams's ideas provide immensely powerful tools for making sense of the increasingly competitive, managerialist, 'networked' and conflicted world of educational policymaking in the contemporary social landscape.

The concluding chapter (Chapter 8) revisits key themes that have been discussed earlier in the book, not least those of history, culture and democracy, in order to summarize Williams's significant, but often undervalued, contribution to education studies. In this reappraisal, some weaknesses in his stance that others have identified, for example in relation to issues of gender and 'race', are discussed. But the message with which the book finishes is one of hope for the future – hope for the power of education indeed to offer, in the title of another of his books, *Resources of Hope* (Williams, 1989a).

Throughout this book, the primary sources used are, of course, Williams's own writings. These are indeed many and varied, and we are also fortunate to have a number of bibliographic resources to draw on, ensuring that the full range of his work is considered (e.g. O'Connor, 1989). Much of his work has been reprinted, often in new editions, with additional commentary by others. To date there have been two book-length biographies, respectively, by Fred Inglis (1995) and by Dai Smith (2008). Inglis's volume covers the whole of Williams's life, whereas Smith's concludes in 1961, while a second volume, covering his later years, is promised. But one especially illuminating source is *Politics and Letters*, a compilation of interviews carried out with Williams by Perry Anderson, Anthony Barnett and Francis Mulhern (Williams, 1979/2015). The distinctive richness of this book is that it gives a clear sense of how Williams spoke, as distinct from how he wrote. The rhythms and cadences of his oral language are fascinating and stimulating. In addition to these sources there are numerous edited collections of Williams's shorter writings and extracts from his longer books, with commentary by editors including Jim McGuigan (McGuigan, 2014), as well as critical essays on his writing, including the fiction such as Tony Pinkney's volume or J. P. Ward's (Pinkney, 1991; Ward, 1981). After Williams's death, one of his former students, Terry Eagleton, edited a collection of essays by a number of his colleagues (Eagleton, 1989). Other collections focus on particular dimensions of his work, such as cultural materialism (e.g. Higgins, 1999; Dix, 2013; McGuigan, 2019) or adult education (e.g. McIlroy and Westwood, 1993).

I only heard Williams speak in person at a couple of events. One was a weekend adult education course held in Bristol, where he and the historian E. P. Thompson were sharing a platform, discussing contemporary issues in linguistics. This experience left a deep impression on me. There are also film sources which capture the man and his work (see O'Connor, 1989). There is a Raymond Williams Society (https://raymondwilliams.co.uk/), which holds a range of events and publishes a journal, *Keywords*, with articles inspired by Williams. This veritable treasure trove of sources and resources has provided a stimulating basis for this attempt to draw out the many insights for education studies and for educational policy, provision and practice embedded throughout Williams's life and work.

1

Biography and Education – Raymond Williams's Educational Experiences

I wish, first, that we should recognize that education is ordinary: that it is, before everything else, the process of giving to the ordinary members of society its full common meanings, and the skills that will enable them to amend these meanings, in the light of their personal and common experience.
(Williams, *Culture and Society* 1958/1989:14)

Introduction

When I try to answer the question of what Raymond Williams was ... my answer is that he was a thinker. When you talked with him, his thinking was almost palpable: a deceptively slow delivery allowed a tremendously impressive body of mental capital to go into action.
(Barnett, 1988, cited by Eldridge and Eldridge, 1994:2)

So said one of his close collaborators, Anthony Barnett, soon after Williams's death in 1988. However, Raymond Williams described himself first and foremost as a writer. The act of committing words to paper was a self-defining process. In spite of his lasting worldwide reputation for his writings on politics, on literature, drama, television and film, his own commitment throughout his life to writing fiction was never in any doubt. Reading the extensive interviews which were published as *Politics and Letters*, it is clear how important to him this creative process was:

> It is certainly true that I have given relatively more time, in comparison with what became visible and valued, to fiction, than to any other forms of writing. In the late forties, I regarded the novels as the work which I most wanted to do. Now I feel differently about them. All along there have been certain things pressing on me, which I simply could find no alternative way of writing; today,

however, fiction is something I'm prepared to work on a long time without feeling any urgency to finish quickly.

(Williams, 1979/2015:271)

During his lifetime five of his novels were published and then, following his death, a final two-volume fictional account of the area of his childhood was completed by his widow, Joy Williams, and published as *People of the Black Mountains* (Williams, 1989d, 1990). Dai Smith, Welsh historian and biographer of Williams, trawled through many of his unpublished or obscure writings, including numerous short stories and several unpublished novels, clearly demonstrating how important this process was to Williams's life and work (Smith, 2008). Williams started writing fiction while still at school and always regarded this – the short story or novel – as the most immediate and powerful way of making sense of human experience and social life. It is paradoxical that he is much better remembered and more highly regarded for his non-fiction than for these novels.

This chapter seeks to explore how Williams understood the connections between biography and identity and in particular how his own educational experiences – in the broadest sense – shaped the person he became. That qualifier 'in the broadest sense' is necessary because Williams understood all personal experience as educational. The environment in which, and through which, we live our lives shapes us as we become who we are. Biography and identity are fundamentally intertwined. It was a profound belief in this idea which would eventually lead to Williams's emphasis on 'structures of feeling' and his adoption of cultural materialism as his analytic method, as we shall see in later chapters. Throughout this writing the influence of place and time – geography and history – on human experience underlies his narrative as well as his analysis. Titles such as *Border Country* and *The Country and the City* demonstrate the former. *The Long Revolution* and *Towards 2000* demonstrate the latter. Here though, in this chapter, the aim is to examine how Williams's own life experiences, including experiences within formal and informal educational settings, shaped his thinking and his actions, shaped his identity. I draw on both strands of his writing, fiction and non-fiction, as well as on analyses carried out by others, to provide this account.

1.1 Childhood and School in Border Country Wales

I come from Pandy, which is a predominantly farming village with a characteristic Welsh rural structure: the farms are small family units. My father began work when he was a boy as a farm labourer. But through this valley had come the railway, and at fifteen he got a job as a boy porter on the railway, in which he remained until he went into the army during the First World War. When he came back he became an assistant signalman and then a signalman. So I grew up within a very particular situation – a distinctly rural social pattern of small farms, interlocked with another kind of social structure to which the railway workers belonged. They were unionized wage-workers, with a perception of a much wider social system beyond the village to which they were linked.

(Williams, 1979/2015:21)

These are Raymond Williams's opening words in response to the first question he was asked in the interviews with the editors of *New Left Review*, published as *Politics and Letters*.

The village of Pandy where Williams spent his childhood lies on the River Honddu, which flows from the Black Mountains down to the valleys of South Wales. The railway line follows much the same north–south trajectory as the river and facilitated the transport of coal and steel from the industrial heartland of South Wales, northwards, beyond the Black Mountains, to the manufacturing centres of the English Midlands. The young Raymond understood the significance of both these natural and human features. His own father, Harry Williams, was employed as a signalman at the signal box in Pandy. In spite of this rural childhood, the young Williams soon became aware of the wider social structures in the world around him. His father was a committed trade unionist and took part in the General Strike of 1926. Raymond became acutely aware of the importance of a strong class consciousness, or what he described as the distinctive self-confidence, of the working people around him.

> We were in no doubt at all about the character of the employers, but the ruling class still did not seem very formidable. The result was to build up a sense, which was very characteristic of the Labour movement at the time, that the working class was the competent class that did the work and so could run society. That was said so much after the General Strike. It was disabling ultimately. But as an adolescent I remember looking at these men even with a certain resentment – they seemed so absolutely confident. I have never seen such self-confident people since.
>
> (Williams, 1979/2015:34–5)

This upbringing, both the society and the physical landscape are portrayed powerfully in his first major work of fiction, published in 1960, *Border Country*.

> The narrow road wound through the valley. The railway, leaving the cutting at the station, ran out north on an embankment, roughly parallel with the road but a quarter of a mile distant. Between road and railway, in its curving course, ran the Honddu, the black water. On the east of the road ran the grassed embankment of the old tramroad, with a few overgrown stone quarries near its line.
>
> (Williams, 1960/1988:33)

This, his most famous novel, evocatively portrays his childhood and surroundings and the title, *Border Country*, also reminds us of another key aspect in Williams's identity. Borders can be both political and social. Welshness was a vital part of his identity, not least when he moved to England. He was always deeply bound to this part of Wales and, later in their lives together, Raymond and his wife Joy enjoyed a second home in the Black Mountains. His intimate love of this landscape comes over most strongly in his final novel *The People of the Black Mountains*, a novel with a deeply temporal dimension, covering the full prehistory, as well as the history, of the area, based on what is actually known as well as imagined in the lives and experiences of those who lived there. But another border which so engrossed Williams in his life was the social border, most frequently conveyed by the term 'class'. Such were his own concerns about the injustices of a society divided by class, with the great disparities of wealth and power existing within western capitalist societies, that challenging these inequalities became a key aspect of his life's work. In many ways he himself did cross these social borders, but his commitments to Wales and to working-class lives were recurrent themes in all that he lived and wrote.

Raymond's parents believed passionately that education and learning can provide routes to fulfilment. As their only child, Raymond became very much the focus of their hopes for the future; they encouraged him to take his learning seriously, and he certainly did. He spent his early years in formal education at the elementary school in nearby Llanfihangel Crucorney, where he stood out scholastically. In 1932, with the support of the headteacher, Tom Davies, he, along with six other pupils from Pandy, won a scholarship to the King Henry VIII Grammar School in Abergavenny, the market town six miles down the valley from Pandy. Here again his academic prowess was evident. This was a selective school and in other communities, perhaps in northern England or in Scotland, attending such a school might have alienated him from his peers and their families, but he recalled that this was not the case. Indeed, there was a strong sense of pride in Pandy at his early achievements as well as his later success.

Apart from Williams's parents, others were deeply influential on his experiences of schooling. In Pandy, the Church of Wales vicar, the Reverend J. A. Hughes, was encouraging and tutored the young Raymond in Latin. This support was provided in spite of the fact that there was relatively little commitment to participating in religious worship in the Williams household, especially among the males of the family. At the grammar school, Williams's imagination was captured by his teacher of English and history, Mr A. L. Ralphs, who identified Raymond as a potential university scholarship boy. Ralphs was a philologist and it may be this that first aroused Williams's interest in the close analysis of particular words. In relation to the wider school curriculum, however, when Williams subsequently reflected on it, he was deeply sceptical about its focus. He came to see it as being fundamentally an imperialist English curriculum designed to foster the subordination of Wales and Welshness and the conformity and obeisance of the working class. It was, he said, 'intellectually deracinating'. In more of his own words:

> What I did not perceive at the time but I now understand is that the grammar schools were implanted in the towns of Wales for the purpose of Anglicization. They imposed a completely English orientation, which cut one off thoroughly from Welshness. You can imagine how this combined with my hostility to the norms of the Welsh nonconformist community. The result was a rejection of my Welshness which I did not work through until well into my thirties, when I began to read the history and understand it.
>
> (Williams, 1979/2015:25)

While at school in Abergavenny, Mr Ralphs, who was a committed internationalist, arranged for Raymond to attend a League of Nations event in Geneva, thus facilitating his first trip abroad. Already by this time he was taking on public speaking roles. He was also writing and taking part in dramatic productions.

In his last years at the grammar school, Williams was taking three subjects for his Higher Certificate (what would now be 'A Levels'): English, Latin and French. It was the headteacher of the grammar school, Mr Newcombe, who wrote to Trinity College Cambridge, proposing that they offer his outstanding pupil a place. Newcombe had consulted Harry Williams, Raymond's father, about this, but not apparently Raymond himself. Raymond was to be financially supported at Cambridge through scholarships both locally and from the university. Subsequently he wondered whether he might have been better suited to attend one of the universities in Wales.

Why didn't the headmaster send me to a university in Wales? That would have been an orientation that would have suited my life much better. It is no use going back over it, but it would have. But that is what he was there for, to find boys like me and send them to Cambridge. I don't say this in an spirit of hostility to him; he thought he was doing the best thing for me.

(Williams, 1979/2015:37)

1.2 'Crossing the Border' to Cambridge University

In late 1939, Williams travelled across England to arrive at one of the most prestigious centres of learning in the world. He was not alone in the crossing of this border from a small, largely rural settlement in Wales to the elite and intellectually competitive environment. Others from working-class backgrounds had also crossed this border at about the same time, but such scholarship boys – and at this time it was very much a male trajectory – were very few. The University of Cambridge was a highly selective institution with the great majority of students arriving from private 'independent' schools, carrying a huge amount of what we might now call social and cultural capital with them.

The experience of arriving at Cambridge was not an easy one (see Williams, 1977, 'My Cambridge', reprinted in Williams, 1989). Williams arrived, already politically aware and committed and soon joined the Cambridge University Socialist Club (CUSS), which was very much dominated by members of the Communist Party. In *Politics and Letters*, he describes the Club as very much his 'home from home' (Williams, 1979/2015:40) and it contrasted greatly with the ethos of his college and the wider university. Even within the club, the members were nearly all from much wealthier backgrounds than him, but they did at least share his cultural and political interests.

> I think I am right to say that I met only one other person from a working-class family at Cambridge, and he was a mature student in his thirties, but had himself been a manual worker as an adult …..The overwhelming majority of people I encountered at the Socialist Club were in terms of education and family very much the ordinary Cambridge mix.
>
> (Williams, 1979/2015:40)

This was a strange time to be at the University of Cambridge. The Second World War commenced in the same year that he arrived there, and this had an increasing impact on 'normal life' at the university. On a personal level for

Raymond Williams, one effect that was to have an enormous influence on his life stemmed from the temporary migration of students from the London School of Economics (LSE) to Cambridge, in order to avoid the blitz that was devastating the capital. Among these LSE students was Joyce Dalling, known as Joy, who was to become Williams's wife in 1942 and who was a major collaborator in much of his work thereafter. In due course they would have three children: Merryn, Ederyn and Madawc.

Williams had gone to Cambridge to study English: a relatively new subject for this highly conservative establishment. An English Faculty was created there only in 1925, and the subject was still in its early days of development. But 'Cambridge English' was already becoming a very particular and widely recognized approach to the study of language and more particularly literature. Under the initial leadership of I. A. Richards, who created an approach which came to be known as 'practical criticism' (the title of one of his books – Richards, 1929), this mantle was later taken on by F. R. Leavis (always known by his initials, rather than his forename) often in collaboration with his wife, Q. D. (Queenie) Leavis. But the undergraduate Williams had very little direct contact with the Leavises at this time.

Practical criticism was an approach to the study of literature which involved close analysis of the ways writing was structured and the ways in which words were used. It focused on – and helped to establish – what would become known as the English canon, including, among others, the novels of Charles Dickens, Jane Austen and the Bronte sisters, the poetry of William Wordsworth and Samuel Taylor Coleridge and the drama of William Shakespeare. Williams was an avid reader of drama and fiction and was well versed in the great poetical works, as can be seen especially in *The Country and the City* (Williams, 1973).

Williams was tutored at Cambridge firstly by Lionel Elvin (later the Director of the London Institute of Education and the author of an early classic in education studies, *Education and Contemporary Society* – Elvin, 1968) and then by E. M. W. Tillyard, described by Inglis in his biography of Williams, as 'a grandee' of the English Faculty (Inglis, 1995:82). Elvin appears to have been culturally much more in tune with Williams's dispositions, whereas Tillyard was a deeply conservative scholar.

As well as providing academic stimulation, Cambridge also provided considerable political and aesthetic stimulation. Through his membership of the CUSS, Williams soon came to know many other students with leftward leanings and became a member of the Communist Party. This was a time of great political debate at Cambridge – and to some extent around the wider country. The rise of German fascism and Soviet communism, and of course, the outbreak of war, had created a febrile international atmosphere and the fertile young minds at Cambridge were feverishly working out their individual and collective positions. Among those with whom Raymond came into contact in these early days were the historians E. P. Thompson and Eric Hobsbawm. On the cultural front, as well as already being a prolific writer for, and editor of, student newspapers, Williams became a frequent viewer not only of film, but also of ballet and theatre. In film, his collaboration with Michael Orrom, with whom he co-wrote one of his early publications (Williams and Orrom, 1954), began during his undergraduate days.

Dai Smith, in his biography of Williams, suggests that here at Cambridge, he was living three parallel lives:

> The three he led over those two years to the summer of 1941 were that of an intermittently conscientious but academically blocked student, that of a full time political activist cum student journalist and, no less deeply, for he was scarcely twenty, that of an incomplete personality yearning for a more defined expression in art and in love.
>
> (Smith, 2008:94)

But Williams did not finish his undergraduate studies without interruption. After his second year he received his call-up papers and was conscripted to the army. In 1941 he was sent off to train as a wireless operator in the Royal Corps of Signals. The following year he was commissioned as an officer in the 21st Anti-tank Regiment. He was appointed to command an anti-tank squad, leading a team of armoured vehicles, essentially mobile guns. After a long period of preparation – training and waiting – his troop joined the D-Day landings and were among the first to land on the Normandy beaches. His guns came under attack and engaged with the enemy. There is no doubt that this experience and the aftermath of proceeding first into Belgium and then into Germany itself had an enormous psychological effect on Williams, as he says in *Politics and Letters*, when asked what the overall effect of the experience of the war was for him:

> It was appalling. I don't think anybody really ever gets over it. First there is the guilt: about moments of cowardice, but also about moments of pure aggression and brutality. Are those really opposites? It is easy enough to feel guilty about when you feel frightened but much worse is the guilt once you've started recovering your full human perspective, which is radically reduced by the whole experience of fighting.
>
> (Williams, 1979/2015:57)

Yet again however, during these stressful times, Williams continued to put his writing to good use, editing the Regimental weekly newspaper, called *Twenty-One*, usually adopting the pseudonym Michael Pope.

He returned to Cambridge in 1945 to undertake his final undergraduate year. He threw himself into intensive study, as well as continuing to write and edit, often returning to Devon at the weekends, where his wife and young child were living with Joy's parents. The university offered a dispensation for returning service people, which enabled them to submit an extended paper as an alternative to one of the final examinations. Williams had become deeply fascinated by the plays of Ibsen and chose to write a 15,000-word paper examining this body of work. This subsequently laid the foundation for another of his early publications: *Drama from Ibsen to Eliot* (Williams, 1952). His other great interest in this final year was in the work of George Eliot, an interest he would build on in his subsequent literary criticism. This was also the period during which he was beginning to work out his own distinctive approach to the study of drama and fiction. As an undergraduate, Williams apparently attended few lectures by F. R. Leavis and, rather, learned about his work through two close friends, Clifford Collins and Wolf Mankowitz, who were following behind Williams, reading English. However, in many ways, the development of his own approach to literary criticism came in response to Leavis's ideas and he always acknowledged his debt to Leavis. But, as Williams's thought became more independent, where Leavis sought to probe and analyse literature within its own terms, closely examining the language and construction, Williams was to develop an approach which would place the writing firmly within its social context, suggesting that literature could be appreciated fully only through recognizing the conditions of its creation. So, while drawing heavily on the tradition of literary criticism that was being established by Leavis, he was developing the strong social and political strands in his analysis which were to form the key distinction of his approach. As his biographer Dai Smith wrote about this emerging original aspect of his work:

> But Leavis' examples, other than in the full revelation of a chosen canon of literature, were impossibly remote from the actual lives of an industrialised working class for whom the fustian antiquity of a non-technological future was as unimaginable as its opposite was desirable. In some of the techniques Williams employed at this time to rid himself and others of the suffocation of cliche, in thought and behaviour, the echo of Leavisite criticism – close reading for practical purposes, pricking of lazy populism and sentiment, insistence on felt experience as prior, even superior, to abstract thought – is self-evident.

> Stronger, though, is the use to which these insights were to be put. For Williams there could be no worthwhile 'politics' without the depth of hinterland behind 'letters' but there was no achievable 'individual' sensibility in the present without a linked 'collective' future of potential.
>
> (Smith, 2008:238–9)

He was also collaborating very actively with his two friends, Mankowitz and Collins, in trying to establish not one but two literary journals: *Politics and Letters* and *The Critic*. These turned out to be fairly short-lived publications but demonstrated yet more evidence of Williams's deep desire to communicate and inform a wider group of people. This was, I am suggesting, indicative of a deep pedagogical urge that ran throughout his life. There was never a time when he was not wanting to engage with others in a process of teaching and learning, whether through writing, lecturing or debating.

These times were crucial in terms of the social and political settlements arrived at following almost six years of severe stress and hardship brought about by the war. The general election of 1945 saw an overwhelming majority for the Labour Party which, under the leadership of Aneurin Bevan, began to create what became known as 'The Welfare State', with public provision of a wide range of health and social services. Formal school education was already in the process of being restructured following the 1944 Education Act. While these were political moves which Williams definitely saw as progressive, indeed essential, he was not greatly enamoured of the ways in which the Labour Party was developing. He remained dubious about the wisdom of accepting loans from the United States and the subsequent Marshall Plan for economic development. He was sceptical about the nature of the Party's commitment to public ownership of essential services; for example he noted his father's reservations about the nationalization of the railways, which he had long supported as a matter of principle:

> When the railways were nationalized, I would talk to my father about the consequences of this move. Within six months he, who had always wanted it, was bitterly against the bureaucratic character of the new structure. It seemed to him the substitution of one kind of directorial board for another. He said that the immediate work discipline became harsher.
>
> (Williams, 1979/2015:71)

Williams's wider view of the range of post-war 'settlements' was to become much clearer and more deeply considered in *The Long Revolution*, published some fifteen years later, in 1960. But in practice, he continued to give political support to the Labour Party throughout his life, invariably seeing himself as well to the left of its centre.

1.3 Williams the Adult Educator

Williams left Cambridge in the summer of 1946. He had been offered the opportunity to stay on as a Senior Scholar, which could have led to a doctorate, probably under the supervision of Leavis. However, perhaps reflecting his continuing ambivalence about the nature of the academy and of academic work, he was keen to follow his two major instincts: teaching and writing. During his last term at Cambridge he became aware of an opportunity to apply for a post working with the University of Oxford Extra Mural Delegacy, serving as a tutor for the Workers' Educational Association (WEA).

He had already undertaken a small amount of work for the WEA in Cambridgeshire and had a strong commitment to the importance of adult education as a social good, providing an opportunity for those who had not had an extended school education.

Williams was interviewed for this post in Oxford and was offered a position in East Sussex, one of the areas in England where the Delegacy and the WEA had a joint arrangement to provide classes. The subjects he was to teach initially focused on key post-war issues such as international relations, but it was not long before he added courses reflecting his literary interests. The growing Williams family (Ederyn was born that year) moved to a flat in Seaford in Sussex, which was to be their home for the next six years.

Raymond would spend every morning writing, always having several projects underway and would travel in the afternoon to wherever he was due to teach in the evening. His biographers suggest that his usual approach to teaching, at this stage of his life, was to prepare some introductory input and then to have a discussion with the students for the second half of the session. However, he gradually came to believe that because he sought to develop the students' critical skills rather than to 'fill them with knowledge', the basis of his classes, especially in literature, should be that the students were provided with reading and that they should then learn through student-initiated discussion. As Smith puts it:

> he reduced drastically the number of texts or extracts to be read over the customary twenty four meetings of two hours per session and he ensured the

texts were read, often in class, with the tutor silent, and remaining so, until discussion was instigated by the students.

(Smith, 2008:235)

Later in this book I will discuss Williams's overall contributions to adult education in more detail (Chapter 4), but this is the period of his life when his distinctive and sometimes controversial approach to teaching really developed. His biographers also note that being based in Sussex, his students did not include many who were working in heavy industry, as he might have preferred, and indeed included a number of students who might well be described as middle class. (Such tensions still exist in WEA provision around the country today.)

While he was based in Seaford (and subsequently Hastings), Williams continued not only his writing but also his political activity. He was continuing to attempt to produce his first novel, which eventually became *Border Country*. But first it went through a series of draft versions with titles including *Brynllwyd* and *Village on the Border* (see Smith's biography for full accounts of the different versions – Smith, 2008). His very first book publication, *Reading and Criticism* (Williams, 1950), was developed very much on the basis of his literature teaching for the WEA. He was also completing his early works on drama and film and laying the foundations of *Culture and Society*, first published in 1958. *Culture and Society* was his 'breakthrough' book, which brought him national and later international attention and was to become one of the most influential books in the broad field of humanities (Williams, 1958/2013).

After sixteen years in Sussex, Williams was invited to return to the headquarters of the Oxford Delegacy at Rewley House in Wellington Square, Oxford. He was effectively being promoted to a senior position in the organization and had been recognized as an outstanding adult educator. So, his family moved to Oxford – and this was where the second volume in his 'Welsh trilogy' of novels, *Second Generation* (Williams, 1964) was largely set. His children – there were three of them by now – attended school in Oxford. However this stay was to be short-lived, for only a year later, in 1961, Williams received an invitation from Jesus College, Cambridge, to take up a Fellowship there, the second time he had been 'called' to Cambridge without initiating the move himself. He swiftly accepted this invitation; he and Joy found a house in Hardwick, a village some four miles outside the city and moved there with their children. Williams's academic reputation, which led to him being offered this post, had been established notably through *Culture and Society*, published in 1958, and significantly enhanced just three years later by *The Long Revolution*. These two works clearly defined

Raymond Williams as a leading literary and political thinker and writer. For himself, however, the publication of his first major fiction work, *Border Country*, was of at least equal significance. This was first published in 1960. These three works between them demonstrate the emergence of one of the most creative and influential minds of the twentieth century.

1.4 Life in the Academy and Beyond

By this stage of his life, Williams had firmly demonstrated his commitment to writing both fiction and non-fiction. He was becoming incredibly productive. Following the success of *Culture and Society*, for some time he had been working on what was to become even more influential in a broader field of politics and sociology, the work he called *The Long Revolution*. Although in many ways a collection of somewhat disparate essays, what Williams achieved in this publication was impressive: a clear delineation of his perspective on social change in Britain, setting out his deep commitment to the steady growth of democracy and equality in society. His emphasis on the public forms of communication and interaction, such as the press and state education, showed how, following the Second World War, he continued to believe in social progress through the steady democratization of public institutions and the steady sharing of resources and wealth. This was a profoundly optimistic view of the world, fostered no doubt by the post-war rise in living standards, the growing strength of the labour and trade union movements and – not least – to the increasing access to knowledge and understanding of all citizens, through radio, television and printed media.

The steady stream of significant publications continued, many of them still recognized as groundbreaking works of lasting influence. *Keywords,* which first emerged as a separate publication in 1976, was a detailed, annotated glossary (Williams described it as 'a vocabulary') of the words which he had identified as playing a key role in social change over the centuries, especially through the industrialization of our society. The ground for this work had been laid in *Culture and Society*, which itself was stimulated by Williams's fascination with particular words, specifically culture, democracy, art, class and industry, and their changing usage in society. *Keywords* gave readers a new insight into the power and symbolism of certain words – even before semiotics had properly emerged as a discipline in its own right. More than twenty years after the publication of *The Long Revolution* Williams wrote what was effectively a kind of sequel, called

Towards 2000 (Williams, 1983), which was far less optimistic, if still hopeful. His collection of essays *Resources of Hope* (Williams, 1989), attempted to offer some positive ways forward.

On the literary side, drawing on a course of lectures he gave in the English Faculty at Cambridge, he wrote *The English Novel from Hardy to Lawrence* (Williams, 1970/1984). The legitimate successor to *Culture and Society*, *The Country and the City*, was published in 1973, demonstrating once again his keen awareness of geography and of history. He traces how literature, especially novels, reflects the real lived experience in which they were created. The theoretical ideas he was deploying in his analyses also came to be represented in a series of articles which were then collected together into books. Notable among these were *Marxism and Literature* (Williams, 1977) and *Culture* (Williams, 1981). The ideas which came to be grouped under the title of 'cultural materialism' are pulled together in such works and demonstrate the ways in which a Marxist understanding of the world may combine with a deeply humane and humanistic understanding of our way of life. These are just some of the significant highlights of his non-fiction output over the years.

In fiction, the third and final volume of the Welsh trilogy, *The Fight for Manod* (Williams, 1988), emerged late in his life and showed Williams's continuing concern for the struggle between 'progress' and 'nature'. In some sense it gave insight to Williams's understanding of environmental politics in the late twentieth century and foreshadowed some of the ecological concerns that have risen more visibly to the cultural surface in the years since his death. Two other novels, independent of the trilogy, had preceded this: *The Volunteers* (Williams, 1978/1985/2011) and *Loyalties* (Williams, 1985/1989). These also develop themes of importance to him. The first is set in his beloved South Wales and sees him engaging with Welsh nationalism in perhaps the most direct way he ever did. He was not an out-and-out nationalist by any means but was a fervent advocate of Welsh distinctiveness and a powerful supporter of cultural developments in Wales (as we shall see in Chapter 3). The second of these freestanding novels, *Loyalties*, is a kind of political thriller, which reflects on the political alliances and allegiances he had encountered at Cambridge. His days as an undergraduate there were the days in which it was not only the Communist Party seeking new members, the secret intelligence services of both the UK and the Soviet Union were also recruiting.

Williams was also prolific as a journalist. For several years he was a TV critic writing a regular column in *The Listener*: a weekly magazine associated with the BBC. It had been clear from his discussions in *The Long Revolution*, that he saw television as a powerful tool in democratization. He pulled these ideas and his reviewing of TV together in a volume published in 1974 called *TV: Technology and Cultural Form* (Williams, 1974), the title demonstrating his interest in the connection between technological and sociopolitical development.

But Williams was also producing works of a more directly political nature during these times. While *The Long Revolution* and *Towards 2000* did provide some kind of a manifesto, he was the lead editor of a key publication of the late 1960s, *The May Day Manifesto*, which was drafted by a group led by himself, Stuart Hall and Edward Thompson who met in Williams's room at Jesus College, Cambridge (Williams, 1968). *The May Day Manifesto* became a significant focus for what was clearly emerging as 'The New Left' in Britain. Here, for example, we begin to see the outlines of a programme for education reform and for further public ownership of key industries, as well as calls for more student power in higher education (see Chapter 5).

1.5 Conclusion: Identity – the Personal and the Professional in Education

Over his lifetime, Raymond Williams engaged in many educational activities and with many institutions and organizations. The interaction between these experiences and his own thinking is evident and we begin to see how his experiences shaped him. What was particularly distinctive in this life was the huge degree of self-awareness, or what we might now call reflexivity, he demonstrated. As his biographers note these qualities were not necessarily manifested in an obvious manner. He was variously described as reserved, introspective or even aloof – 'a private person'. He did not travel internationally very much or even within Britain. The film director Mike Dibb, who worked with Williams on a documentary based on *The Country and the City*, took him to visit some of the places referred to in the literary work covered in that book (as reported by Inglis, 1995:49). Dibbs noted surprise that Williams had not been to most of these places before.

In a very tangible sense Williams was writing his own identity throughout his life. A reading of Smith's biography gives a full sense of how his recording and translation of his life experiences into novels and short stories was a continuous process of self-discovery and personal development from an early age through to *People of the Black Mountains*, at the very end. Much of this work, probably most of it, was never published and, as I noted earlier, he is much better known for his non-fiction than for his fiction. Yet the power of imagination, the creative drive was always at the centre of his life.

If, for Williams, 'culture is ordinary' and also 'a whole way of life', then one might go on to say that in the way he lived his life, experience **is** education, and also life **is** learning. Certainly, however, he engaged with three particular educational institutions of a more formal kind over the course of his life: 'the school', 'the university' and 'adult education'. We will be considering each in more detail in later chapters, but here, by way of summary, we start to map out the significance of each of them in his world.

He attended two schools as a boy: his elementary school near Pandy and the grammar school in Abergavenny. In the first he was 'spotted' as a very promising scholar, supported and encouraged by teachers and later by the local church minister. His progression to the selective grammar school was an early border crossing for him. Here he travelled but a few miles to attend the institution where he had already been picked out from many of his peers in Pandy. Those peers would have continued for another couple of years at the elementary school, before they joined the local workforce. Given his later deep commitment to inclusive education, what came to be referred to in England as comprehensive education, it may seem paradoxical that he himself benefitted from selection at this early age. Not only that, but when he later had his own children, when living both in Oxford and in Cambridge, they too attended selective fee-paying schools. His reflections on the school curriculum are also interesting in the light of him subsequently calling for a common curriculum. The National Curriculum in England came too late for him to directly comment upon, and his ideas for access to knowledge, skills and understanding, as expressed in *The Long Revolution,* might well have led him to be highly critical of what was implemented in England. On school teaching too, he reflected on the importance of the quality, disposition and commitment of teachers in the state sector and was seen as something of an icon by teachers, especially teachers of English. He was also, as we have seen, a key contributor to the establishment of cultural studies as a field of study as well as its subset, media studies, which later became a subject of study in schools.

His relationship to 'the university' as an educational institution was not an easy one. While there is no doubt that his own thinking and incredible influence on humanities and social studies derived from his intellectual encounters at Cambridge and subsequently from a wide range of international university-based scholars, he was never totally at ease in this environment. The early deracination he experienced in relation to both his social class and his Welshness was just a part of the disquiet. He certainly supported the massive expansion of higher education that occurred in Britain (and across much of the 'developed world') from the 1960s onwards, but he was all too aware of the strong connections between the academy and the frequently elitist bastions of power, especially in English cultural and political life. His involvement in the politics of the New Left and his significant engagement with the radical student politics of the late 1960s and early 1970s demonstrate once again how the various dimensions of his life came together.

Perhaps it was in adult education that Williams had the most fulfilling existence, although there were tensions and contradictions there as well, as we will see in Chapter 4. Growing up in South Wales he had seen how educational experiences had been a major shaping force of people's life chances (as we might now call them). His own parents might well have benefitted from staying longer in full-time education, and the towns and cities of the coalfields and steelworks of the valleys were largely populated by men and women whose school education had been curtailed at an early age. He saw the provision of adult education as a fundamental element of social provision in redressing these inequalities. Again curricular and pedagogical questions began to surface for him from his early engagements in adult education tutoring. Initially his classes tended to be concerned with matters of social and political development, especially in the aftermath of the war. But with his own passion for literature, drama and the arts, he believed that provision in what would now be referred to as the humanities should also be a matter of entitlement for those who had been excluded from them in their youth. The tensions between education for employment, for citizenship and for the mind would later be played out in an historical analysis in *The Long Revolution*, but for Williams as an adult education tutor, there was no doubt that all three of these aspects of education were fundamental. His own approach to teaching was significantly developed through his early experiences in adult education. Like many teachers who sought (and seek) an interactive approach with their students, he often found it difficult to provoke responses and engagement, but he continued to maintain this way of teaching and was able to develop a distinctive approach based on his commitment to the development of his students' skills, rather than prioritizing an increase in their knowledge.

The school, the university, adult education have all changed, almost beyond recognition, since Williams's death in 1988. In England most particularly, the impact of neoliberalism can be seen in all three institutions. The schools have become centres for a standardized curriculum, with testing and examinations dominant as a means of measuring educational success. The universities have also been subject to the exigencies of performativity and managerialism in a way that was starting to become evident even during Williams's lifetime. His colleague Edward Thompson edited a scathing attack on these tendencies while based at the University of Warwick, called *Warwick University Limited* (Thompson, 1963/1970). The closure of Birmingham University's Centre for Contemporary Cultural Studies in 2002, a centre for which Williams's work was a key inspiration, is also a clear indication of the vulnerability of the more creative and critical elements of higher education provision. The idea of a university as a centre of critical and independent thought has been under continuous pressure, often associated with economic pressures, throughout the past four decades.

As for adult education provision, it is severely withered. Many universities have curtailed their extra-mural provision altogether, while some continue to collaborate with the WEA or with local authorities. It might be argued that some elements of this provision have been replaced by professionally related development programmes, courses that enhance employees' skills and abilities and may well lead to personal advancement. But such provision may be seen as strictly utilitarian, especially when compared with the range of provision in the 1950s and 1960s. To some extent it might also be argued that the huge expansion of higher education has reduced the need for separate adult education provision and of course the creation of The Open University, a radical outcome of the educational reforms of the 1970s (and in which Williams himself played a significant part), has changed the adult education landscape for the better.

We continue to see some resistance and opposition to the kinds of managerialist tendencies witnessed since the Thatcher and Reagan years. However, populist politics of the twenty-first century on both sides of the Atlantic have continued to erode the humanities in particular and the arts in a wider sense across all educational sectors. The heartfelt warnings from the likes of Stefan Collini (2012) (another Cambridge scholar) or Jon Nixon (2011) in the United Kingdom or Martha Nussbaum (2010) in the United States call for us to remember the centrality of such scholarship in resisting dangerous and malign forces in society. But in a world where economics and productivity are so closely linked, such calls fall all too frequently on deaf ears.

For many who have read his work, Raymond Williams continues to shine a powerful light on these affairs. His writings in literature, politics and social theory show how we may better understand society and social processes through careful close analysis. His novels show how closely related are life experience and personal and social identity. In his life and work he provided a kind of prototype, a model for how to work with people in order to question and challenge destructive forces in society in pursuit of social justice, equality and democracy. Education – in its many forms – is at the heart of this project.

2

Education in Fiction and Fiction in Education – Raymond Williams's Novels and His Analyses of English Literature

Fiction has the interesting double sense of a kind of imaginative literature and of pure (sometimes deliberatively deceptive) invention. These senses have been in the English word from a very early period ...
Novel, *now so nearly synonymous with fiction, has its own interesting history. The two senses now indicated by the noun (prose fiction) and the adjective (new, innovative, whence novelty) represent different branches of development ...*
... we can now sometimes say that novelettes, or bad novels, are pure fiction, while novels (serious fiction) tell us about real life.

(Extracts from *Keywords*, Williams, 1976:111–13)

Introduction

We found in Chapter 1 how Raymond Williams saw himself first and foremost as a writer who, within his own identity, prioritized the writing of fiction, yet today, as noted above, his reputation and legacy rest more on his non-fiction writing, in both politics and letters. We also saw in Chapter 1 how, for Williams, education was a process of becoming: the experiential process through which individual identities are shaped and formed and how these processes are themselves shaped and formed by wider social and cultural influences which change over time and vary between locations. But it was seeking to define and delineate this 'structural' aspect that gave rise to the significance Williams attached to the key concept of 'structure of feeling'. We will return to this concept in a more theoretical way later in this chapter and also later in this book. Here, rather, the initial purpose in this chapter is to start to exemplify and illustrate that concept through looking at ways in which the social institution of education is portrayed in novels, including his own and some of those he analysed in his literary criticism. In particular, we look at how teachers and teaching are portrayed. Part of the wider purpose of this analysis is to demonstrate how fiction can itself be used as a medium or tool for education. Teachers of English literature will already recognize the contribution that such study can make: that the reading of fiction is in itself an educational process, as well as (usually) a pleasurable one.

In one of the few extended discussions of Williams's fiction writing, Tony Pinkney describes him as a postmodern novelist (although Eldridge and Eldridge, 1994, contest this). By using this term Pinkney is drawing attention to Williams's great emphasis on ambivalences in social experience. In reviewing all six of the novels he suggests that in these novels there is a:

> paradoxical interaction of spaces, the local and the global, of an intensely specific, loved place and the multinational worldspace of the late twentieth century is itself a – perhaps *the* – postmodern phenomenon, since a new relationship at all levels to space, place and geography is ... often regarded as a decisive postmodernist trait.
>
> (Pinkney, 1991:17)

I start by taking some of Williams's own fictional writing to see how he portrays teachers and teaching. Then, drawing partly on a work that he and his wife Joy co-edited, we consider the contribution that some of the novels of D. H. Lawrence made in this sphere. Stepping back somewhat, I then consider Williams's approach to literary criticism in a more general sense, offering some reflections on the importance of studying the ways in which novels present and represent the social world to the reader. In conclusion I return to the topic of teachers and teaching to consider other examples, some quite contemporary, of how a range of writers portray schools and educational processes, and what that reveals about their perceptions of education within society.

2.1 Schooling and the Teachers in *Border Country*

Just how much Raymond Williams owed to his teachers in Pandy and in Abergavenny is very clear from reading Dai Smith's biography (Smith, 2008). However, in his own fiction, teachers do not figure largely, even in the 'Welsh trilogy': *Border Country* (1960/1988), *A Second Generation* (1964/1988), *The Fight for Manod* (1979/1988). We learn much more about his family, neighbours, churchmen and businessmen and trade unionists than we do about his teachers. The central character in these books is often the academic, the intellectual, the teacher of adults (each of these is considered here in later chapters), but there is little evidence of the schoolteacher.

In the novel based on his own childhood, *Border Country* (Williams, 1960), the central character is Matthew Price, known at home as Will. Raymond himself was known at home as Jim. We begin to see not only that there will be two lives for the main character, one on each side of the border, but even two corresponding names. There are, as we shall see, some references to elementary and grammar school and an interesting pair of accounts relating to the elementary schoolmaster. However, given the significance of education in *The Long Revolution* (Williams, 1961/2011) (for which *Border Country* is sometimes seen as the fictional forerunner) it is perhaps surprising that more of his fiction is not concerned with schooling. This notable absence of school and of teachers in his own fiction may well reflect the retrospective distaste Williams expressed for the impact of his grammar schooling. Although it was the route that led him to the University of Cambridge and a life of politics and letters, it was also a confusing experience. As he says in interview:

> The history we were taught in the elementary school was a poisonous brand of romantic and medieval Welsh chauvinism given us by the schoolmaster. The reading was dreadful – nothing but such and such a medieval prince defeated the Saxons, and took from them great quantities of cattle and gold. I threw up on that. It wasn't only that it didn't connect. It was absolutely contradicted by how we now were. The irony was that when I entered the grammar school we started to do the history of the British Empire.
>
> (Williams, 1979/2015:28)

> The grammar school was intellectually deracinating, as I can see now. But I was not conscious of it at the time, because in everything that was not schoolwork there was no sense of separation.
>
> (Williams, 1979/2015:29)

The extract from the same interview cited in Chapter 1 also draws attention to the repression of Welshness in the grammar school curriculum. So, if that is Williams's retrospective analysis of his elementary and grammar schooling, what of his actual teachers? If he disapproved of the curriculum, he was ready to acknowledge the profound personal influence of at least one teacher in the grammar school, A. L. Ralphs, as we shall see shortly.

In *Border Country*, there are two passages featuring the elementary schoolmaster, William Evans. The first is a fascinating account of an incident during the General Strike in the 1920s. The scene is set at the village bowling green where Harry Price, the railwayman father of Will/Matthew, the central character based on Williams himself, has been tending the lawns. Harry is awkwardly asking William Evans for an advance of the one pound that he is due to be paid for tending to the bowling green, given the lack of wages coming in because of the strike. Evans seems set to agree this easily when they are interrupted, first by the local policeman, then by Major Blakely, a local landowner, before some troop lorries go by, presumably on their way to control picket lines or demonstrations. Harry and one of his friends are quite clear in the discussion that ensues that the cause of the Strike lies fairly and squarely with the government. Following a very tense discussion, in which the schoolmaster plays only a minor role, the policeman and the major depart.

> Before William Evans could go back to the green, Harry went up to him again.
> 'I'm sorry. We got interrupted.'
> 'The discussion about the strike?'
> 'The money.'
> 'Oh, that, yes. I been thinking, Harry – mind I know how things are – only it seems to me I ought to put it to the committee. It's their money after.'
> 'I need the May wage. You needn't think the work won't be done because I get it in advance.'
> The schoolmaster looked down at Will, who was drawing his boot in the dust.
> 'Would ten shillings advance be any help?'
> 'I could do with the pound.'
> 'Yes, of course, but … ' Evans hesitated, and again looked round. 'Well, perhaps,' he said quickly. 'Seeing it's in a good cause.'
> He took out a big leather purse, and unfolded a pound note.
> 'Come in one day and sign the receipt.'
> 'Aye. Thank you,' Harry said. 'Only what did you mean a good cause?'
> William Evans smiled, and carefully pulled at his nose.
> 'Ask no questions, get no lies. That right, boy?'
> He patted Will on the shoulder.
>
> (Williams, 1960/1988:119)

Williams depicts the schoolmaster as morally dubious, anxious to maintain relations with the strikers but also seeing himself as aligned with state and government. His shifting position over the advance appears very much to represent equivocation and recognition of the schoolmaster's mediating role in local society.

In the second passage we see a much more oppressive aspect of the schoolmaster. Again something of the prevalent structure of feeling is conveyed by the way Williams sets the scene.

> The entrance to the school, Glynmawr Non-Provided, was through an elaborate grey arch, which rose from the dirt playground to announce the porch. A cross was carved in the weathered grey stone, and below it the date of foundation, 1853. Above and below the cross were two scrolls, with the legends, *Laborare est orare* and *Benedicte, omnia opera*, but the carving was now barely legible, for it was filled with dirt and moss. The porch was narrow and dark. Part of its limited space was taken up by an old harmonium, over which William Evans gave his boys their more severe beatings.
>
> (Williams, 1960/1988:162–3)

We read how the boys have a conspiracy that partly undermines the brutality of William Evans. When the schoolmaster wants to undertake a beating, he sends a boy out to cut a stick. Whoever is sent undertakes a special cut of the stick that will weaken it so that it is likely to break when used. Will and his friend Tegwyn Evans are about to be beaten because Will has tried to help Tegwyn Evans sneak into class late (he has been out in the fields, taking his time, bird-nesting or collecting conkers on his three-mile walk to school). Will's friend Brychan has been sent to get a stick.

> 'Discipline,' William Evans said, standing above the boys. 'Discipline, now, in every walk of life is essential. Hold out your hands.'
>
> The boys obeyed. Will noticed that Tegwyn's hand was much thicker than his own. On the end of the fingers there was a smear of bright yellow pollen.
>
> 'You, boy, for lateness,' William Evans said, and swung the stick.
>
> Tegwyn took the cut on his fingers, without cry or movement. The stick did not break. Will saw Brychan anxiously watching.
>
> 'And you, boy, for inattention and disturbance.'
>
> The stick swung again, and Will, looking at Brychan, yelled before it even reached his hand. At the same time he pushed his hand forward, so that the cut came on the bottom of the palm. The stick broke, and Will turned and jumped about, lifting his hand to his mouth and licking. The palm in fact hardly hurt at all.
>
> 'Now, now, boy,' William Evans said anxiously, looking down at the broken stick.
>
> 'It's all right, sir'.
>
> (Williams, 1960/1988:169)

However, Mr Evans was successful in getting several pupils into the grammar school in Gwenton (Abergavenny), among them is Will (Matthew). The exam results are received in the Price household.

> The result was better than Ellen [Will's mother] had expected, though Harry had always been confident. Will passed easily, with very high marks. Harry rode to Gwenton, to buy the local paper, and when he arrived back he was extraordinarily excited, throwing his bike at a run along the hedge under the holly, and shouting the news to Ellen and Will and the neighbours. Will was made a great fuss of by everyone, and several neighbours gave him presents. He himself valued most his father's excitement; he had never before seen him quite like this.
>
> (Williams, 1960/1988:178)

The next day Will's mother goes into Gwenton to buy two books for Will: Euripides' *Trojan Women* and Aeschylus' *Prometheus Chained*. However,

> [t]hey were strange to Will, and he did not understand, either then or later, quite how they had been chosen.
>
> (Williams, 1960/1988)

In his biography of Williams, Dai Smith describes King Henry VIII Grammar School in Abergavenny as having about it 'the architectural air of a miniaturised public school' (Smith, 2008:63). Williams himself recalled a teacher who was to have a profound influence on him, Arnold L. Ralphs.

> For two years he did not teach me in class, but then in the Fourth Form I remember him as a clear and stern critic of our methods in the debates he arranged; half English, half history and International Affairs, in his own characteristic combination of interests. He began a process of critical training which has always remained as a true centre in my own life and in that of many others. He taught English with a genuine passion which his control and quietness only threw into relief. He taught history as an immensely serious and continuing process which was so close to our lives as to be inevitably a moral concern. He extended this work into his devoted care of the school branch of the League of Nations Union. As the 1930s, my years in school, darkened towards war, the firmness and clarity of his own beliefs in law, justice and in peace gave me and others the bearings which overcame despair, and the convictions which could survive even failure, when war at last broke out.
>
> ... In his quiet but articulate witness, he embodied a civilisation; the liberal seriousness of the North. This was unforgettable and is unforgotten.
>
> (Cited by Smith, 2008:66–7)

It is surprising that a character such as Ralphs does not appear in *Border Country*, given the influence he clearly had on the young Raymond, nor is much written about the experience of grammar school. Then, a few years later, Will/Matthew gets a place at Cambridge University – and the impact of this experience on Matthew (as he is known there) is a key theme of the novel. There is some reference though to the unusual way in which he secured his place and some hints at what it might mean in the Price family.

> In Will's fifth year in the grammar school in Gwenton, Harry was called in by the headmaster to discuss future plans. There was a possibility of a university scholarship, but obviously this would be a serious commitment, and a great deal would depend on the attitude at home.
> 'It's what I want,' Harry said.
> 'Well that's something. It's also what we want, here at school. Only you see how it is, Mr Price. This is the local school, the boys come in here and it helps them to get decent jobs. But that's just here, the world they know. Going away altogether, into a quite different world, that would be very much more difficult.'
> ...
>
> 'It's moving,' Harry said. 'None of us is doing what our fathers were doing. None of us is living quite as they lived.'
> The headmaster looked carefully at him.
> 'You may be right, I don't know.'
> 'That's how it seems to me.'
>
> (Williams, 1960/1988:219)

Harry reports this conversation to Will/Matthew. Then, after the Head has written a letter to one of the Cambridge colleges, not only is a place secured for Will, but finances are put in place through scholarships, to make his attendance possible. But Cambridge is indeed a different place and, although Matthew is still deeply connected to his family and his childhood experiences, he recognizes that he has developed a new language and a new way of seeing the world in the abstract and detached way consistent with the view of the academic economic historian he becomes. Many years later, when he returns to his parents' home after his father is taken ill, his mother, Ellen, says:

> He said not to worry you, Will.
> Matthew drew in his breath. As he looked away he heard the separate language in his mind, the words of his ordinary thinking. He was trained to detachment: the language itself, consistently abstracting and generalizing, supported him in this. And the detachment was real in another way. He felt in this house, both

a child and a stranger. He could not speak as either; could not speak really as himself at all, but only in the terms that this pattern offered.

(Williams, 1960/1988:83)

It is only when his father has actually died that he starts to understand what has happened in these border crossings of his life, as he says to his wife, after returning from the funeral:

> the strength was there, the certainty of identity, in a way he had only rarely encountered.
>
> It was as if I stared straight at the sun, as I was learning to see. I had stared as a child, almost destroying my sight. And I was staring again, at the same centre.
>
> Now? In these last days.
>
> 'Yes. In these last days. And Glynmawr station is closing, but I remember when I first left there, and watched the valley from the train. In a way, I've only just finished that journey.'
>
> It was bound to be a difficult journey.
>
> 'Yes, certainly. Only now it seems like the end of exile. Not going back, but the feeling of exile ending. For the distance is measured, and that is what matters. By measuring the distance, we come home.'

(Williams, 1960/1988:351)

The education Will/Matthew has experienced from his school days through university and into work as a lecturer all served to create a sense of a barrier between him and his parents, between him and his home community, with its language, common knowledge and culture. It is only when his father has died that Will begins to make sense of this, just as Raymond Williams achieved this sense-making through writing this novel. If we recognize *Border Country* as a deeply autobiographical 'coming-of-age' novel, then it has taken more than thirty years for Will/Matthew/Jim/Raymond to establish his adult identity. Such a protracted journey is perhaps not unusual, but what gives this particular journey its power and poignancy is the consciousness of class borders and geographical borders that have been so significant. The social milieu in which Matthew/Raymond now moves as a grown man is dominated by a middle-class sensibility rather than a working-class one and by Englishness rather than Welshness. If these differences were experienced as predominantly cultural in nature, it clearly demonstrates why the exploration of culture became so central to Williams's life and work as well as an early indication of the importance of 'structure of feeling'.

2.2 D. H. Lawrence

We know both from *Culture and Society* (Williams, 1958/2013) and from *The English Novel from Dickens to Lawrence* (Williams, 1970/1984) that Williams regarded D. H. Lawrence as a highly significant novelist, whose work effectively captured the structure of feeling of the early twentieth century in England, as the full impact of industrialization – seen by Lawrence as alienating and destructive – was being felt and the ground was being laid for the subsequent burgeoning of the middle class, a process sometimes called embourgeoisement. Teachers figure quite prominently in Lawrence's fiction and there at least two good reasons for this: first, Lawrence himself was a teacher for three years, and second, the teaching profession was a key route for social mobility among working-class men and women.

In one of Williams's lesser-known works, *D.H. Lawrence on Education*, he and his wife Joy collected together a range of Lawrence's writings on education and teaching, drawing not only from his novels but also from a number of essays and short stories. This was published by Penguin in a series of *'Education Specials'* that was very popular with teachers and students in the late 1960s and early 1970s. In his introduction to the collection, Raymond Williams points out that Lawrence was one of 'the first English writers to have direct experience of ordinary teaching. Certainly he was one of the very first to have worked in our modern system of organized schooling for everyone' (Williams and Williams, 1973:7). It is the case that Lawrence captures the nature of teaching in an original way. In an earlier paper (Menter, 2008) I used an extract from Lawrence's *Women in Love* (Lawrence, 1921/1999) to illustrate the depiction of the intensity teaching can involve. This is his depiction, early in the twentieth century, of Ursula Brangwen teaching a botany lesson in an elementary school somewhere near Nottingham:

> A heavy copper-coloured beam of light came in at the west window, gilding the outlines of the children's heads with red gold, and falling on the wall opposite in a rich ruddy illumination. Ursula however, was scarcely conscious of it. She was busy, the end of the day was here, the work went on as a peaceful tide that is at flood, hushed to retire.
>
> This day had gone by like so many more, in an activity that was like a trance. At the end was a little haste, to finish what was at hand. She was pressing the children with questions, so that they should know all they were to know, by the time the gong went. She stood in shadow in front of the class, with catkins

in her hand, and she leaned towards the children, absorbed in the passion of instruction.

(from Chapter 3, *Women in Love* by D. H. Lawrence, 1921/1999:27)

This extract captures the intuitive element of teaching, the spark, the passion. As Williams comments on passages such as this:

> what Lawrence has to say is that the 'personal interests', the 'subjective dreaming', the 'mind wandering to things that are not on the syllabus', these standard complaints of so much educational argument, have to be seen differently: not as distractions but as the often unnoticed and unacknowledged yet in the end decisive realities. And this point is stronger, obviously, when we see it through the eyes of a particular character, whose whole life we know, rather than as an abstract point, where it can be quite quickly forgotten.
>
> (Williams and Williams, 1973:9)

So Williams is making a case not just for a more humane view of teaching but for the novel to convey such a conception. Nevertheless, this view of teaching as a personal mission, as well as a professional occupation, has become familiar in representations of teaching emerging from sociological work later in the twentieth century. For example, the classic studies by Jennifer Nias of English primary teachers, by Michael Huberman of Swiss secondary teachers or Philip Jackson's *Life in Classrooms* in the United States, all share such a perspective on the nature of teaching (Huberman, 1993; Jackson, 1968/1991; Nias, 1989).

However, throughout both *Women in Love* and *The Rainbow* (Lawrence, 1915/2001), we are given insight to the ways in which teachers' personal relationships and working lives connect with broader patterns of social, industrial and cultural change. As (Raymond) Williams puts it, in his introduction:

> his arguments about education are inseparable from his arguments about life and society. Education, for him, is not a separate or specialized subject. It is a set of active decisions about how we shall live.
>
> (Williams and Williams, 1973:7)

There is so much in the selections made by the Williamses which could be used to illustrate this latter point, but let us use an extract from *The Rainbow*, describing Ursula Brangwen's early teaching experience:

> The first week passed in blind confusion. She did not know how to teach, and she felt she would never know. Mr Harby came down every now and then to her class, to see what she was doing. She felt so incompetent as he stood by, bullying

and threatening, so unreal, that she became neutral and non-existent. But he stood there watching with that listening-genial smile of the eyes, that was really threatening; he said nothing, he made her go on teaching, she felt she had no soul in her body. Then he went away, and his going was like a derision. The class was his class. She was a wavering substitute. He thrashed and bullied, he was hated. But he was master. Though she was gentle and always considerate of her class, yet they belonged to Mr Harby, and they did not belong to her. Like some invincible source of the mechanism he kept all power to himself. And the class owned his power. And in school it was power, and power alone that mattered.
(Cited by Williams and Williams, 1973:47)

The social relations depicted in this passage say much about gender, power and the function of schooling in the early twentieth century. Indeed, the discomfort felt so strongly by Ursula conveys a structure of feeling that goes far beyond personal relations, humiliation or embarrassment. We feel here the interface of machine and nature, of brutality and compassion, of male and female, perhaps even of training and education. For women in the early twentieth century, becoming a teacher was a way of earning an independent living and also of moving socially upwards (Widdowson, 1983).

In the introduction to the extracts Williams also urges his reader to study Lawrence's essays on education and other matters. He suggests that Lawrence changed his views significantly during his lifetime but also that he was adept at identifying tensions and contradictions in education. One key tension is between the education of the individual and the education of people for social purposes. In Lawrence's words:

Elementary education today assumes two responsibilities. It has in its hand the moulding of the nation. And elementary school-teachers are taught that they are to mould the young nation to two ends. They are to strive to produce in the child under their charge: 1. the perfect citizen; 2. the perfect individual.

Unfortunately the teachers are not enlightened as to what we mean by a perfect citizen and a perfect individual.
(from *Education of the People,* cited in Williams and Williams, 1973:127)

Furthermore, Williams points out that there is a tension between arguments for the 'self-expression' of the child and the imparting of officially sanctioned knowledge, a tension that was very much part of the discussions in education in England at the time the Williamses' book was published, with many debates about 'free schools', 'deschooling' and 'miseducation' (see Menter, 2016 or Wright, 1977). As Raymond Williams writes in the introduction to the collection:

Lawrence wants people to be themselves, and at the same time, in his social system, in his prescriptions about what should and shouldn't be learned, he has got it all worked out for other people. Both feelings are real, and to follow them through is to arrive at a contradiction which is not only in Lawrence, but in a very wide area of our social and educational ideas.

(Williams and Williams, 1973:11)

The final words of Williams's introduction make the case for the lasting value of Lawrence's views on education. He suggests in his experience of education that Lawrence finds:

> the brightest hopes, the deepest disappointment, the opening possibilities, the dreary and crushing frustrations, and all of these connecting with personal life, with the economy and society, with what it is for men to live at all, we do more than learn a doctrine; we trace, as he would have wanted, a man alive. A man, too, in a time and place that still connect with us. For through all the subsequent changes, many of the problems, contradictions, the illusions, the experiences seem still to be there.

(Williams and Williams, 1973:13)

We see clearly here why Williams was so strongly drawn to Lawrence's writing – their stances not only on education but on the connections between the individual and society have so much in common, even if their political and cultural views were in many respects markedly different.

Both the fictional depictions we have considered, those by Lawrence, written and set early in the twentieth century and those by Williams, set in the 1920s, but written in the 1950s, capture something of the contradictions represented by schooling during the twentieth century. Yes, state schooling was consolidated as a right for all – and was further extended in the post–Second World War era. The structure of feeling in the two depictions is similar in demonstrating the emergent culture of meritocracy at the same time showing elements of the residual culture of constraint, conformity and even oppression. Perhaps the main difference between the two is the element of deracination expressed by Williams, so vividly, as not only a geographical but also a social feature. Matthew Price is the embodiment not just of social mobility through entry into the teaching profession but of a fuller meritocracy that sees a working-class lad being turned into a middle-class intellectual – albeit with a sense of roots still grounded in his humble origins. Williams, of course, was not alone in making this journey. We can find similar tensions in others' (auto) biographies such as Richard Hoggart's

(Hoggart, 1989) or in the purportedly sociological but also autobiographical study, *Education and the Working Class* (Jackson and Marsden, 1962/1966).

What both Lawrence and Williams are capturing through their depictions of the respective structures of feeling is what sociologists of education in the second half of the twentieth century saw as one of the central problems for public education – whether it was a process for social change and development or a process of reproduction and continuity. Furthermore, if we consider the personal motivation of teachers depicted in these works we also get the individualized version of this problem. What, one may ask, is the moral or values basis of these teachers' approach to their work? There is no doubt that in many of Lawrence's teachers, there is a strong moral (or religious) 'calling' that drives them to seek to improve the lives of their pupils. Teaching as a 'vocation' may be seen in historical and sociological studies of the development of the teaching profession in England (see, for example, Grace, 1978; Cook, 1984). Even where teachers are punitive towards their charges they may judge this to be in their better interests. But in both Lawrence and the real teachers, Williams recalls, there is a sense of a wider set of purposes, of striving respectively for the liberation of the inner humanity of young people, against the massification of society represented by industry or in the pursuit of peace and democracy in a turbulent time.

2.3 The English Novel

So far in this chapter we have concentrated on representations of teachers, teaching and schooling in fictional writing by Williams himself and by D. H. Lawrence. We now move to consider wider questions of the significance of the novel and related literary forms in Williams's work. From his first published book, *Reading and Criticism*, through to one of the later theoretical works *Marxism and Literature*, to a collection of essays on the topic, *Writing in Society*, the analysis of writing was at the heart of his intellectual project.

Reading and Criticism was published in 1950 as a volume in the *Man and Society Series*, published by Frederick Muller (Williams, 1950). The series, we are told in the frontispiece, is 'intended for use of students in adult classes, such as those promoted by the WEA and University Extra-Mural Departments, and by other readers requiring new introductory studies in the subjects covered'. The book is dedicated to Williams's parents and was very much a result of his early days of teaching WEA classes in East Sussex (see Chapters 1 and 4 of this book).

Among many debts he acknowledges is one to Mr A. L. Ralphs, the teacher from the grammar school in Abergavenny, mentioned earlier.

Williams opens the book by suggesting that it is 'an introduction to reading' rather than 'an introduction to literature'. He sets out why such a book is needed:

> Since the introduction of free and compulsory education in the last eighty years an immense new reading public has been created. Leisure has correspondingly increased, with the result that the public for serious literature is potentially very large, larger than it has ever been. Step by step with the growth of literacy and education, however, new and broad channels for leisure-time 'activity' have been manufactured: the popular newspaper and magazine, with combined circulations larger than the population; the cinema, which some twenty-five millions attend in Britain every week; the wireless, with audiences for single programmes of between fifteen and twenty million at a time.
>
> ...
>
> Any enquiry into the reading of literature, or into the present position of any of the arts, has a danger of becoming no more than marginal, unless the cultural atmosphere in which all the arts exist is recognised in the discussion.
>
> (Williams, 1950:1)

Here, remarkably, we actually see Williams – who was writing this in 1948, set out a large part of his intellectual agenda for the rest of his life. Indeed, this is, in some sense, a setting out of the area of investigation which became known as cultural studies of which Williams is seen as a central founder (see Chapter 5). Further, we may note that in this immediate post-war context, there was no mention here of television, a medium that deeply fascinated him later on, nor, of course, is reference made to the influence of digital technologies, including social media, which would become so crucial towards the end of the twentieth and into the twenty-first centuries. But what is clearly there, as well as an interest in a range of literary forms, was the recognition of the social significance of the new economic context which had so enormously widened access to these cultural strands. What also shines through in the work is his unstoppable pedagogical commitment: he wants to enable his readers to improve their skills when they are reading, beyond 'the everyday'; otherwise, he says:

> The average man or woman of this country, who has had no special training or opportunity for the attentive reading of literature, will inherit all the negative factors: the routine of mechanical reading; the preconceptions and the prejudices; the lack of guidance; and to these will be added the deadening effect of so much of our material environment.
>
> (Williams, 1950:5)

Throughout the book, he offers examples of how he himself reads literature. There is an appendix which includes forty-five extracts, mostly from novels and poems, which are provided as the basis of exercises in which the reader (or the student in the adult education class) is invited to analyse, using some of the techniques he has described in the book. An outline syllabus for the whole programme of study is another appendix. The final chapter of the book is called 'Literature and Society'. Here we read of the relationships between literature, language and society:

> To the language of a people, which is perhaps the fundamental texture of its life, literature is supremely important as the agent of discovery and analysis. A literary tradition is the record of a large number of important choices. It thus provides a depth of experience on which we may draw on all our choices at our own point in time. The importance to the quality of our lives of a rich, vital and constantly renewed language is inestimable.
>
> (Williams, 1950:107)

So, while in this first book he readily acknowledges and pays tribute to those from whom he has learned and who developed his thinking, there is also evidence of the burgeoning of originality in the ways in which Williams is making connections between language, literature and society, as well as culture. This – culture – was the word which would become a particular signifier of his ideas within a few years, through the publication of *Culture and Society 1780–1950*, often seen as the book that firmly established him as a leading intellectual of the time.

The starting point for *Culture and Society* was Williams's identification of five key words which, while he had been teaching adult education classes in East Sussex, emerged for him as key signifiers of changes in society stemming from the industrial revolution, which, of course, was centred on Britain. In his study of English writing and art over this period he explored how the meaning of these words had changed over the (almost) two centuries. The five words were: industry, democracy, class, art, culture. The book is structured into three parts; the first and third parts focus respectively on the nineteenth and twentieth centuries, with the middle, shorter, part being concerned with an 'interregnum', a period around the turn between these two centuries. Over the book as a whole, the majority of writers and artists discussed are not perhaps best known as novelists but as political philosophers, social theorists or political essayists. We have chapters, for example, on Thomas Carlyle, on J. H. Newman and Matthew Arnold, on R. H. Tawney and George Orwell, although some, such as Orwell and

Arnold were also novelists or poets. There are chapters on 'The Industrial Novel' (considering Mrs Gaskell, Charles Dickens and George Eliot among others), on D. H. Lawrence, a chapter on literary criticism, where he discusses both Richards and Leavis (see Chapter 1 of the present book) and a chapter on 'Marxism and Culture'. It is possible to see again here the early indications of themes that would be central to his life and work. The enormous impact of the book stemmed from the highly original way in which Williams made connections between cultural artefacts and social change.[1] In later chapters we will return to this theme. In this chapter we consider how his reading and analysis of fiction developed during the writing of *Culture and Society*.

Williams had indicated in *Reading and Criticism* how the wide availability of a range of literary forms was changing lives and this 'democratisation' of culture was being widely recognized in the press and in radio and the early days of television broadcasting. It is no coincidence that another key player in the development of cultural studies, Richard Hoggart, had published his own *The Uses of Literacy* (Hoggart, 1957), which addresses similar themes, just a few months earlier. Two key foundation stones of cultural studies had been laid (see Chapter 5).

Williams concludes the chapter on 'The Industrial Novels' (*Mary Barton, North and South, Hard Times, Sybil, Alton Locke* and *Felix Holt*) with this paragraph:

> These novels, when read together, seem to illustrate clearly enough not only the common criticism of industrialism, which the tradition was establishing, but also the general structure of feeling which was equally determining. Recognition of evil was balanced by fear of becoming involved. Sympathy was transformed, not into action, but into withdrawal. We can all observe the extent to which this structure of feeling has persisted, into both the literature and the social thinking of our time.
>
> (Williams, 1958/2013:109)

Taking in words such as these must surely have had a significant impact not only on readers of Gaskell, Dickens, Eliot, and later of Lawrence and Hardy, but also on readers of the romantic poets and of early socialists such as William Morris. None of these writers was simply expressing their individual perceptions and ideas; rather, their words were emerging from the social and technological environment within which they were living.

The 'Conclusion' to *Culture and Society* is a fascinating essay, effectively laying the ground for *The Long Revolution*, to follow two or three years later. This chapter is concerned centrally with culture, communication and community, with the questions of mass, minority and popular culture being raised. The final section has the subheading 'The development of a common culture'. It is all too easy to forget that such terms were hardly used before this time, or at least that they took on very different meanings during this period. One cannot but suggest that Williams (together with a few others) was himself active in shaping the structure of feeling of 1950s and 1960s Britain.

The English Novel from Dickens to Lawrence, originally published in 1970, twelve years after *Culture and Society* and some twenty years after *Reading and Criticism*, was based on a course Williams gave at Cambridge. In its author's voice, it is pedagogically less didactic than *Reading and Criticism* and essentially presents six accounts of important English novelists and their work: the two included in the book's title together with Charlotte and Emily Bronte (together), George Eliot, Thomas Hardy and Joseph Conrad. There are two 'linking' chapters which discuss key breaks in continuity in the development of the English novel. This book is one of the easiest of all Williams's non-fiction works to read and is apparently transcribed from lecture notes and recordings of the lectures.

The book starts with the observation that in a period of twenty months from 1847 to 1848, an incredible number of important novels were published. Williams starts by asking why this occurred. One of the key ideas emerging from this work is that novels are based on their authors' membership of, and account of, a 'knowable community'. Through words on the page the writer conveys what he or she knows about the community of which he or she is a part.

> Most novels are in some sense knowable communities … the novelist offers to show people and their relationships in essentially knowable and communicable ways.
>
> (Williams, 1970/1984:14)

Williams suggests that it was in response to a crisis in 'the knowable community' in the late 1840s that this wave of important novels emerged.

> We can see its obvious relation to the very rapidly increasing size and scale and complexity of communities: in the growth of towns and especially of cities and of a metropolis; in the increasing division and complexity of labour; in the altered and critical relations between and within social classes.
>
> (Williams, 1970/1984:16)

Williams argues passionately at the end of the book for the novel as a distinctive way of making sense of history and of society, in a way that the social sciences cannot do, whilst they are nevertheless valuable.

> It is from this vital area, from this structure of feeling that is lived and experienced but not yet quite arranged as institutions and ideas, from this common and inalienable life that I think all art is made. And especially these novels, these connecting novels, which come through to where we are just because all that life, that unacknowledged life now so movingly shaped and told, is our own direct and specific and still challenging inheritance.
>
> (Williams, 1970/1984:192)

In many ways this book offers the most explicit explanation of why Williams himself continued to write novels all his life. Indeed, he makes a witty self-reference earlier in the conclusion to the book, noting that a number of other writers – he gives George Orwell as an example – undertook both fiction and non-fiction in their work:

> it remains true, looking at it from experience, that there are certain feelings, certain relationships, certain fusions and as relevantly certain dislocations, which can only be conceived in the novel, which indeed demand the novel and just this difficult border country where from Dickens to Lawrence, making its own very varied demands, it has lived and lived with meaning.
>
> (Williams, 1970/1984:190)

Williams's personal experience is clearly a key driver for the next substantial work of literary criticism, *The Country and the City*, published in 1973. He was thinking of his family over several generations. This book is dedicated to the memory of 'the country workers who were my grandparents' and he acknowledges, as usual, the help of his wife Joy, as 'sustaining and irreplaceable'. Furthermore he thanks his daughter, 'Dr Merryn Williams, author of *Thomas Hardy and Rural England*, who was kind enough from her special experience to read the manuscript and the proofs'.[2]

The first chapter opens with the two words of the book's title. He writes:

> 'Country' and 'city' are very powerful words. and this is not surprising when we remember how much they seem to stand for in the experience of human communities. In English, 'country' is both a nation and a part of a 'land'; 'the country' can be the whole society or its rural area. In the long history of human settlements, this connection between the land from which directly or indirectly we all get our living and the achievements of human society has been deeply known. And one of these achievements has been the city: the capital, the large town, a distinctive form of civilisation.
>
> (Williams, 1973/2011:1)

The chapter gives an autobiographical account of how growing up in 'a remote village ... on the border between England and Wales', he became aware of the cathedral city of Hereford, the market town of Abergavenny and the 'industrial towns and villages of the great coal and steel area of South Wales' (Williams, 1973/2011:2). At the time he was living in a village outside Cambridge and having cited William Cobbett,[3] writing in the early nineteenth century about another Cambridgeshire village he offers this reflection:

> whenever I consider the relations between country and city, and between birth and learning, I find this history active and continuous: the relations are not only of ideas and experiences, but of rent and interest, of situation and power; a wider system.
>
> (Williams, 1973/2011)

In a later chapter (7) we will consider Williams's adoption and development of 'cultural materialism', but he states here, in a nutshell, the relation between economics and human experience, together with a reiteration of how he understands education as a lifelong process of learning through experience.

More than any of the previous works discussed, *The Country and the City* is concerned with poetry and examines a wide range of verse to explore how writers have created images of the rural and urban landscapes of England over periods of social change. But, yet again, there are chapters focusing on novels, including a chapter that looks at Dickens's portrayal especially of London. In the chapter entitled 'Knowable Communities' he discusses the educational biographies of George Eliot, Thomas Hardy and D. H. Lawrence. He picks up on a phrase used by an (unnamed) 'British Council critic' who suggested these great novelists were 'our three great autodidacts'. Williams rails at the implicit snobbery of this remark. He recognizes that the three writers' fathers were respectively a bailiff, a builder and a miner, but he points out it is absurd to see them as largely self-taught:

> George Eliot was at school till sixteen and left only because her mother died. Thomas Hardy was at Dorchester High School till the same age and then completed his professional training as an architect. Lawrence went into the sixth form at Nottingham High School and after a gap went on to Nottingham University College. It is not only that by contemporary standards these levels of formal education are high; it is also that they are higher, absolutely, than those of four out of five people in contemporary Britain.
>
> (Williams, 1973/2011:170)

This last sentence may not still hold quite as true in twenty-first century England, but it was certainly accurate in the 1970s. What Williams suggests is revealed by 'the flat patronage of "autodidact"' is that the speaker of this phrase assumed that anyone who had not attended boarding school and then Oxbridge could not be described as properly 'educated'. This 'standard education' is experienced only – then and now – by a tiny percentage of the population – all the rest were seen as 'uneducated' or as 'autodidacts'. In reaction to this he suggests:

> [B]ut to many of us now, George Eliot, Hardy and Lawrence are important because they connect directly with our own kind of upbringing and education.
> (Williams, 1973/2011:171)

The book ends with another deeply fascinating chapter, 'Cities and countries', again with a strongly autobiographical tone. His conclusions are fundamentally political and, as we can now recognize, far-seeing. He suggests major problems arise in society from the continuing divisions of labour that sustain capitalism and the best way to resist this is through cooperative endeavour.

> If what is visible already as the outlines of a movement is to come through with the necessary understanding and strength, we shall have to say what in detail can practically be done, over a vast range from regional and investment planning to a thousand processes in work, education, and community. The negative effects will continue to show themselves, in a powerful and apparently irresistible pressure: physical effects on the environment; a simultaneous crisis of overcrowded cities and a depopulating countryside, not only within but between nations; physical and nervous stresses of certain characteristic kinds of work and characteristic kinds of career; the widening gap between the rich and poor of the world, within the threatening crisis of population and resources; the similarly widening gap between concern and decision, in a world in which all the fallout, military, technical and social, is in the end inescapable.
> (Williams, 1973/2011:306)

The influence of having recently edited *The May Day Manifesto* (see Chapter 5) can be seen here and we also see that some of the ground was being laid for *Towards 2000*, which would follow ten years later. Yet, once again, Williams arrives at these political positions through his study of literature.

Marxism and Literature was first published in 1977 and is a very different kind of text in that it is Williams's attempt to draw together aspects of the theoretical approaches he has been taking throughout his life. In the first section he discusses four 'basic concepts', culture, language, literature and ideology. The second and third sections are discussions respectively of cultural and literary theory. We will return to some of the key themes of the book in later chapters, including his discussion of 'base and superstructure' and of 'dominant, residual and emergent' cultures. There is a chapter on structures of feeling, and we find Williams explicitly naming his position as cultural materialism: 'a theory of the specificities of material cultural and literary production within historical materialism' (Williams, 1977:5). He is defining his approach as a subset or branch of *historical* materialism, a term familiar to most Marxist intellectuals, whereas *cultural* materialism at that time was not. He acknowledges the absence of illustrative material in the book, but refers his readers to all the exemplary material included in his earlier non-fiction works, in drama, literature and television,

> as a reminder that this book is not a separated work of theory; it is an argument based on what I have learned from all that previous work, set into a new and conscious relation with Marxism.
>
> (Williams, 1977:6)

I might respectfully suggest that it is actually a separated work of theory, in that there is no attempt to integrate the material of analysis (as there was, for example, in *Culture and Society* or *The Country and the City*), but we can concur that the book does make most meaning – the ideas become clearer – when it is read in the mirror of his other work.

In 1983, Williams collected a number of his own articles and lectures together and published them in a collection entitled *Writing in Society* (Williams, 1983/1991). The volume covers a wide range of literary topics including drama and prose, as well as reflections on the subject 'English Studies', especially at Cambridge University. The book as a whole provides the strongest possible confirmation that, for Williams, writing was the most critical and creative activity in his working life. In the introductory chapter, with typically wide-ranging historical perspective he reflects on changes in writing:

> I was concerned with a major cultural shift in our own period, in which the relations between writing and speech, between writing and dramatic action, and then, in quite new ways, between writing and the composition of images, were changed or were newly developed in radio, television and film. It was clear that these new relations and forms were important in themselves. But, also, in their increasing centrality, they allowed us to see, in some new ways, the historically specific relations between writing, print and silent reading which had been taken for granted, and at the same time privileged, in the four centuries in which

these relations were dominant and were often, in specifically 'literary' studies, assumed to be universal.

(Williams, 1983/1991:6)

The significance of these 'relations and forms' will be revisited in later chapters here (especially 5 and 6), but now, in the twenty-first century, we must also acknowledge how new forms of writing have emerged, through the development of social media, with many important communications being written on electronic devices and despatched on digital platforms, technologies that could only be alluded to by Williams.

The final chapter in *Writing in Society* is a deeply personal and reflective article based on lectures he gave at Aberystwyth University in 1978. It is called 'The Tenses of Imagination' and in it he reflects on the power of fiction to relate to the past, the present and the future. He refers both to his Welsh trilogy and to the three volumes of *People of the Black Mountains* he was then engaged in writing. As we have noted earlier, this fictional writing has not only an incredible sense of place but is also fundamentally concerned with processes of change over time. In a world of rearmament and mass unemployment, he suggests, imagination is more important than ever, both in understanding the past and the present and in creating a better future:

> there are deeper forces at work, which perhaps only imagination, in its full processes, can touch and reach and recognize and embody. If we see this, we usually still hesitate between tenses: between knowing in new ways the structures of feeling that have directed and now hold us, and finding in new ways the shape of an alternative, a future, that can be genuinely imagined and hopefully lived. There are many other kinds of writing in society, but these now – of past and present and future – are close and urgent, challenging many of us to try both to understand and to attempt them.
>
> (Williams, 1983/1991:268)

We will return to these themes, hope for the future and the importance of creativity and imagination in later chapters.

2.4 Conclusion: The Reality of Fiction

The concept of structure of feeling emerged early in Williams's work through his study of film and drama. He was concerned to develop an alternative conception to the Marxist notions of the relation between culture and economy, frequently referred to as the base – superstructure relationship, which he found to be over-deterministic, hence the combination of hard and soft represented respectively by 'structure' and 'feeling'. In *Keywords* (Williams, 1976:253) he suggests that 'structure' is one of the most significant words in modern thought 'and in many of its recent developments it is especially complex'.

But it should be emphasized that structure of feeling initially emerged as an *analytical* concept to be deployed in the study of cultural forms such as drama and literature, as well as film and television. Indeed, it was in *Preface to Film*, published in 1954, that he first used the term:

> In the study of a period, we may be able to reconstruct, with more or less accuracy, the material life, the social organization, and, to a large extent, the dominant ideas ... To relate a work of art to any part of [the] observed totality may, in varying degrees, be useful, but it is a common experience, in analysis, to realise that when one has measured the work against the separable parts there yet remains some element for which there is no external counterpart. This element, I believe, is what I have named the *structure of feeling* of a period and it is only realisable through experience of the work of art itself, as a whole.
>
> (Cited by Higgins, 1999:38)

In the interviews that *New Left Review* carried out with Williams, published as *Politics and Letters*, there is a long passage (Williams, 1979b:156–74) where this concept is being put to the test. In his responses it becomes clearer that he believes the use of the idea will enable readers to detect significant patterns of social as well as cultural change and to get a sense of the dominant class powers within the society under scrutiny.

Williams's fullest written account of structure of feeling appears in *Marxism and Literature*. Again, we see an emphasis on the way in which the concept may be used to reveal insights into social relations in a state of flux within a given culture. He stresses that the term relates to emergent social formations rather than to residual or indeed dominant social formations (Williams, 1977:132). 'Methodologically, ... ' he writes, 'a "structure of feeling" is a cultural hypothesis, actually derived from attempts to understand such elements and their connections in a generation or period, and needing always to be returned, interactively, to such evidence' (Williams, 1977:132–3). The elements he is referring to here are those of: 'impulse, restraint and tone; specifically affective elements of consciousness and relationships: not feelings against thought, but thought as felt and feeling as thought: practical consciousness of a present kind, in a living and inter-relating continuity' (Williams, 1977:132).

The way I now read fiction is profoundly affected by Williams's concept of structure of feeling. The great novelist for me is one who implicitly captures something of the dynamics of society through character, dialogue, emotion and plot. It is indeed 'the element for which there is no external counterpart'. To me, this is the kind of literary equivalent of *The Sociological Imagination* set out by C. Wright Mills (1959), which is so eloquent about the connections between the individual and society or between the private and public.[4]

The effects of formal education on a learner's identity was well understood by Williams as indicated above – the way in which his own trajectory began to put a boundary between his home community and the wider world of literature and a different kind of language (section 2.1). Intriguingly the same theme – but with a different outcome – is picked up in Lewis Grassic Gibbon's trilogy *A Scots Quair*, a book which Williams says he came to rather late and discusses in *The Country and the City*. Set initially in rural parts of Aberdeenshire, the protagonist Chris Guthrie, the daughter of the house, shows academic promise and excitement in school learning.

> So that was Chris and her reading and schooling, two Chrisses there were that fought for her heart and tormented her. You hated the land and the coarse speak of the folk and learning was brave and fine one day and the next you'd waken with the peewits crying across the hills, deep and deep, crying in the heart of you and the smell of the earth in your face, almost you'd cry for that, the beauty of it and the sweetness of the Scottish land and the skies. You saw their faces in firelight, father's and mother's and the neighbours', before the lamps lit up, tired and kind, faces dear and close to you, you wanted the words they'd known and used, forgotten in the far-off youngness of their lives, Scots words to tell you to your heart, how they wrung it and held it, the toil of their days and unendingly their fight. And the next minute they passed from you, you were English, back to the English words so sharp and clean and true – for a while, for a while, till they slid so smooth from your throat you knew they could never say anything that was worth the saying at all.
>
> (Gibbon, 1946/1986:37)

This kind of schism between home and the wider world, between country and city, between Scotland or Wales and England is perhaps far less apparent in contemporary society for reasons – including the development of mass media – to be discussed later. But in the early to mid-twentieth century it is clear that the possibility of border crossing was not limited to Williams. In Chris Guthrie's case however, although it was anticipated that she would go on to train as a teacher, her mother died in tragic circumstances and she did not leave home in the way that Will/Matthew Price did.

In a chapter in *The Country and the City* called 'The Border Again', Williams offers a more general insight into the way in which *A Scots Quair* reveals important processes of social change: the relationships between the rural and the urban, the agricultural and the industrial. He does this by contrasting Gibbon's work with that of D. H. Lawrence. Gibbon, Williams suggests, wholeheartedly connects with the rural and agrarian society being transformed during the early twentieth century. Lawrence, however, by contrast, does not see the significance of this past but only of the industrial present. While acknowledging Lawrence's genius as a writer, he calls into question his understanding of contemporary society. He concludes with these words about Lawrence:

> His is a knot too tight to untie now: the knot of a life under overwhelming contradictions and pressures. But as I have watched it settle into what is now a convention – in literary education especially – I have felt it as an outrage, in a continuing crisis and on a persistent border. The song of the land, the song of rural labour, the song of delight in the many forms of life with which we all share our physical world, is too important and too moving to be tamely given up, in an embittered betrayal, to the confident enemies of all significant and actual independence and renewal.[5]
>
> (Williams, 1973/2011:271)

Fiction can provide powerful insights into the nature of teaching and educational processes. Because education and teaching provide key sites, at certain times and places, for social change and, at other times and places, for social stability, it is no wonder that diverse and well-written fiction offering representations of teachers lends itself so well to an analysis based on structure of feeling. What happens in schools and other educational institutions is a key indicator of social patterns and social relations. Developing such ideas derived from Williams's thinking, how might our understanding of teacher identity and national culture/s be aided by a consideration of teachers in fiction? We may consider a few examples.

In his novel *A Disaffection*, James Kelman (1989) describes the experience of a teacher in a Glasgow secondary school:

Patrick Doyle was a teacher. Gradually he had become sickened by it. (p. 1)

> Dinnertime crept up on him. The bell went and he was sitting on his stool having a laugh with something one of the boys was saying. This was very unusual these days. He had definitely been enjoying the class, a bunch of stupit fourth-yearers, they were all stupit; fourth-yearers. What was it about fourth-yearers. A couple

of them were smiling at him as they headed for the door, instead of the usual avoiding the eyes. It was like how things used to be. They really did, they did use to be like that, things – back when the spark still existed. Before it had been extinguished. But it hadn't been extinguished; it still existed, it was just fucking dormant.

(Kelman, 1989:15)

If extracts such as these and the earlier ones from Lawrence, convey, in their different ways, a sense of the individual professional identity of some teachers in particular times and places, we should also acknowledge that in literature we may also be powerfully reminded of the influence of culture and tradition (cf. Leavis, 1948). Indeed, we could invoke further literature, from Mr Gradgrind in England (Dickens's *Hard Times,* 1854/1994) to Jean Brodie in Scotland (Muriel Sparks's *The Prime of Miss Jean Brodie,* 1961/2000) and no doubt we could come up with many more examples – such as E. R. Braithwaite's *To Sir With Love* (2005), or somewhat less romantically, and more recently, the two main teacher characters in Zoe Heller's *Notes on a Scandal* (2003). Any of these novels could be taken for analysis, as a means to identifying the contemporary structure of feeling through the depiction of the teacher(s) portrayed and their work.

Drama too can provide important insights. *The History Boys*, Alan Bennett's play, set in a northern English boys' grammar school in the 1980s also provides an acerbic view of the early encroachment of performativity into education in England (a theme we shall return to in Chapters 3 and 7):

> **Headmaster:** Shall I tell you what is wrong with Hector as a teacher?
> It isn't that he doesn't produce results. He does. But they are unpredictable and unquantifiable and in the current educational climate that is no use. He may well be doing his job, but there is no method that I know of that enables me to assess the job that he is doing.
> There is inspiration, certainly, but how do I quantify that? And he has no notion of boundaries. A few weeks ago I caught him teaching French. French!
> English is his subject. And I happened to hear one child singing yesterday morning, and on enquiry I find the pupils know all the words of 'When I'm cleaning Windows. George Formby. And Gracie Fields. Dorothy, what has Gracie Fields got to do with anything?

(Bennett, 2004:67)

In fact Dorothy has already warned us about the Head, a few scenes previously:

Mrs Lintott: One thing you will learn if you plan to stay in this benighted profession is that the chief enemy of culture in any school is always the Headmaster. Forgive Hector. He is trying to be the kind of teacher pupils will remember. Someone they will look back on. He impinges. Which is something one will never do.

(Bennett, 2004:50)

What extracts such as these convey is a sense of the individual teacher within society. These teachers are connecting with pupils, but also with the wider society in which they are fulfilling their role. The structure of feeling in which these events take place is captured in a way which could not be captured in social science.

Equivalent insights may also be gained from moving image representations of the teachers. We might consider the teachers in *Kes* (north of England) (Loach, 1969) or in *Gregory's Girl* (Scotland) (Forsyth, 1981) or the more contemporary teachers such as Roisin in Ken Loach's *Ae Fond Kiss* (a teacher in a Glaswegian Roman Catholic secondary school) (Loach, 2004) (see Ellsmore, 2005 or Chennault, 2006, for fuller examinations of teachers and schools in screen culture). Each of these cultural works presents us with a particular version or versions of teachers as individuals but also as a member of the teaching workforce at a particular time and place.

To possible concerns about the fictional nature of these novels and films leading to distorted or partial views of teachers, we can offer three responses. First, each of these creations is likely to carry 'truths' that are richer and may be more accurately conveyed through creative forms than is possible through social science, as Williams suggests in relation to Lawrence. Second, it may be noted that 'factual' screen portrayals of teachers, such as the 'fly on the wall' accounts of life in contemporary secondary schools (e.g. 'Educating Essex' on Channel 4), sometimes appear to be the least authentic genre on the small screen. Insightful though they may be, they rarely communicate the wider social, political or cultural contexts in which schooling is taking place. Third, we can turn to auto-/biographical accounts in order to 'validate' the creative accounts. Memoirs such as those by R. F. McKenzie (1970, *State School*) or Sybil Marshall (1963, *An Experiment in Education*), Beryl Gilroy (1976, *Black Teacher*) or Brian Simon (1998, *A Life in Education*) each conveys the nature of the authors' experience. Accounts such as these provide an important complement to the fictional work described above and could provide another important complement to social scientific study.

Whether in novels, drama or biography, film or TV, these creative or personal accounts of teachers remind us of the teacher as an individual as well as an occupational group member. We certainly see human agency in such accounts, even if it is sometimes a reactive form of agency rather than proactive, as well as often seeing the constraining parameters of a profession which is part of the institutional structure of society. It seems likely that through a more thorough study of such literature and other cultural forms, it could be possible to start to detect significant differences in the ways in which teachers are depicted within particular contexts and their respective education systems. These differences, once identified, may then lead us to a better understanding of the relationship between teacher identity and national culture. In conveying a strong sense of time and place, of the material and the cultural, these cultural representations are capable of conveying a structure of feeling, as well as the specifics of teachers' experience and lives. However, these insights should best be seen to be complementing rather than replacing those we may gain from social science.

The study of the links between national culture and teacher identity is vital; education systems are a key symbol of national culture and also a key means of reproduction of that culture. The 'knowledge workers' who represent that system, and whose function is also to carry out the intellectual labour that will lead to the re/creation of that culture, are teachers. Put simply therefore, we might argue that the condition of teachers' identities – collective and individual – is an indicator not only of the condition of an education system, but to some extent, of the condition of democracy within a society. Indeed, in Williams's terms, the condition of teachers and teaching may be seen as a significant element in the contemporary structure of feeling.

In this chapter we have explored how fictional accounts in a variety of media may bring critical aspects of the world of education to the fore, most notably through the lives and experiences of teachers. Having explored such real-life concerns mainly through considering imaginative and creative cultural forms, we turn in the next chapter, to consider the way Raymond Williams examined schooling in Britain using socio-historical analysis, another means of making sense of social experience, of 'real life'.

3

The History of Schooling in England – Education in *The Long Revolution*

Instead of the sorting and grading process, natural to a class society, we should regard human learning in a genuinely open way, as the most valuable resource we have and therefore as something which we should have to produce a special argument to limit rather than a special argument to extend.

(Williams, 1961/2011: *The Long Revolution*, p. 178)

Introduction

In this chapter we turn from the imaginative portrayal of schools and teaching in fiction to Raymond Williams's socio-historical account of the development of education in Britain, especially England. This draws heavily on his influential chapter about education in *The Long Revolution*, the book published in 1961 and which concluded his first major phase of work, following *Culture and Society* and *Border Country*. That chapter was an extended essay powerfully combining sociological and historical analysis. Recognizing the significance of education to social development in Britain in the second half of the twentieth century, Williams exposed some of the underlying tensions and divisions reflected in the way public education was developing. In the wake of this, and other contemporary analyses, many sociologists began to study the ways in which social divisions and education were interacting. The tradition of large-scale quantitative studies of educational outcomes began to emerge, from the 1960s onwards.

In the first section of this chapter I review how Williams discussed education and how he located it within the wider pattern of social change in Britain, his long revolution. I argue that his central concern in this educational discussion was with the school curriculum and the way it was shaped and contested. In the next section I discuss the contribution this analysis made to the emergence of curriculum studies, a new sub-discipline in educational studies. His contribution, I argue, was especially important to the development of the sociology of the curriculum. Such work in turn laid the foundations for another subfield of education studies to emerge later, indeed around the time of Williams's death, which became known as education policy sociology. Questions about who makes policy, and how, flourished from the late 1980s onwards, not least in response to the radical upheavals of that period, particularly in England. The final section of the chapter picks up again on the question of the 'United Kingdom'. The driving force for education policy reform in this period lay in Whitehall in London. In the jurisdictions of Wales, Northern Ireland and Scotland there were indeed many 'reforms', but as time went on, and not least after the devolution 'settlement' at the turn of the century, we saw increasing divergence around education across the four UK nations. There is little doubt that this phenomenon would have concerned Raymond Williams and using some of the work he did offer – especially on the relationship between Wales and England – we consider what these divergences signify in the wider context of 'the Union' and indeed in a post-Brexit Britain.

3.1 Education and British Society

The chapter in *The Long Revolution* most often referred to by educationists is 'Education and British society' (although it is mostly concerned with English education). The careful analysis of the development of public education provides original insight into the sociological function of schooling in a particular context. But this chapter about education is also set in the context of the general thesis of a long revolution. In the introduction to the book, Williams identifies three elements of this revolution – which will be picked up again in the chapter on education. These three are respectively the democratic revolution, the industrial revolution and the cultural revolution but might also be described as respectively the political, technological and communications revolutions. The first of these concerns the growing demands for 'self-governance' by the people. This relates not only to Britain but to the growing pressures around the world for decolonization and political independence. The industrial revolution also is a historic reference not only to the growth of manufacturing industry in the nineteenth century but to the continuing influence of science and technology on the economy. The consequences of these developments are significant not only for the organization of capital but also for the organization of labour. As Williams points out, there is an interaction between the political and the industrial elements which creates tensions within contemporary societies. The third revolution, Williams suggests, is the most difficult to interpret, but is, of course, the one which, in much of his work, most powerfully interests him. He writes:

> We speak of a cultural revolution, and we must certainly see the aspiration to extend the active process of learning, with the skills of literacy and other advanced communication, to all people rather than limited to groups, as comparable in importance to the growth of democracy and the rise of scientific industry.
> (Williams, 1961/2011:11)

So while this revolution is indeed cultural, incorporating many aspects of social life and communication, and while at this point in *The Long Revolution*, he is clearly thinking on a global basis about change around the world, nevertheless we can see how he is positioning organized forms of education as a fundamental aspect of this revolution, which underpins his subsequent analysis of the British (or English) case.

In his preface to the 2011 edition of *The Long Revolution*, Anthony Barnett (one of the three *Politics and Letters* interlocutors) also uses a threefold typology to explain the distinctiveness of Williams's long revolution; this offers a helpful backdrop to our discussion of education. He says that Williams's distinctive approach is based on the recognition of: difficulty, a complex unity and humanity. The first of these refers to the difficulty of making sense of something we are part of – we cannot separate our own experience from the phenomena we are investigating. This leads, Barnett suggests, to Williams opposing easy answers 'whether in politics (especially on the left), in the market place or culture at large' (Barnett, 2011:viii). The complex unity indicates that we cannot understand any part of the long revolution without considering its relationship to other parts. 'There is a constant, gritty stress and working through of both the separate processes and their simultaneous shaping influence upon each other, which "taken as a whole" releases the energy of change' (Barnett, 2011:ix). Third, Williams's humanity is a recognition of the significance of human agency and his opposition to many established political institutions:

> Profoundly loyal to the potential humanity of his side but determined to repudiate the cynical inhumanity of its various political forms, whether mandarin paternalism, bureaucratic trade unionism or police-state Communism, perhaps

the deepest motivation behind Williams' argument is his insistence of the creative potential of self-government.

(Barnett, 2011:xi)

In the chapter to be examined here we see evidence of all three of Barnett's themes. This, together with the three elements of revolution identified by Williams himself, was what made it such an original analysis of state education in Britain.

The chapter begins with the assertion: 'There are clear and obvious connexions between the quality of a culture and the quality of its system of education' (Williams, 1961/2011:153). He then immediately goes on to point out a difficulty with making assumptions about any education system:

> Yet we speak sometimes as if education were a fixed abstraction, a settled body of teaching and learning, and as if the only problem it presents to us is that of distribution: this amount, for this period of time, to this or that group … It is not only that the way in which education is organised can be seen to express, consciously and unconsciously, the wider organisation of a culture and a society, so that what has been thought of as a simple distribution is in fact an active shaping to particular social ends. It is also that the content of education, which is subject to great historical variation, again expresses, again both consciously and unconsciously, certain basic elements in the culture, what is thought of as 'an education' being in fact a particular selection, a particular set of emphases and omissions.
>
> (Williams, 1961/2011)

The rest of Williams's chapter is in effect a detailed socio-historical justification of this – at the time – radical thesis. The recognition that any curriculum is a selection from a wider culture and that education systems have 'particular social ends' were among themes picked up by educationists and sociologists in particular, as we shall see later in this chapter. But first we examine in more detail how Williams himself supported these insights and explore some of their then contemporary implications.

He starts by suggesting that there are three 'general purposes' of education systems. First is the 'training' (his word) of members of a group to an accepted 'social character'. Second, there is the 'teaching' (again, his word) of particular skills. The third is what he calls a 'general education', or drawing on a term used by Fred Clarke (one of the first prominent twentieth-century English 'educationists'), 'education for culture'. We see here again that now-familiar triumvirate of politics, economy and culture. In his dated, gendered language Williams summarizes these purposes thus:

> Schematically one can say that a child must be taught, first, the accepted behaviour and values of his society; second, the general knowledge and attitudes appropriate to an educated man; and, third, a particular skill by which he will earn his living and contribute to the welfare of his society.
>
> (Williams, 1961/2011:155)

We are then provided with an historical account of the development of formal education in England, starting in the sixth century with schools associated with cathedrals and monasteries, the purpose of which was to train monks and priests. These schools taught either Latin or religious singing, and the former were known as grammar schools – a term that would continue to be important in English educational parlance. These grammar schools later came to teach a wider range of subjects, for example: grammar, rhetoric, law, poetry, astronomy, natural history, arithmetic, geometry, music and the Scriptures. The idea of a university emerged in England in the thirteenth century in Oxford, with the establishment of early colleges. Williams suggests that here were the beginnings of the concept of a liberal education, albeit within a strongly Christian framework. By the end of the fifteenth century, several independent schools had been established, including the colleges at Winchester and Eton, associated with colleges at Oxford and Cambridge universities. This provision was almost entirely for boys from the wealthy classes in society, although parallel systems of apprenticeship and chivalry also existed. 'The labouring poor', Williams notes, 'were largely left out of account' (Williams, 1961/2011:180).

The next section of Williams's chapter discusses the impact of the Reformation. Grammar schools continued to be important, but were often less directly tied to the Church. In terms of what was taught in these schools, Williams notes: 'Greek and sometimes Hebrew were added to the main Latin curriculum, and the main gain was an expansion of the study of literature' (Williams, 1961/2011:181). In the seventeenth century, nonconformists, feeling discriminated against by the existing traditional institutions, started to set up their own. Williams suggests that the best of these schools and universities led the way in defining a new form of education. He says:

> Here, for the first time, the curriculum begins to take its modern shape, with the addition of mathematics, geography, modern languages and, crucially, the physical sciences.
>
> (Williams, 1961/2011:163)

He also makes brief reference to what would now be called primary education, with a range of provision from preparatory schools for the elite schools, through to 'Charity Schools', the purpose of which was often the 'moral rescue' of the poor. Then he notes:

> By the last quarter of the eighteenth century, with the quickening pace of the Industrial Revolution, the whole educational system was under new pressures which would eventually transform it.
>
> (Williams, 1961/2011:164)

Indeed, this is the point, he suggests, at which 'a new kind of class-determined education' emerges, in parallel with the contemporary development of the class system itself, as society was transformed by the growth of industrial capitalism – the wider impact of which Williams was so fervently interested in with his analysis of literature.

Higher education had become exclusive; the new educational institutions available included industrial schools and Sunday schools (for adults as well as children). Here students would mainly learn to read the Bible – all other subjects were seen as dangerous, unnecessary and/or harmful to the working class. Williams tracks the development of these schools through the nineteenth century, and finds a broadening of the curriculum, to include writing (as well as reading) and arithmetic – this then was the period during which the now somewhat arcane notion of 'the three Rs' was established.

The selective and elitist nature of what we now refer to in England as 'the public schools', actually private, independent (largely) fee-paying schools, was consolidated through the Public Schools Act in 1868. The Taunton Commission of 1869 envisaged three grades of secondary schools essentially along social class lines: the top grade for upper- and upper-middle-class boys, providing a liberal education to the age of 18; the second grade for the bulk of the middle class up to the age of 16, preparing boys for the Army and the Civil Service and newer professions; and the third, preparing lower-middle-class boys as tradesmen or 'superior artisans'. Girls' secondary education, Williams notes, started in Wales in 1889. Local Education Authorities were established in 1902. When the leaving age for elementary schools was raised to fourteen, there was no longer any need for the third-grade secondary school. Several more university colleges were established in the late nineteenth century, and this leads Williams to say:

> The nineteenth-century achievement is evidently a major reorganisation of elementary, secondary and university education, along lines which in general

we still follow. Both in kinds of institution, and in the matter and manner of education, it shows the reorganisation of learning by a radically changed society, in which the growth of industry and democracy were the leading elements, and in terms of change both in the dominant social character and in types of adult work.

(Williams, 1961/2011:170)

It is here that Williams defines the three ideologies that have shaped the form in which education in England was emerging. He suggests that there were those who believed that the whole population should be educated to a basic level; this was argued for not only by the working class itself who demanded education but also by those who saw that only this would help to meet the needs of the expanding economy. This alliance of forces he called 'the public educators'. The second grouping, 'the industrial trainers', saw the need for actual preparation for work as essential, including not only necessary skills but also the development of the 'required social character – habits of regularity, "self-discipline", obedience and trained effort' (Williams, 1961/2011:171). Then the third group, the 'old humanists', persisted in stressing the importance of a 'liberal education' as a 'civilizing' influence. These three groupings were not necessarily discrete, but there were nevertheless frequent strong tensions between them and the ways in which structures and curricula of education were developed in the twentieth century very much reflect the struggles between these forces. Williams suggests that at the end of the nineteenth century, the industrial trainers were dominant. As we shall discuss later, the same dominance may very well be present in the state education provided in England in the early twenty-first century. The final section of 'Education and British Society' considers developments in the twentieth century. From the 1930s, primary schools had largely replaced the elementary school provision and now took pupils until eleven years of age. Williams notes that this signified the success of the public educators – this was a universal, comprehensive provision with a common curriculum, albeit for younger children only.

At the time Williams was writing, the Education Act of 1944 was only about fifteen years old. In the wake of the Second World War and as part of what is often referred to as 'the social democratic settlement' (see Hennessy, 1992; Centre for Contemporary Cultural Studies, 1981) state-provided secondary education (there was still, of course, a significant private sector) was to be universally available and was to be restructured in a tripartite manner: grammar, secondary modern and technical schools. These categories roughly correspond to the three grades proposed by the Taunton Commission all those years ago. In reality very few of the third-grade schools were ever established and the system became mainly a dual or bipartite one of grammar and secondary modern schools. Admission to the grammar schools was selective, with children sitting the '11plus' examination during their last year of primary school. The curriculum of the grammar school was predominantly within the liberal education mode favoured by the old humanists, whereas the secondary modern curriculum was much more in line with the priorities of the industrial trainers. These two approaches to curricula remind us that, in Williams's terms, different cultural selections were being made for each sector. The fact that secondary education was now provided for all students up to the age of fourteen (and soon fifteen) may be seen as a success for the public educator lobby.

Williams was in no doubt that the fundamental organization of secondary schooling at this point was along social class lines – he was anticipating many more technical schools than were actually established and so the three types of schools were in essence: (1) the grammar school for the upper and middle classes (although many upper-class children would still be in the independent private sector); (2) the secondary modern for the more 'upwardly mobile' working class and (3) the technical school for the rump of the working class (my words, not Williams's). Significantly, Williams notes that the language and rationale used to support the tripartite system are not based on social class but rather on the language of 'intelligence'. These different types of school were being provided to offer children of different 'levels of intelligence' an education appropriate to that level. Considerable controversy developed during the 1960s about the use of 'intelligence' and 'IQ' as a basis for sorting children into different groups (see Simon, 1971). Drawing partly on the work of the psychologist P. E. Vernon, Williams asserts:

> To take intelligence as a fixed quantity, from the ordinary thinking of mechanical materialism, is a denial of the realities of growth and of intelligence itself, in the final interest of a particular model of the social system. How else can we explain the very odd principle that has been built into modern English education – that those who are slowest to learn should have the shortest time in which to learn, while those who learn quickly will be able to extend the process for as much as seven years beyond them? This is the reality of 'equality of opportunity', which is a very different thing from real social equality.
>
> (Williams, 1961/2011:177)

Williams is prescient here – the arguments he is developing became particularly important during this period and, by the later 1960s, led to the proliferation of 'comprehensive' schools, promoted especially by the Labour Party (see Jones, 2003). Arguments about intelligence persisted, however, with many schools that were described as comprehensive dividing their students into 'streams' or adopting 'ability grouping', based on the continuing influence of ideas about fixed intelligence (Jackson, 1966).

The chapter concludes with Williams offering not only a critique of the school curriculum of the day, and an attack on examinations based on memory tests, he also calls for the school leaving age to be raised (which it subsequently was – to 16) and actually sets out proposals for what we would now call a core curriculum, which I abridge here for the sake of brevity. As a basis for discussion, he suggests these are the essentials:

a) English and mathematics;
b) general knowledge of ourselves and our environment, drawing on:
   i biology and psychology;
   ii social history, law and political institutions, sociology, descriptive economics, geography including actual industry and trade;
   iii physics and chemistry;
c) history and criticism of literature, the visual arts, music, dramatic performance, landscape and architecture;
d) extensive practice of democratic procedures and in the use of libraries and media;
e) introduction to at least one other culture.

(Williams, 1961/2011:184–5)

He also calls for much more imaginative provision through a greater variety of institutions for the post-16 age group, suggesting schools are not necessarily the best environment for these students.

His final words, anticipating that his ideas will be described as Utopian, clearly put education at the centre of the long revolution which will bring class divisions in British society to an end.

> The privileges and barriers, of an inherited kind, will in any case go down. It is only a question of whether we replace them by the free play of the market, or by a public education designed to express and create the values of an educated democracy and a common culture.
>
> (Williams, 1961/2011:186)

If Williams had lived to see the full realization of neoliberalism and its impact on social policy, including education, he would no doubt have been distraught.

He might also have been angry enough to lead opposition against the many 'reforms' that have increased division and in many ways returned us to those elements of the nineteenth-century traditions in education he was so keen to replace with community-based, inclusive initiatives such as common schooling and a core curriculum. In the subsequent sections of the present chapter we will examine in more depth how Williams's thinking on the public provision of education, even though largely expressed through this one chapter in *The Long Revolution*, has inspired other educationists in their thinking.

Williams's chapter is indeed powerful but has two significant weaknesses. The first is that it does not fulfil its title – it is not about education and British society – it is almost entirely about education in England. Wales is mentioned a couple of times as one might expect, but sadly, Scotland – neither its universities (ancient and modern) nor its much more universal approach to secondary schooling – is discussed, and they could well have been given as examples of how alternative approaches might actually be possible in England. Second, the issues around gender in education are largely ignored. Education has an important contribution to make to our understanding of democracy, not least through links between provision of schooling for girls (which he does touch on) and universal suffrage. But there are also important issues about gender and the teaching profession, which link with social mobility as well as with questions around the feminization of the teacher workforce.

3.2 Understanding the School Curriculum

The influence of the chapter on education in *The Long Revolution* was profound. The 1960s was a period of considerable development in the field of education studies in Britain and indeed elsewhere. Part of the reason for this development was the increasing 'academicization' of teacher education. Trainee teachers were undertaking prolonged periods of study at colleges of education and, increasingly, at universities. By the end of the decade it was common for intending primary school teachers to follow a three-year programme of study leading to a Certificate in Education or a Bachelor of Education degree. Some of these students were extending their studies by an extra year in order to complete an honours degree. At the beginning of the 1960s, many secondary teachers still entered the profession without any specialist training, but by the end of the decade studying at a university or college for at least a year had become the norm.

In Britain, four particular fields of study were established during this period as the 'foundations' of education studies, respectively, the philosophy, history, psychology and sociology of education. It was a period of prolific publication in these fields including, for example, a series of books edited by J. W. Tibble, called *The Students Library of Education* (sic), published by Routledge and Kegan Paul.[1] Many of the authors were based in universities with education departments, including London, Leicester and Bristol (see Tibble, 1966).

Teacher education programmes developed into a mixture of applied and theoretical studies. For example, courses on the teaching of reading, physical education and health education on the one hand were offered at the same time as courses on 'great ideas of the twentieth century', 'education and equality' and 'the social psychology of learning' on the other. Among the more theoretical courses were some which related directly to the issues around the school curriculum. These might well be called 'Curriculum Theory' or 'Curriculum Studies'. Such a subfield had developed strongly in the United States and many of the initial reference points were located there. This interdisciplinary field drew on all four foundation disciplines in asking questions such as: What determines the nature of a curriculum and how are the aims and objectives of education translated into the curriculum? What were less common in these US studies though were questions about *who* determines the school curriculum and with what authority, the very questions that arise from Williams's analysis of education in England.

It was thus during the 1960s that the subfield of curriculum studies developed in Britain and when Williams's account became so influential. Questions about the purposes of education had been raised by many scholars (e.g. Nisbet, 1957) and social commentators throughout the twentieth century and had been the subject of major government reports. But the more specific focus on the way in which the curriculum is determined and shaped really came to the fore in the 1960s. By the end of the decade a range of radical ideas, for example about free schools[2] and the 'deschooling' of society, were beginning to be passionately debated (see for example Illich, 1970; Dennison, 1969; Goodman, 1971). The 1960s were a critical time in the development of education studies in Britain and elsewhere.

The sociology of education during the 1960s was largely within the large-scale quantitative tradition of analysing the connections between social class and educational outcomes. The kinds of studies undertaken by A. H. Halsey with Jean Floud and others were highly influential and represented the application of mainstream sociology to education (see Floud, Halsey and Martin, 1956, or, for later follow-up, Halsey, Heath and Ridge, 1980). But during the 1960s there was increasing interest in the processes of education, that is, what was actually happening in schools and classrooms which led to the differential outcomes so well identified by the sociologists of the day. Influences from anthropology were important as well, as were research methodologies such as symbolic interactionism and phenomenology that led to groundbreaking studies of language within education and the processes of social differentiation

By the beginning of the 1970s the so-called New Sociology of Education had been established with the defining text being a collection edited by Michael F. D. Young at the London Institute of Education, with the provocative title of *Knowledge and Control* (Young, 1971). With the subtitle of 'New Directions for the Sociology of Education', *Knowledge and Control* has become a seminal text in education studies. Included in it are a long introductory essay by Young himself; the important paper by the sociologist of education Basil Bernstein, called 'On the classification and framing of educational knowledge';[3] two contributions by the French sociologist Pierre Bourdieu and an innovative account of 'Classroom knowledge' by Nell Keddie. It is difficult to overstate the significance of this collection in education studies as a field. We find the first reference to Raymond Williams early in Young's introductory essay where he is bemoaning the lack of consideration given to the content of education by sociologists either in Britain or in the United States. He notes that non-sociologists have given some consideration to such matters; however, he suggests:

> Even Raymond Williams, who comes nearest to finding a sociological alternative [referencing here *Culture and Society* and *The Long Revolution*], has not been able to develop a framework for analysing how styles, media and forms of presentation in the 'arts' are socially constructed, and are the historical products of the shared activities of those involved.
>
> (Young, 1971:10)

In response to this we might point out that Williams never claimed to be a sociologist, and second, that even if he did not provide a 'framework' he certainly did provide vitally important starting points for sociologists to build upon – as we shall see.

In the subsequent chapter 'Curricula as Socially Organised Knowledge', Young returns to Williams in a more positive way. He suggests Williams identifies four (rather than three as I suggested) 'distinct sets of educational philosophies or ideologies which rationalize different emphases in the selection of the content of curricula, and relates these to the social position of those who hold them'. Young presents these in the following table:

	Ideology	Social position	Educational policies
1	Liberal/ conservative	Aristocracy/gentry	Non-vocational – the 'educated' man, an emphasis on character
2	Bourgeois	Merchant and professional classes	Higher vocational and professional courses. Education as access to desired position
3	Democratic	Radical reformers	Expansionist – 'education for all'
4	Populist/ proletarian	Working classes/ subordinate groups	Student relevance, choice, participation

(Young, 1971:29)

'In placing curricular developments in their historical context,' Young goes on to say, 'Williams's chapter is original and insightful though inevitably lacking in substantive evidence. It is only regrettable that in the intervening nine years no sociologist has followed it up' (Young, 1971:29). The first of Pierre Bourdieu's two chapters on 'Intellectual field and creative project' makes reference to the same pair of Williams's books, but draw on Williams's more general cultural and aesthetic theory rather than on the chapter on education in Britain. The final chapter in Young's collection, by Ioan Davies, also makes passing reference to Williams's 'Marxist critique of culture' in discussing ideologies in education.

Class, Culture and the Curriculum (Lawton, 1975) was published in the Students Library of Education series. It was written by Dennis Lawton, another curriculum specialist at the London Institute of Education. Lawton draws heavily on Williams's chapter from *The Long Revolution* to discuss the links between culture and the curriculum. He contrasts Williams's ideas with those of G. H. Bantock and Paul Hirst, both also contemporary curriculum theorists. Lawton's thesis is that 'how one sees culture determines one's attitude to education and to curriculum planning' (Lawton, 1975: 25). Where Bantock distinguished high and low culture and called for different curricula for different social groups, Hirst saw knowledge as 'culture-free' and distinguished different 'forms of knowledge' that should be drawn upon to create the curriculum. Williams, by contrast, called for a common curriculum, which is radically different from the prevailing largely nineteenth-century models existing at that time. Lawton's book turns into a call for the introduction of 'a common culture curriculum' for all schools and sets out proposals that are closely aligned to those set out by Williams, discussed in the previous section.

In the 1985 book *Sociology and School Knowledge*, Geoff Whitty offers a critique of Lawton's curriculum model but also again draws heavily on Williams at several points (Whitty, 1985). One distinctive contribution he makes is to link Williams's three groups of interests in the curriculum with the debates emerging in relation to the contemporary curriculum and to contemporary political groupings. The 'Black Papers' on education – a series of short publications in the 1970s – had provoked considerable hostility within the education community, with their claims that education in England was being taken over by radical, progressive and even subversive liberals. Whitty links the industrial trainers to those who were calling for greater 'relevance' in the curriculum to meet the needs of the modern economy. The universities, however, he suggests, are closely aligned to the old humanist lobby, wishing to preserve traditional subjects and disciplines. This leads to them supporting the independent schools where such a curriculum was still very much dominant. Whitty also implies some overlap here with the Black Paper writers and with some sections of the Conservative Party. The contemporary manifestation of the public educators, he suggests, 'consists of the teaching profession, the labour movement and those parental pressure groups that are part of the state education lobby' (Whitty, 1985:115). Later in this book, Whitty also spells out an issue that Williams did not, the exclusive effects of the mainstream curriculum. While Williams certainly recognized the class basis of the curriculum, Whitty points out other ways in which it excludes significant groups:

> When one considers the wealth of sociological work that documents the social bases of these curriculum models, it is scarcely surprising that working-class groups, blacks and women have gained so little of value from exposure to such curricula. The academic curriculum reflects what Williams (1965)[4] called a 'selective tradition' and much of it still represents the traditional culture of an elite as the only worthwhile knowledge.
>
> (Whitty, 1985:173)

Michael Apple, a leading US curriculum scholar (and a close associate of Whitty's), also drew heavily on Williams's work in several of his publications. As early as 1979, he was referring to Williams's work to explore the hegemonic aspects of state education systems, and seeking to both expose and oppose injustices in these systems. He says:

> In my discussion, I shall often draw upon the work of the social and cultural critic Raymond Williams. While he is not too well known among educators (and this is a distinct pity[5]) his continuing work on the relationship between the control of the form and content of culture and the growth of economic institutions and practices which surround us all can serve as a model, both personally and

conceptually, for the kind of progressive arguments and commitments this approach entails.

(Apple, 1979:3)

Apple draws on several of Williams's later works (to which we will be turning in later chapters of this book) to underpin his arguments about the point that schools act as 'agents of cultural and ideological hegemony' (Apple, 1979:6). Frequently he pairs Williams's name with that of Antonio Gramsci (see Chapter 5) – two key sources for making links between hegemony, education and the selective tradition in curriculum construction, which, he argues, demonstrate, in capitalist societies, how schools serve to reproduce existing social relations, with all of their iniquities. In *Education and Power*, an analysis of how education systems can promote (or counter) hegemony, he draws on the idea that the curriculum is founded in a 'selective tradition', pointing out that to consider what is omitted from a curriculum is as important as examining what is in it (Apple, 1982:31).[6]

In reviewing the emergence and development of education studies, in England and the United States, we can see that the contribution of Williams's critical analysis of English education, most explicitly in *The Long Revolution*, but also developed in other places, is indeed significant. He played a major part in alerting us to the significance of the history of schooling, the processes of selection in constructing a curriculum and the influence of powerful interest groups on education policy. It is to policymaking in education that we now turn.

3.3 The Construction of Education Policy

If the chapter on education in *The Long Revolution* did much to stimulate the development of curriculum studies in the United Kingdom, United States and elsewhere, it also provided a stimulus for another significant development in education studies. The study of education policy had been an interest of historians of education, economists and political scientists for many years, but from the 1960s onwards, there was considerable academic interest in the way in which education policy was made and by whom. Historians such as Brian Simon and Harold Silver traced the ways in which education was being reshaped during the nineteenth and twentieth centuries (see, for example, Simon, 1994 and Silver, 1980). The economics of education in the second half of the century were examined closely by John Vaizey (e.g. Vaizey, 1958) and, although this subfield of education studies has become less visible since that time, there is still important work being undertaken which links education and employment (e.g. Brown and Lauder, 1992). In political science the most influential work in England before the 1980s was arguably that carried out by Maurice Kogan, a civil servant in the (then) Department of Education and Science (DES) before taking up a post as Professor of Government and Social Administration at Brunel University. Using his insider knowledge as a starting point, he demonstrated the way in which education policy was made and in particular how a range of interest groups were able to influence and shape the policy that emerged through the parliamentary process (Kogan, 1975). Kogan is especially well known for his thesis that education policy was being made – at that time – through what he called 'a partnership' between central government, local government and teachers. His analysis was not based on a view of a class-divided society, but rather that of a continuing contest between interest groups, which, in the end, would lead to some kind of consensus.

However, such a view of the policy process began to look increasingly inappropriate as the consensus started to break up in the 1980s after the Conservative Government led by Margaret Thatcher came to power in 1979. In fact, during the 1970s, the orthodoxy of a partnership model was already being questioned by sociologists such as Roger Dale, Jenny Ozga and Martin Lawn (Dale, 1989; Ozga and Lawn, 1981), who were bringing a neo-Marxist perspective to the analysis and, in particular, examining the role of the state in serving particular class interests. By the end of the 1980s a combination of this perspective, together with a strong sociological analysis of the people actually making policy, had developed as a way of seeking to understand not only how policy was being made but who was making it and in whose interests. Important work in Scotland by McPherson and Raab (1988) had provided an impressive model for this kind of approach. They had shown the ways in which a 'policy network' of civil servants, politicians, local authority officers and teachers' leaders largely shared a common set of values, a shared 'assumptive world', which informed their approach to policymaking.

In England, where education policy had become far less consensual than in Scotland, what was of interest to sociologists was how the power struggles between different sectors of the policy community played out. In particular, the work of Stephen Ball came to the fore. Having started with an interest in the social processes internal to schools, he rapidly built a further interest in what he came to call – and this was an original term at the time – *the policy process* in education. There is no doubt that one of his inspirations was Williams's triumvirate of public educators, old humanists and industrial trainers. Much of Ball's early work was carried out in response to the radical education act of 1988, the Education Reform Act (ERA). In his study of the origins, purposes and effects of that Act (Ball, 1990) he makes extensive reference to Raymond Williams, especially *The Long Revolution*.

In the very first chapter of *Politics and Policy Making in Education*, Ball uses Williams's typology as a starting point:

> I still see Williams' basic typology of definitions as relevant to understanding contemporary struggles over the meaning and purposes of schooling, and especially the curriculum. I shall argue later that in the 1980s the public educators are in disarray and that the field of education policymaking is overshadowed by the influence of the old humanists and industrial trainers. The former are vociferously represented both in the ranks of the Conservatives' New Right, and, more modestly, are crucially ensconsed in the DES. The latter consist of a shifting and often indistinct alliance of representatives of business and finance, politicians and curriculum developers ... with a crucial power base in the DTI (Department of Trade and Industry).
>
> (Ball, 1990:5)

It is Ball's aim to develop an elaboration of the Williams typology. He also notes a suggestion made by Salter and Tapper (1981) that a fourth category of 'educational bureaucrats' should be added, although he points out that, while this grouping clearly plays a significant part in the policy process, it is not always apparent what their ideological interest is – which is the rationale for Williams's original threefold categorization. In other words the educational bureaucrats as a group may be of a different type from the original three, perhaps having the greatest commitment to some form of 'efficiency' and/or 'effectiveness' in the design and implementation of policy.

In going on to suggest that policy scholars might develop a more theoretical approach to their work, Ball invokes Michel Foucault as providing one useful set of resources from his work on the way in which 'discourses' can exert power and influence in social affairs through their promotion of forms of knowledge as truth. Foucault has continued to be a key influence on Ball's work since that time and has led him very much towards postmodern interpretations of policy. He explores the way in which, during the 1970s and 1980s, the New Right successfully promoted 'a discourse of derision' in education, targeted particularly at teachers. This, he proposes, has facilitated an upheaval in education policy:

Some aspects of the once unproblematic consensus are now beyond the pale, and policies which might have seemed like economic barbarism twenty years ago now seem right and proper.

(Ball, 1990:38)

Ball carried out a series of interviews with key stakeholders in the education policy field, whose names are listed in an appendix to his book. Through analysis of their perspectives and experiences he comes up with a reworking of Williams's categories. He suggests the DES itself maintained a stance towards 'reformist old-humanism'. But, he writes, this stance:

> can be set in antagonistic relation to three other positions within the curriculum field: the *cultural restorationism* of the New Right, the *industrial-training* lobby of the schools/industry movement and the DTI, and the *new progressivism* of the education intellectuals.
>
> (Ball, 1990:211, my emphases)

Ball concludes his analysis by reminding us of Williams's point about an education curriculum expressing 'a compromise between an inherited selection of interests and the emphasis of new interests' (Williams, 1961/2011:172). However, Ball points out, these struggles in the 1980s are not only about school knowledge, they are also about 'control over teachers and teachers' work'. He adds, '[T]he 1988 Act can also be read as signalling the break-up of a national education system' (Ball, 1990:211).

The influence of Williams on Ball is clear. As Michael Apple, whose curriculum analyses we have already considered, says, the wider impact of Williams's work in education studies, especially 'critical' education studies, is apparent.

> By providing some of the most important foundational components that led to a strengthening of the broader cultural Marxist tradition, his work has had an impact in a more indirect way as well. Thus knowingly or not, the development of educational scholarship that rests within this tradition owes a major debt to Williams.
>
> (Apple, 1993:91)

In the same essay from which this extract is taken, Apple explores the success of the New Right in establishing hegemony in education policy, especially in his own country, the United States. He ends his analysis with a call for scholarly and political action. Invoking Williams's 'journey of hope' from *The Long Revolution*, he says:

One of the places that journey of hope continues is in the real lives and experiences of those politically active teachers, parents, and students who are now struggling in such uncertain conditions to construct an education worthy of its name.

(Apple, 1993:114)

In a fascinating essay published in the same book as that in which Apple's chapter appears, Fazal Rizvi explores the contrast – what he describes as 'the fundamental incompatibility' – between Williams's concept of a self-governing democracy and what occurred in the implementation of the 1988 ERA in England. Rather like Apple's demonstration of the success of the New Right in the United States, he demonstrates how particular ideological rhetoric has been used. The Thatcher government, he writes:

> has fed on the discontent, anger, and fear of the people. Its anti-bureaucratic, anti-hierarchical, and anti-authoritarian rhetoric has sought to give people a sense of control over their lives. Its rhetoric has stressed many of the virtues that Williams celebrates – self-reliance, self-management, decentralisation, and democratic control. But ERA's *articulation* of these values has rested upon assumptions about the nature of human beings, social relations, and political organisation which are diametrically opposed to those which Williams espouses.
>
> (Rizvi, 1993:143)

We have seen the ways in which Williams's ideas have fed into 'critical education studies' and how so many of the fundamental insights he offered have now become embedded in our thinking. If we take a more recent example – and fewer educationists nowadays explicitly cite Williams – we can still detect this profound influence. Adrian Hilton was a policy adviser to the leading Conservative politician Michael Gove, who was to become Secretary of State for Education in the Coalition Government that came into being in 2010. Hilton subsequently undertook a careful analysis of the origins and development of the academies and free schools in England. The first of these had been introduced by the Labour Government of Tony Blair and the latter were developed under Gove's reign at the DfE. In seeking to tie down the ideological origins of these policies for 'self-governing' schools (and we should bear in mind Rizvi's comments above), Hilton examines the ways in which politicians on both sides of the left/right divide can apparently come to agree about some principles of school management in the contemporary world. Looking at the schooling and university backgrounds of key policymakers, many of whom he also interviewed, he comes to this conclusion:

there is manifestly a high degree of elite social reproduction through a dominant system of independent and/or selective education which inculcates the structures and values of an essentially Christian ethos, focusing on moral/character education ... While there may be inter- and intra-party differences on how to enhance democratic legitimacy, improve accountability or propagate social justice, there is an identifiable and distinct epistemic community controlling the strategy.

(Hilton, 2019:101)

This idea of a policy community with some shared and some different values and ideologies stems very much from the analysis that Williams provided on English education in the 1960s.

In 1967–8 Williams was the lead editor of *The May Day Manifesto*, which sought to set out an alternative programme of political action to that being followed by the Labour Government of the day (and we will revisit this in Chapter 5). Within that short book, there are two pages on education. The first page or so offers a sharp critique of existing provision in England, particularly highlighting the links between schooling and inequality. The last section, however, sets out an alternative vision, which one can see clearly builds on Williams's analysis in *The Long Revolution*. It is worth quoting at some length:

> The socialist alternative, of education as preparation for personal life, for democratic practice and for participation in a common and equal culture, involves several practical and urgent measures. We need to abolish a private educational provision which perpetuates social division. We need to create a genuinely comprehensive system of nursery, primary and secondary education which will be more than a matter of 'efficiency' or 'streamlining' but will break through the existing, self generating system of a class-structured inequality of expectancy and achievement. We need to shift emphasis, within what is actually taught, from the transmission of isolated academic disciplines, with marginal creative activities, to the centrality of creative self-expression and an organic inter-relation between subjects, between theory and practice.
>
> (Williams, 1968b:34–5)

3.4 Conclusion: Education in a Disunited Kingdom

The historical struggles over the curriculum in England have continued into the twenty-first century. In spite of the introduction of a National Curriculum in 1988, through the ERA, and the continuing overall dominance of the industrial trainer lobby – at least in relation to state schools – there are still major differences in the educational experiences and opportunities provided for different groups of pupils. England may be less obviously divided by social class than it was in the 1960s, but the impact of poverty on many children is still very evident (Smyth and Wrigley, 2013), while the private school sector continues to offer a predominantly old humanist curriculum and continues its strong association with ancient universities.

One of the criticisms made earlier about the chapter on education in *The Long Revolution* was the misnomer in its title 'Education and British Society', for it was almost entirely about England. In the final section of the present chapter I want to explore what Williams might have gained from considering the full implications implied in his title. He was after all deeply interested in the relationship between England and Wales, the country of his birth. This interest comes through strongly in his novels but also in *Politics and Letters*, where he recalls the colonializing tendencies of his grammar school education in Abergavenny. In some of his later writings he does discuss questions about 'Welshness' and Welsh culture and language and indeed described his own identity as 'Welsh European'.[7] In an article originally published in 1983, called simply 'Wales and England' (reprinted in *What I Came to Say*), he reflects on these matters and draws attention to the problematic nature of such discussions right at the outset:

> It can be said that the Welsh people have been oppressed by the English State for some seven centuries. Yet it can then also be said that the English people have been oppressed by the English State for even longer.
> (Williams, 1989:64)

He goes on to draw from earlier work such as *the Country and the City* and *Border Country*, to remind us of the ways in which he has explored these matters in terms of culture, language and literature, as well as politics and economics.

In the light of such views about the significance of national difference within the UK, it remains surprising that there was no serious recognition of these questions in the education chapter of *The Long Revolution*. Two major political developments that have occurred since Williams's death relate directly to these questions. The first is the devolution settlement that occurred at the end of the twentieth century, giving Wales, Scotland and Northern Ireland new levels of self-rule. Certainly the autonomy granted was 'relative', but education was one of the policy areas that was devolved to the three countries' own governments. The second is the tortuous process that the 'United Kingdom' (*sic*) has been going through in attempting to leave the European Union. While this process has fewer direct implications for education in the four nations, its cultural implications are potentially enormous, and there is little doubt that Williams, whilst being largely opposed to large-scale governmental organizations and bureaucracies, would nevertheless have argued for some communal form of remaining in the Union.

However, there is a third, rather more, insidious political question that plays into questions around education: the rise of new forms of national populism (Eatwell and Goodwin, 2018). This has been most apparent in several 'advanced' western nations, including the United Kingdom, where it has been a major factor in the debates about Europe, and in the United States, where it led to the election of a billionaire 'reality TV' presenter, Donald Trump, as President, from 2017 to 2021. In Stephen Ball's (1990) terms, such populism applied to education most obviously links to what he called the 'cultural restorationists', whose influence could be detected even during the debates around the National Curriculum in the late 1980s. The combination of neoliberalism in politics and economics with the growth of popular nationalism in the culture, notably in sections of the media, has undoubtedly shifted the terms of educational debate since Williams's time and has significantly different manifestations in each of the four major UK jurisdictions.

Williams was clear about links between education and the economy – links best represented by the industrial trainers and the public educators. But the links to national identity were in some ways underplayed in his work on education, although he was keenly alert to it in more general cultural affairs. In England the old humanists represented a particular form of national identity that was most closely associated with 'the best that has been said and thought in the world', in Matthew Arnold's terms (Arnold, 1867). But we can easily detect the importance of education in the development of national identity by considering the historical development of state education systems, as Andy Green has done in his two important socio-historical texts, *Education and State Formation* (Green, 1990), which looks at England, France and the United States, or in *Education, Globalization and the Nation State* (Green, 1997). The latter work includes consideration to how newly 'democratic' nations, whether in the former Soviet Union or in formerly colonized nations in Asia (and there are similar patterns in Africa), have prioritized their education systems as part of 'nation building'.

In Williams's later work, *Towards 2000*, there is a chapter entitled 'The Culture of Nations' in which Williams discusses questions of nationalism and national identity. This is one place where he explicitly refers to the significance of schooling in unusually acerbic language:

> When children start going to school they often learn for the first time that they are English or British or what may be. The pleasure of learning is attached to the song of a monarch or a flag. The sense of friends and neighbours is attached to a distant and commanding organisation: in Britain, now, that which ought to be spelled as it so barbarously sounds – the United Kingdom, the 'Yookay'. Selective versions of the history underlying this impressed identity are regularly presented, at every level from simple images and anecdotes to apparently serious textbook histories. The powerful feelings of wanting to belong to a society are then in a majority of these cases bonded to these large definitions.
>
> (Williams, 1983/1985:182)

The chapter is concerned with a close examination of nation, nationhood, nationalist and other related terms and – in line with the wider analysis of *Towards 2000* – concludes that the idea of the nation-state is one which effectively helps to sustain capitalist modes of production in the Western world and limits authentic forms of democracy.

Williams was very much in favour of further political devolution within Britain, not only to the four nations but also to the regions of England. In a wide-ranging and fascinating book *After Raymond Williams: Cultural Materialism and the Break-Up of Britain*, Hywel Dix (2013) examines all of these issues and links them to Williams's interest in literature, both novels and drama.[8] In calling for self-rule in Wales, Dix argues that for Williams:

> It is important to emphasize that he advocated this kind of nationalism not out of abstract chauvinism or ethnic pride, but out of a strong sense of the need for democracy. Williams was interested in finding the means by which people can direct their own lives. The question has then to be seen less as a matter of how English imperial institutions frustrate national aspirations in the peripheral areas of Scotland and Wales, and more as a matter of how the ruling-class version of nationhood hinders effective democracy at every level, including within England itself.
>
> (Dix, 2008/2013:134)

It is indeed the case since devolution at the turn of the twenty-first century that Wales has created an increasingly distinctive approach to its educational provision, interestingly appointing a Scottish former inspector of education as a chief adviser on curriculum reform. Whereas prior to devolution the education policy being determined in Whitehall at the education department was usually aimed at 'England and Wales', Scottish education policy had historically been determined through the Scottish Office, a separate government department and, although often following the English and Welsh pattern, had always had several distinctive elements, in relation to both curriculum and assessment. Northern Ireland was also usually fully in line with England and Wales, although since the escalation of internal strife in the late 1960s there had been several distinctive elements, including the provision of 'Education for Mutual Understanding'. Patterns of education provision both in schools and in terms of teacher education haven seen increasing divergence since devolution (see Paterson, 2003, on Scotland; Jones and Roderick, 2003, on Wales; Donnelly, McKeown and Osborne, 2006, on Northern Ireland; and, covering all four nations: Menter, Gallagher, Hayward and Wyse, 2015, or, on teacher education, Teacher Education Group, 2016).

The most extreme version in the UK of Williams's worst-case scenario, depicted in *The Long Revolution,* has undoubtedly occurred in England. It is here that we have come closest to the 'free play' of the market in the public provision of education, while in the other three jurisdictions, albeit with significant variation and some exceptions, we have much more evidence of 'a public education designed to express and create the values of an educated democracy and a common culture' (Williams, 1961/2011:186). But in coming to such a judgement, we are informed by Williams's highly original analysis of these matters and the insights he provided, especially into curriculum construction and into the processes of educational policymaking. The conceptual tools that he provided will be revisited in Chapter 7 and his contribution to the provision and development of adult education is the subject to which we now turn in the next chapter.

4

The Significance of Adult Education

Popular education, in any worthwhile sense, begins from a conception of human beings which, while recognizing differences of intelligence, of speed in learning, and of the desire to learn which is clearly affected by differences of environment, nevertheless insists that no man can judge for another man, that every man has a right to the facts and skills on which real judgement is based, and that, in this sense, all education depends on the acknowledgement of an ultimate human equality. This has been the guiding idea of our English adult education, and the right of students to control the processes through which they learn has, from the beginning, been central and fundamental.

(Williams, 1959b, from *The Highway* pp. 183–8,
reprinted in McIlroy and Westwood, 1993:123–4)

Introduction

We know Raymond Williams's interest in and commitment to adult education began while he was still at school and was at least partly awakened by his involvement in the International League. He gave talks and took part in other educational activities while still living at home in Pandy. Then, at Cambridge, when he returned to his undergraduate studies after the war, he gave a number of classes in towns around the Cambridgeshire fens. We have seen how, in spite of being encouraged to stay on at Cambridge to undertake a higher degree, he opted to apply for, and was appointed to, a post working for the WEA through the University of Oxford Delegacy for Extra-Mural Studies. His years in Sussex working as an adult education tutor were deeply formative in both his approach to teaching and the way in which he was able to combine his own writing with the classes he was offering. Indeed much of his early writing was derived from and aimed at the adult education classes he taught. His friend and collaborator Stuart Hall, in his own memoir, suggests Williams's time as an adult education tutor in Sussex, 'in a quiet and provincial corner of southern England', gave him 'a happily offbeat relation to the intellectual establishment' (Hall, 2017:250).

In the first section of this chapter we consider why Williams was so deeply committed to the provision of education for adults, indeed how he saw such provision as a fundamental part of the long revolution. We turn then to consider his own approach to teaching, considering the pedagogy he developed and exploring the way in which it links with, and is similar to, approaches developed elsewhere. In the third section we consider the developments in adult education which occurred during his lifetime, not least the creation of the Open University (OU), a radical departure in higher education when it was initiated in the 1960s. In the final section we explore what has happened to adult education in the years since Williams's death. Much has been lost in terms of the kinds of provision that existed during the twentieth century but we also consider whether some of the new forms of communication that have developed during the twenty-first century provide any real kind of alternative.

4.1 Education for Democracy

In gathering together much of his writing about adult education, John McIlroy, working together with Sallie Westwood, suggests that Williams's motivation for taking up the Oxford Delegacy post in Sussex as his first full-time post was as follows:

> In intellectual terms he wanted to combine the cultural radicalism of Leavis and his own 'intoxication' with practical criticism with the development of a socialist cultural position; he saw adult education as an ideal forum for this. Williams wanted very much to work in adult education because of class loyalty and identification; because of a desire as an intellectual to make a new bonding with the class that had produced him; because of the specific form his passage from the working class had taken, which focussed his attention on culture; and, because of the four years of army life had provided a pause for pondering his origins and his passage from them.
>
> (McIlroy, 1993a:273)

Williams's involvement in adult education stemmed from his personal background and from his politics. As McIlroy says:

> For Williams, involvement in adult education was first and foremost about the working class, his own relationship with the class he came from and the collective

emancipation of that class. Both directly, in terms of how adult education could help provide workers with emancipatory knowledge for the extension of working-class democracy and the best of working-class culture and, indirectly, by providing a site for his own work which would, he believed, ultimately serve the interests of those workers. The complex interrelations between education and class were to haunt his work for the rest of his life.

(McIlroy, 1993c:14)

The invaluable collection of writings gathered by McIlroy and Westwood in this volume leads McIlroy to say:

> His writings resonate with the belief in the power of education and the centrality of communication in the making of a new 'knowable' community. They are impregnated with the values of spontaneity, voluntarism, democracy, the self-governing community. The emphasis on the political importance of the personal, the ordinary, the woof and warp of people's lives, the quality of life in a society, informed both his work and the politics of the New Left – many of whose leading protagonists were involved in adult education.
>
> (McIlroy, 1993c:17)

This was a period during which there was unprecedented enthusiasm for the 'cause' of adult education as well as optimism about its potential influence. In the wake of the Second World War and the creation of the Welfare State, high-quality education for those who had missed out on earlier opportunities was seen as a key plank in the modernization of society and the promotion of a wider, more inclusive democracy, all of which were aspects of the long revolution.

However, within the work of the Oxford delegacy there seem to have been two significant tensions. One was political, the other educational. In relation to the first tension, in *Politics and Letters,* Williams referred to Thomas Hodgkin, who was in charge of the Oxford department. He said that Hodgkin ran the department:

> with a very strong and principled conception of how to develop a popular working-class education. He believed that essentially the people to do it were committed socialists. He fought hard to say that tutors had the right, when it was relevant, to declare their position in the class, but to ensure within the open structure of the class that this position was always totally challengeable, naturally subject to opposition and discussion. That approach was attacked very bitterly, of course. The whole Delegacy was seen as a Communist cell.
>
> (Williams, 1979/2015:80)

Williams is himself clear that there could be a danger of teaching 'declining into a propaganda exercise' (Williams, 1979/2015). But he was more worried about a tendency for a reverse kind of process: a takeover of adult education by the middle classes, who would use WEA provision as a form of leisure and education, rather than education leading to action. The late Roger Fieldhouse, who became Professor of Adult Education at the University of Exeter, has written more extensively about these political struggles and the factionalism that sometimes emerged within the adult education community arising from these tensions (Fieldhouse, 1993). Accusations of bias and propaganda were certainly coming to the fore during these post-war, Cold War times when forms of 'McCarthyism' were influencing discourse in Britain and indeed these anxieties and allegations continued to be propagated, especially by right-wing think tanks throughout the rest of the century, affecting mainstream education and teacher education significantly (see Jones, 1989). In his historical account of adult education in the UK, Stevens notes:

> The history of adult education is punctuated by political conflict, often bordering on outright hostility that has threatened careers and even the future of institutions themselves.
>
> (Stevens, 2015:2)

The second tension in the Delegacy had some links with the first and was really concerned with whether adult education offered by a university, especially a high-status one, should or should not replicate the forms of education offered to its resident students. Even though Williams recognized the considerable autonomy he and other tutors had, in their physical detachment from the university, he still experienced:

> constant pressure from the university: you must improve academic standards, you must get written work, there must be no crossing of subject boundaries.
>
> (Williams, 1979/2015:80)

Williams reports his experience of such criticism concerning the first class in which he started 'discussing the themes of *Culture and Society*', presumably because it was not 'straight' English literature. There was actually quite tight control of the syllabi, both by the university and by the Ministry of Education. But as well as pressures from the university to ensure high academic quality, there were also those in adult education who, with one eye on finances, wanted a more utilitarian approach, with classes that were more directly related to employment. Indeed, after he moved to Oxford in 1960 for a short period before going back to Cambridge, Williams was somewhat disillusioned to find a plan to turn Wellington Square – Rewley House, the headquarters of the Delegacy – 'into a residential college .... whose focus would be on refresher courses for young graduates who had gone into industrial management' (Williams, 1979/2015:81). It was also true that for Williams, as for adult education tutors all around the country, the number of students from working-class backgrounds attending the courses and classes provided had been falling steadily. Adult education was increasingly becoming a place of leisure and recreation for the middle classes, including a high proportion of women.

4.2 Curriculum and Pedagogy in Adult Education

Williams's approach to teaching in adult education at this stage of his life, in relation to both the curriculum and the pedagogy he practised, is in many ways most clearly demonstrated in *Reading and Criticism*, his first published book, which emerged from the classes in Sussex. The curriculum, set out in that book, was based on his own literary education, focussing on poetry, drama and fiction, mostly from English writers. He claims that the ideas and methods within the book are not new (Williams, 1950:ix), although this is not strictly true. In its close focus on reading, Williams is emphasizing the importance of skills in textual analysis. It is not his students' knowledge of literature, its history or its social significance on which he is concentrating; he is more concerned with the development of their skills. However, somewhat paradoxically, in building upon his 'intoxication' with practical criticism, Williams was beginning to develop his distinctive ideas about the ways in which literature could be read, ways which revealed much about the society from which it was drawn. This would underlie what he would come to term the 'structure of feeling'. Following Leavis and others working under the umbrella of 'practical criticism', he was committed to the idea that meaning and significance could be derived almost entirely from the text itself. He argued that 'contextualising' writing through separate readings of history or biography was unnecessary. His almost obsessive examination of particular words had started by this time (and, as we saw in Chapter 1, was the basis of *Culture and Society* and then later the entire focus of *Keywords*), with one word – culture – emerging as having special significance (more of this later, in Chapter 5).

In an appendix to *Reading and Criticism*, Williams sets out a suggested syllabus for a four-year programme of study. The first year, called 'An Introduction to Reading', consists of four sections. In the first section, newspaper extracts and advertisements are introduced for 'pre-literary analysis'; then short extracts of poems and prose are analysed before shorter and then longer complete literary works. The second and third years of the syllabus are both headed 'Reading in Practice'; the second year is concerned with 'Modern Literature' and the third year with 'General Literature': poems and plays written before the twentieth century. In the fourth year a 'Special Study' is undertaken, either 'a special period of literature' – examples include Elizabethan drama, the novel since Henry James, 'Study of a special form over a longer period' or 'Correlated study of the literature and social history of a period'. Intriguingly, he says of this last topic for special study:

> This has been attempted for Literature and Society 1789–1832. The subject is obviously too large, but under certain conditions it might profitably be undertaken.
>
> (Williams, 1950:140)

If this gives us a sense of *what* he was teaching, we turn now to the question of *how* he taught. McIlroy describes Williams's approach to classroom teaching in adult education.

> In the classroom he was usually a close listener, courteous and restrained, suggestive, reflective, undogmatic: 'The objection as a matter of fact is not to telling anyone anything. It is a question of how one tells them, and how one would expect to be told oneself'. Williams saw teaching as the guiding of discovery; if possible, collective discovery. His later writings were freighted with the lessons he learned in the classroom. Pedagogy was organic to philosophy.
>
> (McIlroy, 1993c:6)[1]

McIlroy notes the tension in adult education between 'lecturing' and student-led discussion. In his literature classes, Williams went beyond the approach he had experienced at Cambridge:

> by supplementing set texts with duplicated poems and prose extracts which were discussed in class and used as the basis for written work. The tutor became far more passive and the class more active and student-centred, with the tutor summarising, distinguishing between what he thought to be valid and invalid approaches and offering his own judgements before handing back to the group.
>
> (McIlroy, 1993a:288)

It is reported by McIlroy that this approach could lead to extended periods of silence in the classes which would nevertheless eventually be broken by sustained animated discussions among the students. He describes Williams's view of students:

> What made Williams the adult education tutor *par excellence* was his deep and abiding understanding that adult education was for its students, not for its professionals. It induced in him a combination of respect for rigour regarding content and disrespect for established and often ossified forms which came between the student and learning. Having established mastery over the orthodox literature curriculum, he was not content to teach this in orthodox ways and sought to transform literature teaching and to develop its techniques for use in related areas. He did this by focusing on the method which would enable him to connect with his students and make knowledge and skills available to them.
> (McIlroy, 1993a:298)

Other than in shorter articles written for adult education journals and a few remarks in his later work, including *Politics and Letters*, Williams did not offer any extensive views on teaching and learning, or any theoretical insights on pedagogy. This gave rise to some criticism within the adult education community, but has been firmly rebutted by Westgate (2010) and McIlroy (1993a), among others, mainly on the grounds that his actions were demonstrably and positively influential on the practices that were developing at the time. It is clear that his approach to teaching was distinctive and grounded in his personal and political values. He did not relish the institutionalization of teaching and learning. He made this clear writing in *The Guardian* newspaper in 1968, when he contrasted the constraints of in-house university teaching with his experiences of adult education:

> I have tried in my own teaching – lectures, classes and supervisions – to use methods I learned in adult education. But the difficulty of which everyone is aware is the examination system, which exerts its own, often separate disciplines. To have been free of that in adult education, was of course, an advantage.
> (Williams, 1968b:244)

These words were written at a time of crisis in British universities, with great student unrest, mirroring that in France, the United States and elsewhere, but for Williams, students' concerns confirmed the deep significance of adult education:

> I think the student movement has been right to identify the present educational and administrative structure with the values of the bourgeois society which, in the

nineteenth century, created it: the rigid selection and distribution of specialised minority roles, as against the idea of public education, in which the whole society is seen as a learning process, and in which, consequently, access is open, not only for all people but for all their questions, across the arbitrary divisions of quotas and subjects. This is what adult education embodied, as a demand, at once educational and social; in fact political; and there is good evidence to show that, in its genuine form, this extending education makes higher rather than lower demands, not only in intellectual quality (which a specialism can protect but not extend) but also, and crucially, in human recognition and response.

(Williams, 1968b:245)

Another great socialist and educator, Paulo Freire, although working in a very different context from Williams, contrasted 'banking education' with 'problem-solving education'. By 'banking education' he was suggesting that students become a kind of passive depository into which the teacher deposits information, often learned through rote. Freire's work came to attention in Britain (and in the United States) in the wake of these student uprisings and has inspired many radical educators ever since. In books such as *Cultural Action for Freedom* and *Pedagogy of the Oppressed*[2] (Freire, 1972a, b), Freire set out his approach. Working with illiterate villagers in Brazil, Freire had developed pedagogical principles similar in their essence to those adopted by Williams. Through this learning, many of the workers became politicized and challenged their landowners and employers. Freire was exiled from Brazil but continued to work in a number of other countries.

Hywel Dix (some of whose work was referred to earlier in this chapter) has developed the comparison between Williams's and Freire's pedagogy, in an essay with the title 'The pedagogy of cultural materialism: Paulo Freire and Raymond Williams'.[3] Drawing a number of parallels between them (including the fact they were both born in 1921) and acknowledging the very different contexts, Dix suggests:

The ultimate goal of both Williams and Freire was to inaugurate a kind of educational practice that would overcome the hierarchical distinction between teacher and taught, and therefore overcome also the social and political practice of dividing people up into leaders and led, masters and men. Achieving this requires an educational practice where the teacher does not exercise unquestioned authority over the student body. Rather, it requires that the distinction between active teacher and passive student be broken down, and that the teacher enter into dialogue with the students.

(Dix, 2010:87)

Such an approach is challenging for both the teacher and the student, requiring skilful judgement about the content and approach which will preserve this egalitarian relationship; nevertheless, it is one which has inspired many a radical educator over the years (see for example Apple, 2013).

McIlroy suggests that Williams's contribution to adult education was immense. He wrote:

> *The Long Revolution* was an inspirational book and it is difficult now to experience its powerful impact in the early 1960s. To the idea of culture as *a way of life* and the struggle for a *common culture* Williams now added the central idea of a *learning community*, the cultural empowerment of the majority of the population, the excluded and the disinherited who through the third phase of revolution would achieve enfranchisement in the cultural powers of meaning generation. The Learning Community reflected his experience of the democratic educational participation of the WEA but its realisation would close the existing gap between education and life. These three central, intertwined ideas represented a fresh restatement of radical adult education and a programme to which existing adult education could contribute.
>
> (McIlroy, 1993a:306)

To reiterate Williams's own way of putting this, as quoted above: 'the idea of public education, in which the whole society is seen as a learning process'. While, as with his proposal that 'culture is ordinary', so this view of the whole society as a learning process may be seen as too diffuse to be of great analytical value; nevertheless it is a key underpinning idea for Williams's work, demonstrated through his fiction as well as his critical writing on culture and communication.

4.3 The Defence of Adult Education

Williams's book *Communications* was originally published in the early 1960s as a 'Penguin Special' (Williams, 1962/1966). Penguin Specials were books commissioned by the publisher and brought out speedily in response to particular cultural or political moments (*The May Day Manifesto* of 1968 was brought out under this imprint). *Communications*, as much as any book written by Williams, plants the seeds for his contribution to the development of cultural studies; it is significant that it grew out of his adult education work for the WEA.

One of the reasons Williams felt that adult education was so important during the 1950s and 1960s was because of the rapid growth of 'mass communication'.

He was greatly concerned at what he saw as a threat to democracy in the heavily commercialized interests behind the popular press and television, especially independent television, supported as it was – and is – largely by advertising revenue. In an article published in the WEA's magazine *The Highway,* he wrote:

> There is thus a constant pressure on all those who control and use these media, not to engage in the slow and careful process of popular education, but rather to seek the quick results, the easy influence, the continual simplifications and distractions of the alternative conception – the exploitation of human weakness and natural inexperience, for profit or power.
>
> (Williams, 1959b:125)

> Perhaps what we learn, finally, from our study of the contemporary mass media, of the press as of other forms, is that a conception of education is inseparable from a conception of society, and that now these great powers have been loosed, we are launched too far from any kind of compromise. We can no longer afford either partial education or partial democracy. Neither has the strength to stand against the new powers. The only strengths that will be adequate are the strengths of full democracy, of a full and wholehearted popular education, which we are learning to conceive, and which we must, with urgency, go on to bring to life.
>
> (Williams, 1959b:126)

It has been suggested by some commentators that Williams, somewhat isolated in Sussex during this period of his life, was not politically active. Extracts such as the two above surely give the lie to this – his political energy and passions were being invested in his calls for popular education and adult education available to all at a time of great threats to democracy.

In *Communications,* building on such concerns, Williams outlines a way to study the media and reveal the interests, power and ownership which lie behind the public forms of television, film, radio and the press. In the book he sets out some proposals for the teaching of these matters, writing:

> We already teach communication, in certain ways, and we also teach some practice and appreciation of the arts. Some of this work is good, but some of it is limited by assumptions taken over from old-fashioned ideas of culture and society, and some of it is even harmful.
>
> (Williams, 1962/1966: 127)

He then offers thoughts on the teaching of, respectively: speech, writing, creative expression, contemporary arts and 'the institutions', finishing with a section on 'teaching criticism'. In this final section, he writes:

I am sure that we are neglecting the world of ordinary[4] communication to which all of us, after education, go home or go on. Yet this has crucial bearings on the whole social process which education is supposed to prepare us for.

(Williams, 1962/1966:134)

He then suggests that 'There are many ways of including this ordinary world', listing nine examples:

- regular comparative reading of the range of national newspapers;
- discussion of the range of comics;
- discussion of advertisements of a particular commodity;
- discussion of selected stories in women's and teenagers' magazines;
- a comparative study of 'social images' of particular kinds of professions;
- comparative visual studies of kinds of modern architecture and design;
- regular discussions of comparable television programmes;
- repeat sessions of television programmes;
- writing reviews of a current film.

For Williams, modern forms of communication can be thought of as education in its most open sense. What these media do is 'centrally, ... teaching, and teaching financed and distributed in a much larger way than is formal education' (Williams, 1962/1966:14). In an essay on this topic, Westgate (2010) cites this statement and says:

> The culture industries have become resources for permanent education. Pointed critique of educational communicators and their means of expression required an instructor with clearly articulated methods to engage learners from their own life-worlds. Williams inspired a kind of independent inquiry from his adult education students.
>
> (Westgate, 2010:71)

Westgate then suggests that Williams's approach to teaching and learning is imbued with what has become known as 'critical pedagogy', an approach which seeks to open students' eyes to and raise their awareness of their social and political contexts. Westgate suggests that Henry Giroux, one of the best-known proponents of critical pedagogy, was clear in his acknowledgement of Williams as a key influence (see Giroux, 1983, for example).[5]

During Williams's lifetime, two major developments in post-school education appeared to begin to fulfil some of the educational ambitions for adults that were important to him. The first of these was the enormous expansion of higher education in Britain which commenced most notably in the wake of the Robbins Report of 1963 (Committee on Higher Education, 1963). The second was the creation of the Open University in the 1970s.

The Robbins Report on Higher Education was commissioned under the Conservative government led by Harold Macmillan and was welcomed and accepted by a later Conservative government led by Alec Douglas-Home (see Simon, 1991). It led to a massive expansion of provision in the sector, albeit as a binary system with two major groupings – the universities and the colleges/polytechnics. Robbins had advocated a unitary system very strongly, but the subsequent Labour Government (from 1964) maintained the division. This expansion of places, however, led, over the next two or three decades, to a vast increase in the numbers of people undertaking higher education. By 1997, and following the ending of the binary divide in 1992, the new prime minister, Tony Blair, could set a target of 50 per cent participation of 18- to 30-year-olds in English HE (the target was not actually met – although that level was reached in Scotland).

Also inspired by the Robbins Report, the Open University was a fine example of opening up higher education to a much wider community and was the first national and systematic development of the use of television for the purposes of adult education. As Williams said in *Politics and Letters*:

> the Open University, ... combined my interests in communications and in Adult Education. I supported [it] very strongly, but I also thought it could be combined with a reshaping of adult education, which ... had run into new kinds of difficulty. There could be a connection between education by television, radio and correspondence courses, and the kind of tutorial class education which had been so well developed by the WEA ... But Jennie Lee told me ... that as the Minister responsible she had decided to steer clear of the old types of adult education and set up what looked as much as possible like a conventional university, including the 'trimmings'. So that was it, that kind of assimilated even where radical initiative, and the Open University still has no properly based tutorial organization, and little of our old educational democracy.
>
> (Williams, 1979/2015:271)

Williams thus saw the Open University as an important missed opportunity for the democratization of adult education, even while supporting its premise of wider access to higher education. It was a case of an 'assimilated even when radical initiative' – you can almost hear the sigh! This was another example of his disillusionment with the Labour Party, which he usually supported in general elections.

It is curious that Williams seems to have said or written very little about the general process of widening participation in higher education. This, one might speculate, perhaps reflects his continuing ambiguity about the formal, institutionalized patterns of higher education we have already discussed. In his discussion of Williams's views on higher education, Dix suggests a distinction between 'hard' and 'soft' conceptions of a university.

> A hard university practises a programme of banking education and contributes to the continual reproduction of the dominant ideology through mobilization of a competitive ethic and selective promotion ... This is not how Williams imagined a university. Williams' concept of the university can therefore be referred to as a 'soft' university. A soft university is not restricted to one location, like a hard university. On the contrary, if it is really to be democratised, then what happens in the university must have an active relation with all the rest of society.
>
> (Dix, 2013:98)

Dix suggests that the Open University was the clearest example of such a soft institution.

4.4 Conclusion: Whatever Happened to Adult Education?

Williams expressed his concern about the state of education, including higher and adult education in *Towards 2000*. Having referred to the success of the Open University he argues:

> There can be a new range of formal learning systems, which people can use in their own time and at their own pace. This will be especially important in a period in which there are new needs for permanently available education. Yet what is now happening, in the existing institutions, is a steady pressure from a late capitalist economy and its governments to reduce education both absolutely and in kind, steadily excluding learning that offers more than a preparation for employment and an already regulated civic life.
>
> (Williams, 1983/1985:151)

In other words the Industrial Trainers were in the ascendancy. If that was the case in the 1980s what has been the experience of educational provision for adults since that time in England? Adult education provision – with the exception of the Open University – has been severely curtailed around the UK, perhaps especially in England, with local authorities and many universities withdrawing their provision. In 2020 there were just twenty-five universities in Britain offering adult education to external students. This conclusion will consider the implications of this and whether any alternatives have moved into the void created.

The language of adult education has changed and new technologies have emerged which provide opportunities and challenges. As well as continuing use of the term 'adult education', we also see reference to 'Lifelong Learning' and 'Continuing Education'. The Department at the University of Oxford, which in Williams's time it was known as the Oxford Delegacy for Extra-Mural Provision, is still based in Rewley House, but now called the Department for Continuing Education (see Goldman, 1995, for a full history).

In 2019 a report was brought out recognizing the centenary of the 1919 report on adult education, which had described provision as '*A Permanent National Necessity* ... ' This phrase became the title for the 2019 report, along with the sub-title, '*Adult Education and Lifelong Learning for 21st Century Britain*' (The Centenary Commission on Adult Education (CCAE), 2019). This report was produced by a group of leading adult educators and gives insight into the state of adult education today. It is clear that the tensions within adult education provision today are similar to those evident in mid-twentieth-century Britain:

> It has always been a challenge to most effectively balance provision for adult education and lifelong learning in support of economic prosperity, on the one hand, and for individual flourishing, social and community development and democratic engagement on the other. Over the last 20 years at least, we have got that balance wrong, focusing resources on the former and running down support for the latter. This has had damaging consequences for personal development, social fulfilment, community engagement, and the health of democracy.
> (CCAE, 2019:6)

We see here very similar themes to those with which Williams was grappling during his time working in Sussex. The following priorities are identified by the twenty-first century commission.

We have identified six areas for our focus which we explore in this Report:

i. framing and delivering a national ambition;
ii. ensuring basic skills;
iii. fostering community, democracy and dialogue;
iv. promoting creativity, innovation and informal learning;

v. securing individual learning and wellbeing; and
vi. attending to the world of work.

(CCAE, 2019:6)

But this Commission goes on to argue that, in the context of such developments as longer lifespans, political instability, economic and social inequality, threats to jobs arising from the development of artificial intelligence and the threats arising from climate change, adult education provision is more necessary than ever. They say:

> There has never been a 'golden age' of provision. However, there was steady progress until the beginning of this century. Around 11% of working age adults participated in 'learning' in the early 1990s; ten years later, it was over 20%. That put the UK clearly at the top of the European league – outstripping even the Scandinavian countries, with their long traditions of adult education.
>
> But by 2018 we were back down to under 15% participation. While the number of *full-time* entrants into Higher Education rose by 9% between 2009/10 and 2017/28, the number of *part-time* entrants fell from 470,000 to below 240,000 – a drop of 49%.

(CCAE, 2019:7)

In coming to their conclusions and setting out a list of recommendations for governments in the UK and other bodies to consider, they argue that:

> Our quality of life in the future will depend on averting a climate catastrophe. If any justification is required for providing increased educational opportunities for all, surely this is it – the importance of enabling educated discussion of such grave issues and problems, and how to go about tackling them, as individuals, communities, workplaces – and as a society.
>
> Provided such catastrophe is averted, we can expect lifetimes of up to a hundred years, with increasing numbers remaining mentally and physically fit into their 90s. Lifelong learning needs to be about individual benefit and fulfilment as well as productivity at work and social engagement – although the enhanced mental and physical health that is associated with education will in turn benefit the economy and society. A far greater investment in lifelong learning will pay off in every sense. There is no benefit to be had from further delay.

(CCAE, 2019:51)

The report makes frequent reference to the WEA, including a very interesting case study about a Green branch that has been formed. It does seem that the continuation of the WEA as a significant provider of adult education is a huge achievement and one that Williams would have applauded. In 2003 the WEA celebrated its centenary (Roberts, 2003). Its survival has been against the odds of draconian financial cutbacks and appears to have been dependent both on the decentralised nature of the organization (the internal 'democracy', as Williams put it) and on continuing support from the labour movement, including trade unions and the Labour Party. The language of social class is not evident in its discourse to any extent these days, having been replaced by phrases such as 'disadvantaged' and 'raising aspirations', these perhaps being more attractive buzzwords for the present time, especially when it comes to building political as well as financial support:

> We also have a special mission to raise aspirations and develop educational opportunities for the most disadvantaged. This includes providing basic maths, English and IT skills for employment; courses to improve health and wellbeing; creative programmes to broaden horizons and community engagement activities that encourage active citizenship.
> (From: https://www.wea.org.uk/about-us, June 2020)

The WEA currently works with a range of partner organizations, including the Open University and 'Local Enterprise Partnerships' in delivering its courses.

What of the Open University itself? Although it has experienced various difficulties of management and finance over the years, the OU continues to provide a wide range of courses – some vocationally oriented, others offering more general aspects of science, humanities and arts. The track record in the field of education is an interesting one. Initially the OU offered higher-level postgraduate programmes in education studies. This provision came under sustained attack during the 1970s for its perceived infiltration by Marxists. An account of this period – not dissimilar to the McCarthyite-like experiences at the Oxford Delegacy in the 1950s – is given by Weinbren (2010). Since that time education courses have been less radical and have included a range of initial teacher education courses as well as school leadership courses. Throughout its existence the OU has continued to specialize in distance and online learning. When the global coronavirus pandemic of 2020 developed, all British universities had to close down their face-to-face provision and rapidly develop their electronic forms of engagement with students. The OU had to make far fewer such adjustments.

It is impossible not to speculate on what Williams would have made of the great 'advances' in electronic technology made over the last thirty years. The development of the internet and the World Wide Web, the ready availability of search engines and the speed of contact and communication now available with mobile technology and platforms such as Facebook, Twitter and Instagram have all dramatically changed the face of communication (Castells, 2000). These changes have had huge social, cultural and political impacts, but have also opened up possibilities for informal learning that could barely have been foreseen in the 1960s. With these new opportunities, considerable ethical challenges around data secrecy, privacy and new forms of harassment and abuse have also arisen (Barrett-Maitland and Lynch, 2020).

In the same way that Williams saw television and radio as providing opportunities for greater democracy in adult learning, so we can see equivalent avenues of learning opening up now. The accessibility of structured courses provided in 'virtual learning environments' (VLEs) or through 'Massive Open Online Courses' (MOOCs – and these are referred to in the CCAE report) – have become important elements in educational provision. Furthermore the ease with which we can 'call up' television programmes, films and podcasts on screens – large and small – at any time, means that anyone in possession of the appropriate technology can 'self-educate'. But again, the potential for abuse and misuse of such systems must be borne in mind. As Williams taught us, we must continue to ask questions about who is creating these resources and why. What are their motives and interests?

Writing in 1993, John McIlroy suggested:

> the challenge facing adult educators has never been greater. Adult education, too, has felt the winds of privatisation, commercialisation and the market economy. The emphasis is not on the public education Williams espoused – despite the crying need for it – but on education seen as a consumption good or help up the vocational ladder. Courses about work proliferate, but are centred on professional techniques, not the social and personal meanings of work. Williams would have hated the way that education dealing with the rich, complex experience of life suggests all problems can be solved by a speedy subjection to counselling technique.
>
> (McIlroy, 1993c:19)

The attraction and occasional obsession with counselling which seems to have irked McIlroy so much in the early 1990s has not disappeared,[6] as demonstrated by the proliferation of 'self-help' literature available in bookshops, but there is evidence that cultural interests have broadened, for example, through the growth of a range of literature and music festivals, through local history groups, book groups and many other small-scale and local community-based organizations. 'Health and well-being' is one of the 'phrases for today' that reflects greater interest than ever before in personal fitness, mental health, the outdoors and nature. These all exist alongside a range of work-related provision for learning, both formal and informal. Adopting Williams's view that education is inseparable from life experience, we can propose that the range of learning opportunities across society has proliferated.

In terms of organized adult education, it is not only the OU and the WEA that continue to offer programmes of study. Some universities still offer significant provision, as do some local authorities. There continues to be a range of organizations that support such work – each with their own acronym – such as the National Institute of Adult and Continuing Education (NIACE), the Standing Conference on Universities' Teaching and Research on the Education of Adults (SCUTREA), the Universities' Association for Lifelong Learning (UALL) and journals such as *The International Journal of Lifelong Learning* and *The Journal of Adult and Continuing Education*.

It remains true that adult education is frequently marginalized in discussions about education, with schools and universities being the dominant sectors in public discourse. Nevertheless, the kinds of insights that Williams gave us, both about the importance of adult education and the ways in which popular education could influence society and culture, are as relevant as ever. As McIlroy (1993c,b) complains, the considerable scholarship derived from Williams's work all too rarely focuses on this aspect of his contribution, but in this chapter we have seen how his placing of adult education within the long revolution and his recognition of the significance of forms of communication and the influences of technology continue to provide us with fresh and important insights. The importance of adult education may never have been more important than it is today, as Stevens suggests in the contemporary context:

> Given [the] unashamedly divisive measures in schools and with so many working-class men and women in alienating jobs on poverty-level wages and zero-hours contracts, adult education is as important today as it was in the mid-nineteenth century.
>
> (Stevens, 2015:7)

So while there is little doubt that adult education provision has changed significantly since Williams's time, and continues to be under considerable economic pressures, it can be demonstrated that its actual and potential contribution to reinvigorate the long revolution remains, and indeed may be more important than ever.

5

Culture, the Academy and the Role of the Public Intellectual

> ***Intellectual*** *as a noun to indicate a particular kind of person or a person doing a particular kind of work dates effectively from eC19,[1] though there were some earlier isolated uses .... Nor can we overlook a crucial kind of opposition to groups engaged in* **intellectual** *work, who in the course of social development had acquired some independence from established institutions, in the church and in politics, and who were certainly seeking and asserting such independence through C18, C19 and C20.... Within universities the distinction is sometimes made between specialists or professionals, with limited interests, and* **intellectuals**, *with wider interests. The social tensions around the word are significant and complicated, ranging from an old kind of opposition to a group of people who use theory or even organized knowledge to make judgments on general matters, to a different but sometimes related opposition to ELITES (q.v.), who claim not only specialised but directing kinds of knowledge.*
>
> (*Keywords*, Williams, 1976:140–2)

Introduction

By whatever definition one might choose, Raymond Williams was indisputably an intellectual. In the words of his colleague Robin Blackburn, he was 'the most authoritative, consistent and original socialist thinker in the English-speaking world' (Blackburn, 1989:ix). He achieved this accolade not only through being 'an intellectual' but through his contributions to the academy and to politics. The range of his work and activity was phenomenal. Not only was he a novelist, but through his literary critical work in drama, film, television, poetry and fiction and most notably through his exploration of the very notion of 'culture', he was one of the key founding figures of the field of cultural studies – and also media studies. Beyond that, he was a significant contributor to debates on economics and politics. His deep commitment to socialism motivated his activities in these fields; he wrote and published during his lifetime many books and articles on these topics, but he was also a political activist, while, for most of his life, holding full-time academic posts, first in adult education and later at the University of Cambridge. Perhaps above all, we can see him throughout his life as a 'public educator'. Alternatively, he might be referred to, in Hilary Wainwright's term, as a 'writer-agitator' (Wainwright, 1994:78).

In this chapter we consider this extraordinary range of contributions, commencing with a discussion of the ways in which Williams examined culture and helped to develop public understanding of the term as well as its significance in our society. In so doing we pick up the educational implications of this exploration, some of which have only emerged more fully since Williams's death. We then go on to consider Williams's role as not just 'an intellectual', but as a public intellectual, or, to use Gramsci's term, an 'organic intellectual'. In the third section we focus on Williams's political activity and engagement within a number of organizations and publications as well as his commentary from outside such recognized groupings. This section also includes a discussion about his treatment of issues of 'race' and gender, areas where there has been some criticism of his position. Finally we consider how the role of the public intellectual has changed in the twenty-first century and, building on the previous chapter, noting how significant changes have been wrought in the functioning of 'the academy', in particular the university as an institution.

5.1 Culture and the Problem of 'Cultural Capital'

'Culture', Williams writes in *Keywords* (Williams, 1976:76), 'is one of the two or three most complicated words in the English language.' It is the single word, more than any other, that preoccupied Williams during his lifetime and for which he is best known in the wider academic community. In *Keywords*, using his favoured historical analytic technique, he explores its origins and changing usage, most frequently as a noun describing a process, in its early days most often relating to agriculture. He notes its increasing association with other words, such as 'cultivated' and 'civilisation', as it increasingly came to be used in relation to societies and social processes. He suggests that there are three main meanings of the word in its modern usage:

(i) the independent and abstract noun which describes a general process of intellectual, spiritual and aesthetic development, from C18;
(ii) the independent noun, whether used generally or specifically, which indicates a particular way of life, whether of a people, a period or a group, from ... C19;
(iii) the independent and abstract noun which describes the works and practices of intellectual and especially artistic activity.

(Williams, 1976:80)

Williams suggests that the third use is the most common in contemporary life, with culture often being taken to refer to music, literature, painting and sculpture, theatre and film. He suggests that the first and third uses are often closely connected, as in Matthew Arnold's *Culture and Anarchy* (Arnold, 1867).[2] The second use of the word is the one favoured by anthropologists and the one Williams himself proclaimed in such key essays as 'Culture Is Ordinary' (see Williams, 1989a). In concluding the *Keywords* analysis he notes the distinction that is often made between 'high' art as culture on the one hand, and popular art and entertainment on the other, implying the latter tend not to be seen as culture. These tensions reflect 'a real social history and a very difficult and confused phase of social and cultural development'. However, the anthropological use of the word has, he suggests, 'bypassed or effectively diminished the hostility and its associated unease and embarrassment' (Williams, 1976:82).

One of Williams's students, Terry Eagleton, pursued *The Idea of Culture*, in a book with that title, published more than twenty-four years later than *Keywords*. Here, in spite of the enormous influence Williams's work had had on his own work, he suggests that Williams's use of the word was too inclusive to be meaningful. He wrote:

the complexity of the idea of culture is nowhere more graphically illustrated than in the fact that its most eminent theorist in post-war Britain, Raymond Williams, defines it at various times to mean a standard of perfection, a habit of mind, the arts, general intellectual development, a whole way of life, a signifying system, a structure of feeling, the interrelation of elements in a way of life, and everything from economic production and the family to political institutions.

(Eagleton, 2000:36)

Perhaps the endurance of Williams's influence in the field of cultural studies demonstrates that Eagleton's criticism has had little effect. Williams's 1976 threefold definition remains useful to this day and the word has now entered common parlance in British society in a way that might even surprise him. It is a word that came to considerable prominence in the field of Education Studies from the 1970s onwards, as we shall see. Culture can now attract a wide range of adjectival forerunners such as: 'mass', 'elite', 'high', 'low', 'working class', 'common', 'youth', as well as a number of prefixes, such as 'sub-', 'counter-' and 'multi-'. All such attachments reveal further social developments and some will be explored later in this chapter. But for Williams himself, all three main definitions have significance and his work can in some ways be seen as a continuing exploration of how each relates to the others. This exploration can be traced through *Culture and Society, The Long Revolution, Communications* and *Towards 2000*. But a fuller, more explicit treatment is given in the 1981 book, called simply *Culture*, which was published in the 'Fontana New Sociology' series. Here he offers a broadly sociological view of the word. He writes:

> Cultural sociology, ... is concerned with the social processes of all cultural production, including those forms of production that can be designated as ideologies.
>
> (Williams, 1981:30)

The word 'ideologies' is important because it provided one of the connections with Marxist cultural theory and because it became a key component of the field of cultural studies then emerging, partly through the influence of Gramsci (see below). Williams acknowledged that this sociology of culture had several disciplinary starting points, namely: 'history, philosophy, literary studies, linguistics, aesthetics and social theory' (Williams, 1981). Of particular interest to educationists is his assertion that a sociology of culture must concern itself with processes of social and cultural 'reproduction'. This theme was significantly developed by educational sociologists from around the time of this publication.

In the chapter in *Culture* called 'Reproduction', Williams refers explicitly to education:

> In societies like our own there can be an effective kind of cultural reproduction within the very processes of knowledge. An educational system can promote rigorous training in reliable procedures of knowledge and analysis, so that many of us can then know and analyze. Or (as I think now commonly) it can be directed to induce an endlessly knowledgeable helplessness, in the sheer scale of what is to be known and its virtually infinite exceptions. And then at this level (but only at this level, for at some prescribed leaving age we are expected to go on and take up positions in the world) nothing is certain enough to be realisable,

and there is only the (highly specific and complex) inertia of the (relatively unknowable) 'way of the world'.

(Williams, 1981:182)

This is – for Williams – an unusually acerbic and carefully qualified attack on contemporary education at this time, written perhaps in the wake of what became called 'The Great Debate' in England following from Prime Minister James Callaghan's oft-cited 'Ruskin speech' (see Jones, 1983). Williams appears less cynical when discussing education again a few pages later in the same book:

> It is characteristic of educational systems to claim that they are transmitting 'knowledge' or 'culture' in an absolute, universally derived sense, though it is obvious that different systems, at different times and in different countries, transmit radically different selective versions of both. Moreover it is clear, as Bourdieu (1977)[3] and others have shown, that there are fundamental and necessary relations between this selective version and the existing social relations. These can be seen in the disposition of a curriculum, in the modes of selection of those who are to be educated and in what ways, and in definitions of educational (pedagogic) authority. It is then reasonable, at one level, to speak of the general educational process as a key form of cultural reproduction, which can be linked with that more general reproduction of existing social relations which is assured by existing and self-prolonging property and other economic relations, institutions of state and other political power, religious and family forms.
>
> (Williams, 1981:186)

But he cautions us about pushing the metaphor of 'reproduction' too hard and acknowledges that education systems can change 'internally' and in relation to 'other systems'. This is Williams warning us again about the pitfalls of over-determinism in our thinking about education.

Nevertheless, in writing about British society in the 1960s, whilst acknowledging that features of social class are changing, Williams stresses that our society continues to be divided by class and by culture, with the links between the two forming a major barrier to social reform (this is a key premise of *The Long Revolution*). He roundly rejects romanticized notions of working-class culture but stresses the importance of collective organizations such as the trades unions and the churches. This rejection he shared with Richard Hoggart, whose seminal text *The Uses of Literacy* was published just months before *Culture and Society*. Hoggart opens his book by saying, 'This book is about changes in working-class culture during the last thirty or forty years, in particular as they are being encouraged by mass publications' (Hoggart, 1957:9).

The overlap between this text and Williams's (and indeed the subsequent *The Long Revolution*) is remarkable. Hoggart offers definitions of the working class and proceeds to examine how the development of mass communications is reshaping the normal experiences of working-class families. The many common points of reference, including Thomas Hardy, D. H. Lawrence and George Eliot, make it hard to credit that Hoggart and Williams did not actually meet each other until August 1959, by which time their respective volumes had been completed. They had a discussion which was transcribed and published in *New Left Review* (and is reprinted in McIlroy and Westwood, 1993). In this they compared their personal experiences growing up in working-class families in respectively the Welsh borders and a northern industrial town. They also discuss the changing nature of class and the need for the development of theory by which to make sense of these changes. Hoggart has a section in his book where he writes about 'the scholarship boy', that is, the young male who is academically successful and experiences some kind of physical and social deracination, in terms that are not dissimilar to Williams's autobiographical passages, discussed in earlier chapters here. Hoggart, whose early career was also in adult education, was to become recognized as another prominent founding figure in cultural studies. Later he was to establish the Centre for Contemporary Cultural Studies (CCCS) at the University of Birmingham, a research centre at the heart of the development of cultural studies for many years until it was controversially closed down in 2002.

In education studies there are a number of pertinent developments worthy of careful consideration. In Chapter 3 we considered issues around the school curriculum being 'a selection from the culture'. But there are two further particular developments which seem especially significant and relate to the examination of culture. They both connect with the theme of social class but one is specifically concerned with language, the other with a broader conception of 'cultural capital'.

The connections between language and social class and how these connections play out in education systems have been a matter of debate and discussion within education in England (and in many other places) since at least the 1960s (e.g. Lawton, 1968). One principal issue of debate arose from the sociolinguistic work of the sociologist Basil Bernstein published in the early 1970s (Bernstein, 1971b). In analysing the speech of children from different social class backgrounds, Bernstein suggested that different linguistic codes were deployed within different social groups. He went so far as to suggest that children from working-class backgrounds tended to use a 'restricted code', while those from middle-class backgrounds tended to use an 'elaborated code'. Whilst this terminology immediately implied some deficiency or defect in language use among working-class children, this was not Bernstein's intention. Rather, as a sociolinguist, he was seeking to demonstrate how schooling, with its clear adoption of more elaborated forms of communication, was likely to favour those children who were already familiar with it from their home background. Nevertheless, these distinctions were picked up in the wider public discourse as demonstrating the inherent weakness of working-class language – and culture. How could you expect children from working-class backgrounds to be successful at school when their very language and culture were in some way deficient? Other sociolinguists reacted strongly to this implication, some suggesting that working-class language was really just as complex and nuanced as middle class (e.g. Labov, 1973); others made more direct attacks on Bernstein's work (e.g. Rosen, 1972). Keddie was among those who coined the related notion of 'the myth of cultural deprivation' (Keddie, 1973). Williams, however, did not especially connect with these debates in sociolinguistics being more interested in structural linguistics and in some of the related psychological work being undertaken in the Soviet Union at this time. In a chapter in *Marxism and Literature* called simply 'Language', he cites Vygotsky (among others) and concludes:

> What we can ... define is a dialectical process: *the changing practical consciousness of human beings*, in which both the evolutionary and the historical processes can be given full weight, but also within which they can be distinguished, in the complex variations of actual language use.
>
> (Williams, 1977:44)

Second, in education studies, specifically the sociology of education, the idea of 'cultural capital' became popular in the 1980s and thereafter. Largely derived from the work of the French sociologist Pierre Bourdieu (and referred to by Williams in the extract above on p. 101 – also referred to in Chapter 3 of the present book), it was an idea that helped explain the continuing inequalities in educational outcomes related to social class. The idea is that schools reflect a particular cultural orientation that effectively favours, and leads to success for, children from cultural backgrounds aligned with this orientation (see Reay, 2017). This idea is closely linked to that of language codes. Indeed Bernstein (1977), after his early sociolinguistic work, went on to suggest that schools often used an 'invisible pedagogy' which favoured middle-class children and more than one empirical study sought to explore the processes which gave rise to these differential experiences (Sharp and Green, 1975).

But we may note that 'cultural capital' was not a term that Raymond Williams used and it is pertinent to consider why this may have been. He clearly knew Bourdieu's work[4] so why did he not use these metaphors of 'capital'? It would appear to be difficult to use these concepts as explanations of differential achievement in schooling without at least implicitly suggesting that working-class culture is in some way deficient. This Williams would reject absolutely. The kinds of deficit views of culture that so irked some sociologists in the 1970s and 1980s in the wake of the misinterpretations of Bernstein's work, as discussed above, must have been an anathema to Williams. His emphases throughout any discussion of education systems were on the ways in which those in power influenced the curriculum and the pedagogy of schooling. In other words, the deficit lay in the system, not in the pupils the system was intended to serve.

However, in *Towards 2000*, Williams did come close to using the related, more general, term of 'social capital'. A key term he uses in discussing working-class communities in industrial societies is 'bonding' (Williams, 1983:167–8), a word that was to become significant in the theorization of social capital (see Baron, Field and Schuller, 2000). It could be argued that Williams's concept of 'structure of feeling' provides a much richer, more nuanced and subtler understanding of these social and cultural processes. While we will be discussing this concept in greater detail later (Chapter 7), we can say at this point that processes others might describe sociologically as 'reproduction' may be represented far less deterministically and with far greater human agency as 'structure of feeling'.

5.2 The Role of the Organic Intellectual in Society

Throughout his life, as we have seen, Raymond Williams engaged not only with his students in adult education and in the university but also with a much broader community. In pursuing his particular commitment to 'public education' and putting into practice his views that both culture and education are 'ordinary', he developed a range of activity, or, as we might put it now, an increasingly public profile. As we saw from the extract from *Keywords* at the beginning of this chapter, Williams was well aware of some of the difficulties with the word 'intellectual', not least in British society. We have already noted how every public activity he undertook had a distinctively educational character. His writing and his engagement in debate with others were always aimed at developing his own and others' understanding of the subject under discussion. His deep interest in the processes and technologies of communication was undoubtedly at the core of this aim and led him to become an epitome of what Antonio Gramsci called 'the organic intellectual'.

In his *Prison Notebooks*, Gramsci uses this term in his analysis of social processes. The editors of the English translation explain it in this way:

> Intellectuals in the functional sense fall into two groups. In the first place there are the 'traditional' professional intellectuals, literary, scientific and so on, whose position in the interstices of society has a certain inter-class aura about it but derives ultimately from past and present class relations and conceals an attachment to various historical class formations. Secondly, there are the 'organic' intellectuals, the thinking and organising element of a particular fundamental social class. These organic intellectuals are distinguished less by their profession, which may be any job characteristic of their class, than by their function in directing the ideas and aspirations of the class to which they organically belong.
> (Hoare and Nowell-Smith, 1971:4)

Williams was clearly a member of both these groups. Holding a position as an academic at the University of Cambridge, he was, like F. R. Leavis, a traditional professional intellectual. But because of his clear class consciousness he was also, like Paulo Freire (see Chapter 4), an organic intellectual in attempting to bring about social and political change. Though for Williams there was often a tension between his respective memberships of these two groups, it is apparent that he was most deeply committed, indeed loyal to the second group.[5] We may note that even today, although manifestations of social class may have changed, we can still identify these two groups of intellectuals in our midst, including a number of organic intellectuals who do not hold academic posts but use speaking, writing and social media to communicate ideas for social change and betterment. For those working in the academic establishment, the tensions that Williams experienced may now be felt even more keenly perhaps, owing to the deep encroachment of managerialism and performativity within the academy (see 5.4, below).

In spite of his prolific writings in newspapers and journals such as *The Guardian* and *The Listener*, and although he was clearly one of the best-known supporters of socialist causes, it is interesting to note that Williams was rarely called upon to take part in official government reviews or even to offer advice to the Labour Party. The only exception to this generalization was his membership of The Arts Council for a relatively brief period in the late 1970s. While his contribution here does seem to have been appreciated, he felt very ambivalent about the ways in which the Council worked as he wrote in an article originally published in 1979 (republished in Williams, 1989a). The tensions and contradictions in the notion of creative activity being managed, even controlled, by a bureaucratic state-funded organization gave him cause for considerable concern. We will return to his engagement with the arts in Chapter 6.

Many of the writers whose work Williams examined in his cultural and literary analysis might well be considered as organic intellectuals of a sort, but a brief examination of two, about whom he wrote short single volumes (as well as referring to them in longer works), raises interesting questions. The earlier of the cases is that of William Cobbett (1763–1835), included as a subject in *Culture and Society*, but also later the subject of one of these short volumes (Williams, 1983b). Williams's interest in Cobbett lies in his social analysis and in a kind of incipient socialist politics he developed. In *Culture and Society*, he refers to Cobbett as 'the first great tribune of the industrial proletariat' (Williams, 1958:23). Cobbett was many things during his life, often referred to as a 'gentleman farmer', but also at various times a soldier, journalist and political activist. Williams reads Cobbett's writings closely to demonstrate how he was becoming aware of a new kind of ruling class emerging as the Industrial Revolution took hold. Cobbett described the 'rentier culture', which, in Williams's words, is 'the whole way of life based on profit from the work of others' (Williams, 1983b:74). Cobbett was one of the first to recognize the exploitative and alienating nature of these changes in social and economic relations. In much of his writing he sought to reveal these iniquities and encourage campaigning against them. Even in the last two years of his life, as Williams says, he 'continued to campaign, over a wide range of causes: for a reduction in the working day to ten hours (it settled at twelve); against the new Poor Law and its workhouses; for relief and political change in Ireland' (Williams, 1983b:27).

From the perspective of the present book, it is also interesting to note that Williams gives credit to Cobbett's early insights into the significance of education and its ideological, even hegemonic, function. Cobbett first looked at 'traditional education' as it had 'come down from the Renaissance grammar schools to the privileged education of the modern period'. He saw this education as being provided not only to sustain the privilege of 'The Aristocracy' but also as a way of excluding the poor. Even the 'poor scholars' who were given access to this form of education were there, Cobbett said, in order that 'the needy learn in their youth to crawl to the rich and powerful' (Williams, 1983b:45). Williams quotes Cobbett at some length before offering the view that:

> Contemporary arguments against the fee-paying schools are most frequently cast in terms of their social privileges, which are indeed still real. But the central

argument against them, in Cobbett's time as in our own, is *intellectual*: it is against the *kind of mind*, the mental habits and signals, which they indeed so efficiently reproduce.

(Williams, 1983b:46)

Williams acknowledges several problems and contradictions with Cobbett's views on education, but is clearly very impressed by his overall percipience. His conclusion indicates that he found him inspiring in his own life and work. In spite of his 'quirkiness', his desire to make a difference could not be contained:

In fact, he keeps getting up: 'that they might see the man'. He does not ask permission or approval, least of all from the privileged or worldly-wise. There is a challenge and it has to be made. There is an argument, and it has to be carried out.

(Williams, 1983b:81)

These words suggest a model for the way in which Williams himself saw his responsibilities as an intellectual. Whether we can actually describe Cobbett as an organic intellectual is perhaps a moot point. 'Radical' is perhaps the better term to describe him as his writings and campaigning were most often a criticism of the class to which he himself belonged – the rentier class – rather than fitting Gramsci's definition of one who is working intellectually in support of their own class in opposition to the dominant class.

The second case of a public intellectual is George Orwell, or 'George Orwell' as Williams sometimes refers to him, not least to remind us that this was a pseudonym for Eric Blair, his birth name. Orwell is probably much better known to today's generations, including young people, than Cobbett. Orwell went to Eton College for his later schooling and, Williams suggests, very consciously created a new persona with his new name. He took Orwell as the final case study in *Culture and Society*, and also wrote a freestanding short volume called simply *Orwell*, published in the *Fontana Modern Masters* series edited by Frank Kermode (Williams, 1971). Williams has also quite a lot to say about his somewhat complicated views on Orwell in *Politics and Letters*. From the outset we may say that while Orwell was very much a public intellectual whose essays, novels and journalism have had enormous influence around the world (not only in Britain) and are often seen as highly critical of contemporary culture and politics, the common use of the adjective 'Orwellian' proves this point. We cannot say though that he was an organic intellectual in the Gramscian sense, not only because of his own class origins but also, in the light of Williams's many doubts about his views, because of the contradictions in his work.

Orwell's two best known books are both satirical novels: *Animal Farm* (1945/2000) offers a sharp satirical critique of a Stalinist communist society; *Nineteen Eighty-Four* (1949/1989), completed only shortly before his early death in 1950, sounded a warning about the dangers of technological 'mind control'. In his earlier writings however, Orwell had written about poverty in (*The Road to Wigan Pier*, 1937/1989; *Down and Out in Paris and London*, 1933/1940). He also wrote about his experience of the Spanish Civil War (*Homage to Catalonia*, 1938/1989), in which he fought as a member of one of the communist groups. Williams explores the ways in which Orwell's experiences and writing led to him changing his views during his lifetime, becoming best known politically as what Williams calls, an 'ex-socialist'. His account is careful and respectful and acknowledges the lasting influence of many of Orwell's ideas but, in the final analysis, Williams sees deep elements of class superiority emerging from his writing. Williams, with his deep humanism, came to reject Orwell to such an extent that he could no longer read his work.

> The recruitment of very private feelings against socialism becomes intolerable by *1984*. It is profoundly offensive to state as a general truth, as Orwell does, that people will always betray each other. If human beings are like that, what could be the meaning of a democratic socialism?
>
> (Williams, 1979:390)

In Williams's view, Orwell was the traitor, the one who had betrayed socialism and his former comrades: 'I am bound to say, I cannot read him now: at every point it is these bad moves that he made that stick in my mind' (Williams, 1979:392).

But in his concluding critique of Orwell, Williams manages (as ever) to offer an optimistic prospect. Reflecting on the political and social changes over Orwell's lifetime he suggests:

> The affiliation he tried to make, that he was ready to die for, was prevented by the political contradictions of those years and was lost, finally, in illusion and terror. The writer had to split from the political militant. Faith in the people had to be projected to an evolutionary distance: much farther than would ever have been necessary if his original class idea of unthinking sub-humans had not translated so readily into a disillusioned view of the apathetic and tolerant mass. Beyond and past him, in and through many of the contradictions he experienced, real popular forces have continued to move, and the fight he joined and then despaired of has been renewed, has extended, and has gained important new ground.
>
> (Williams, 1971:94)

The great irony is of course – in spite of Williams's hopes in 1971, but actually bearing out his critique – that Orwell's *Nineteen Eighty-Four*, written as a warning against the tyranny of populism, has now been so well incorporated into Western culture that the dominance of the corporate culture, advertising, branding and sloganizing (i.e. hegemony, see below) has severely undermined the kind of organic community culture and organization for which Williams always hoped.[6]

We have considered here two cases of public intellectuals who in their different ways have been influential and whose work deeply fascinated Williams, but who could not be called organic intellectuals in the authentic Gramscian sense. Williams, on the other hand, I would suggest, does very much suit such a title. His public activity, albeit with some weaknesses (and some of these we will consider later in this chapter), was consistently aimed at the liberation and enrichment of his own class, the working class, and at moving us all, by the process of the long revolution towards a participatory democracy which recognized the importance of community, culture and education. He himself did not use the term 'organic intellectual' and would almost certainly have demurred from accepting the term being attached to him.

Another of Gramsci's areas of work which was a clear influence on Williams was the concept of hegemony. This word was analysed in *Keywords* and is used quite frequently by him in many of his more political writings. It also became important in Marxist sociology of education in the 1970s. For Williams, the word was often taken to refer to the dominance of particular world powers; indeed, 'superpower' is a term coined in the aftermath of the Second World War, but it is in a more precise and nuanced way that the word 'hegemony' was becoming significant for Williams:

> The word has become important in one form of C20 Marxism, especially from the work of Gramsci. In its simplest use it extends the notion of political predominance from relations between states to relations between social classes, as in **bourgeois hegemony**. But the character of this predominance can be seen in a way which produces an extended sense in many ways similar to earlier English uses of **hegemonic**. That is to say, it is not limited to matters of direct political control but seeks to describe a more general predominance which includes, as one of its key features, a particular way of seeing the world and human nature and relationships. ..... Thus an emphasis on **hegemony** and **hegemonic** has come to include cultural as well as political and economic factors; it is distinct, in this sense, from the alternative idea of an economic *base* and a political and cultural *superstructure*, where as the *base* changes the *superstructure* is changed, with whatever degree of indirectness or delay.
>
> (Williams, 1976:118)

We will revisit Williams's later work on base and superstructure in Chapter 7, but here we begin to see the significance of hegemony in democratic societies and to see some of its educational implications. He goes on to say:

> The idea of **hegemony,** in its wide sense, is then especially important in societies in which electoral politics and public opinion are significant factors, and in which social practice is seen to depend on consent to certain dominant ideas which in fact express the needs of a dominant class.
>
> (Williams, 1976)

These ideas were developed particularly strongly in the work of Stuart Hall, for whom the creation of cultural hegemony was a powerful, if incomplete, explanation of the continuing existence of deep and structural inequalities in Western societies. It was through the hegemonic creation of forms of 'common sense' that true class interests became obscured and thus failed to be recognized and, in Hall's term, why 'authoritarian populism' became so dominant (Hall, 1988). A key social institution for establishing such hegemony was state schooling, the education establishment.

Gramsci's thinking on hegemony had a particularly strong influence on the group of sociologists of education who converged at The Open University (OU) in the 1970s (mentioned in Chapter 4). OU textbooks such as *Schooling and Capitalism*, edited by Roger Dale, Geoff Esland and Madeleine MacDonald (later Arnot) and published in 1976, included extracts from the work of Michael Apple (whose contribution is called 'Commonsense categories and curriculum thought'), as well as from Michael F. D. Young and Pierre Bourdieu, in a section headed 'Curriculum and cultural reproduction'. The final section of the book is called 'Consciousness and change' and has four contributions, from respectively: Raymond Williams ('Base and superstructure in Marxist cultural theory'), Herbert Marcuse ('New forms of control'), Antonio Gramsci ('The intellectuals') and Paulo Freire ('A few notions about the word "conscientization"'). Of these four, one might note that it is Freire alone who might be described as primarily an educationist. The shaping of educational sociology by forms of Marxism in the 1970s is apparent. The editors' introduction gives a clear exposition of the kind of critique of education being offered which is somewhat sharper and more politically informed than Williams's historical analysis in *The Long Revolution*. Their rationale for the collection is to offer a critique of the dominant 'liberal' ideology of education:

> Perhaps the single most important plank of the liberal ideology of education is that education creates and sustains progressive social change. This faith

rests in a number of critical assumptions. It is basically from a belief that these assumptions are not valid that we have assembled this collection of readings, the majority of which start from a similar belief.

(Dale, Esland and MacDonald, 1976:1)

They list three such assumptions:

- 'schooling critically affects the level of economic growth and social progress through its link with technology';
- education is 'capable of redressing social inequalities, of overcoming – through the equalisation of educational opportunity – the unfair distribution of life chances';

and

- 'education and the culture it both produces and transmits are viewed as independent and autonomous features of our society'.

(Dale, Esland and MacDonald, 1976:1–2)

They then seek to demonstrate how all three of these claims are fallacious. In passing, we may also note how the three claims relate to Williams's three categories of interest groups (in *The Long Revolution*): respectively, the industrial trainers, the public educators and the old humanists.

Critical perspectives such as these and the concept of hegemony, applied more widely beyond education, were central to the creation of the Centre for Contemporary Cultural Studies (CCCS). The CCCS was established in Birmingham in 1964, under the leadership of Richard Hoggart; Stuart Hall later became Director. These ideas were equally influential in such journals as *Marxism Today*, where Hall played a significant role (see Hall and Jacques, 1983, 1989), and in which the critique of 'Thatcherism' as a cultural as well as political phenomenon was developed. The CCCS volume which is most relevant to our concerns here is that called *Unpopular Education*, published in 1981 (CCCS, 1981). Hall himself was not directly involved in this work (he had moved to the OU by this time), although his influence is apparent.

In some ways the critique of state education advanced in this book has many similarities to the OU collection referred to previously, though it tends to take a more historical stance. The book has a subtitle of 'schooling and social democracy since 1944', this signalling an examination of the place of state-funded education as part of the post-war social democratic settlement. The collective of authors state early on that they are seeking to develop 'a more adequate socialist politics of education' than was available at the time. The book offers a critique of state education and suggests that Labour as well as Conservative governments have played a part in effectively undermining state education as a progressive force in society. It is a detailed and important analysis which in many ways foreshadowed the real impact of Thatcherism and neoliberalism on British (especially English) state education. Raymond Williams is mentioned positively in several places, though mainly in what might be described as passing references.

5.3 *The May Day Manifesto* and *New Left Review*

As we have seen, Williams partly achieved his personal and political aspirations through his educational practice, including his work within the adult education sector and through other public engagement, but he was also directly involved in overtly political movements. He was the lead editor of *The May Day Manifesto*, published in 1967–8, and strongly supported radical student action during this period. Although there were student 'sit-ins' in many English universities in the late 1960s, with the focus frequently being on greater self-determination in the curriculum and pedagogy of the university, it was the events in Paris in May 1968 which attracted the greatest attention. Here there was sustained fighting between student-led groups and the French police and military. Williams recalled that there were many connections between the New Left in Britain and the radical groups in France.

He was already a leading light in the New Left, working closely, for example, with Perry Anderson, E. P. Thompson and Stuart Hall. Williams had been a member of the Communist Party while a student at Cambridge but did not remain a member for long (see Chapters I.2 and I.4 of *Politics and Letters*). Although he usually supported the Labour Party, and campaigned for it in some general elections, he was deeply ambivalent in this support – and was frequently disappointed by the Party when it was in government (see Section V.1 in *Politics and Letters*). Indeed, he was generally sceptical about British parliamentary democracy and came increasingly to support calls for new forms of voting, including some kind of proportional representation, with increased devolution to national and regional forms of government. For him, meaningful participation by citizens was the real test of democracy and this he found to be severely lacking in British politics.

Later in his life he also indicated strong support for Plaid Cymru, the Welsh independence party, as well as showing increasing interest in green politics, although the Green Party itself was only just emerging in Britain at the time of his death and was not actually founded until 1990. Nor did he live to witness the establishment or re-establishment of parliaments or assemblies in Wales, Scotland and Northern Ireland.

Williams's commitment to socialism was solid and enduring, born out of his childhood in rural Wales and his family's commitment to community and organized labour. As he matured and developed his political and economic analysis of Britain, which emerged very clearly in *The Long Revolution*, his network of similarly minded activists steadily increased. He became a leading voice in what was emerging as the British 'New Left', although he was not happy about the use of 'New', pointing out that new inevitably becomes old at some point. David Widgery's analysis of left-wing politics in Britain from 1956 to 1968 attributes to Williams a distinctive voice:

> What Williams ... offered was the replacement of a conflict model of society (of the sort which has been traditional among socialists and even radicals) with a communications model, in which the unity of humankind is primordially broken, not by the clash of rival social interests, but by blockages and faulty linkages in moral perception. Society is conceived as a kind of mental organism whose warring faculties, in the shape of sectional or partial value-systems, eventually, if effortlessly, knit together in a single communications net or 'common culture'.
> (Widgery, 1976:137)

While some of this language is clearly not Williams's own (e.g. 'a kind of mental organism'), this extract does nevertheless capture some of the originality of his political thinking. Widgery goes on to suggest that Williams's style is 'peculiarly idiosyncratic and cloudy' (Widgery was not alone in this opinion) and suggests that this may reduce the wider influence of his work.

In 1960 Williams was to play a pivotal role in the establishment of the journal which would significantly represent the intellectual development of this movement: *The New Left Review (NLR)*. He describes in *Politics and Letters* his crucial mediating role in guiding the creation and development of this journal through a difficult birth (see Williams, 1979/2015:363–6). Williams contributed several important articles to the journal over many years, including some of his seminal theoretical outputs (see Chapter 7). It was the then editors of *NLR* (Perry Anderson, Anthony Barnett and Francis Mulhern) who interviewed him at length in creating the testament that became *Politics and Letters*.

The 1960s were a febrile time in British as well as European and global politics. We have seen in earlier chapters how educational politics and the sociology of education went through a period of rapid development, with the emergence of a strong radical progressivism, sometimes under a banner of the 'counter-culture'. This reflected the wider disquiet in society about the dominance of commercial culture with strong colonialist and oppressive elements. Many nations around the world had been struggling for independence (see Fanon, 1967) and 'Black Power' in the United States was challenging the deeply embedded racism of that society (see Baldwin, 1963; Carmichael and Hamilton, 1967). This was a different sense of resistance from the earlier movements of the industrial working class. Although the wider Labour Movement usually sought to align itself with much of the protest, it was more actively or visibly led by young people, including a large number of students, as well as by feminists and black community groups.

It was out of this turbulent environment that Williams, working with Edward Thompson and Stuart Hal, set about compiling *The May Day Manifesto*. This was planned as an explicit 'political intervention' seeking to respond to the perceived failure of the Wilson-led Labour Government of the mid-1960s and to offer some positive socialist alternatives. Earlier (in Chapter 3) we explored what this publication had to say about education, but the book as a whole covered a full range of economic, social and political matters. Williams took the lead role and wrote a good many of the words himself. Thompson and Hall played a significant part and Williams also acknowledged a much wider range of contributors, regarding it very much as a collective creation with him in the coordinating and lead editing role. The analysis in the book starts from a reassertion of the inequalities in British society, including data about poverty, in order to counter common claims in the 1960s that poverty had been eradicated. Among the proposals in the manifesto are calls for the establishment of a minimum wage, a policy eventually enacted in Britain, some decades later, albeit with serious flaws (Williams, 1968a).

One of the main criticisms which have emerged around Williams's politics relates to his continuing central and almost sole focus on social class as the basis of inequality in society. During the 1960s, as indicated earlier, radicalism was strongly associated with feminism and anti-racism. Williams has been challenged on both counts of failing to recognize the structural social inequalities related to 'race' and gender, and the significance of what would now be described as intersectionality.

In relation to 'race' the most developed attack came from an alumnus of CCCS, Paul Gilroy. Following a discussion of the 'new racism' that had emerged during the 1970s in Britain, Gilroy examines the connections that Williams made between 'race' on the one hand and patriotism and nationalism on the other, within *Towards 2000*. For Gilroy, Williams falls into the error of accepting links between national identity and whiteness, in exactly the same way as the new racism expresses that connection. He argues:

> Quite apart from Williams's apparent endorsement of the new racism, the strategic silences in his work contribute directly to its strength and resiliance (*sic*). The image Williams has chosen to convey his grasp of 'race' and nation, that of a resentful English working man, intimidated by the alterity of his alien neighbours is ... redolent of other aspects of modern Conservative racism and nationalism.
>
> (Gilroy, 1987:50–1)

In relation to gender and the women's movement, Williams does acknowledge at times the importance of feminism but rarely draws on it as a central plank of his social criticism. Juliet Mitchell played with Williams's title, when she called her collection of essays on feminism, literature and psychoanalysis, *Women: The Longest Revolution* (Mitchell, 1984), although she makes no explicit criticism of Williams in the book, referring to him only in passing, citing his 'humanism' (Mitchell, 1984:128). The title of Mitchell's book is taken from her article of the same name, originally published in *New Left Review* in 1966. These publications were an important stimulus to the ensuing debates about the links between socialism and feminism (see also Barrett, 1980). Mitchell's main reference points are works by Marx and Engels.

Williams's interest in ecological politics had been increasingly visible in his novels (*The Fight for Manod*, 1988, and *The Volunteers*, 1978/1985/2011, for example) but by the time *Towards 2000* was published it was becoming apparent in his non-fiction work as well. If *The May Day Manifesto* set out a political vision in 1968, *Towards 2000* is effectively Williams's manifesto for the 1980s and beyond (Williams, 1983). It commences with more despair at the dishonesty in British political life, in particular how party manifestoes presented before elections are rarely implemented and how what actually determines policy once a party is in power may much more accurately be described as 'crisis management'. He cites the 1972 report entitled *Limits to Growth* (Meadows, Randers and Behrens, 1972) to underpin his belief that the prevailing system of capitalism is bound to collapse at some point and is not sustainable. *Towards 2000* includes the chapter from *The Long Revolution* called 'Britain in the Sixties' as a starting point; further chapters ensue on society, democracy, culture and technology, and politics. In other words, Williams is revisiting his long-standing interests and updating his analysis. In the next part of the book he extends the analysis to look at nations (where the views Gilroy found so problematic about 'race' are expressed), global politics and war. The final chapter is called 'Resources for a Journey of Hope' and this is where we see Williams's deep humanism and optimism returning to the fore, in spite of his anxiety about ecological concerns.[7]

One of the few explicit references to education in *Towards 2000* is in the chapter on culture and technology. Here Williams is concerned about the ways in which education is being stifled at a time 'where there are new needs for permanently available education' (Williams, 1983:151). He writes:

> Yet what is now happening, in the existing institutions, is a steady pressure from a late-capitalist economy and its governments to reduce education both absolutely and in kind, steadily excluding learning which offers more than preparation for employment and an already regulated civic life ... [U]se of new technologies can add diversity and permanent availability to the most comprehensive institutions, above all in making them outward-looking, taking their own best knowledge and skills to a wider and more active society.
>
> (Williams, 1983:151)

We may wish to reflect on the extent to which educational institutions of today have effectively and successfully responded – or not – to this challenge from the 1980s.

Williams does make an acknowledgement of gender issues in the chapter on politics, where, referring to the industrial working class, he says:

> we have certainly to move beyond conceptions of this class which are centred on the male wage-earner at work. This not only neglects the internally subordinate position of employed women, but the radically different and more general subordination of women (including above all the 'non-employed') within wider social relations.
>
> (Williams, 1983:170)

Shortly after this he notes how the nature of politics has been changing in other ways:

> All significant social *movements* of the last thirty years have started outside the organised class interests and institutions. The peace movement, the ecology movement, the women's movement, solidarity with the third world, human rights agencies, campaign against poverty and homelessness, campaigns against

cultural poverty and distortion: all have this character, that they sprang from the
needs and perceptions which the interest-based organisations had not room or
time for, or which they had simply failed to notice.

(Williams, 1983:172)[8]

But, he goes on to insist, an examination of all of these issues leads us 'into the central systems of the industrial-capitalist mode of production and among others its system of classes' (Williams, 1983). It is interesting to reflect on this in the twenty-first century and to consider movements such as anti-capitalism and Extinction Rebellion as social movements whose concerns may also arise from the continuing underlying systems of production.

The final chapter of *Towards 2000*, while ending optimistically, nevertheless recognizes the rise of neoliberalism (not a term Williams actually uses) in what he somewhat quixotically dubs 'Plan X', 'a new politics of strategic advantage' (Williams, 1983:243). He discusses how the peace, ecology and feminist movements have all become significant political forces but yet, while the political systems remain as they are, may not bring about the kinds of radical change needed to build a safe, sustainable and equitable future. He concludes:

> It is only in a shared belief and insistence that there are practical alternatives that the balance of forces and chances begin to alter. Once the inevitabilities are challenged, we begin gathering our resources for a journey of hope. If there are no easy answers there are still available and discoverable hard answers, and it is these that we can now learn to make and share. This has been, from the beginning, the sense and impulse of the long revolution.
>
> (Williams, 1983:268–9)

One might add, this also confirms why public education is such a critical element of the long revolution.

After his death, taking the title of the final chapter in *Towards 2000* the publisher Verso brought out an outstanding collection of Williams's articles, edited by Robin Gable, entitled *Resources of Hope: Culture, Democracy, Socialism* (Williams, 1989a). This includes an introduction by Williams's NLR colleague Robin Blackburn, which stresses the importance of his political work:

> for a full understanding of Williams's work it is essential to attend to its political meanings. An understanding of, and commitment to, a radically transformed social order were integral to his vision and achievement. Williams's directly political interventions were a natural outgrowth of his concern for a democratic

culture, just as the experience and commitments they reflect themselves helped to inform his major critical studies.

(Blackburn, 1989:ix–x)

In summing up the political influence of Williams (and of his collaborator E. P. Thompson), we may also concur with Hilary Wainwright's view:

> Essential to … an egalitarian culture, and hence a thoroughgoing democracy, is a mutuality of intellect and experience. A problem within the working-class movement, in England at least, has been a counter-position of the two, often in reaction to the class-ridden character of educated culture. The obvious common response to this has often been anti-intellectualism, whether in the form of reckless militancy or a complacent sentimentalism. Thompson and Williams tried instead, both by practical personal example and in their writing, to explore a creative dialectic between experience and theory, intellect and feeling.
>
> (Wainwright, 1994:77–8)

5.4 Conclusion: Fighting Performativity in Higher Education Today

Some organic intellectuals have a university base and, for a good twenty years of his life, this was the case for Raymond Williams. Given his political position and his own experiences from childhood to his arrival as a Cambridge undergraduate in 1939, his relationship with the university – whether Cambridge specifically or the wider institution – was not always an easy one. In concluding this chapter we examine some of his own encounters with the university establishment as well as giving consideration to the ways in which universities and the higher education they offer have changed in recent years.

In his essay 'My Cambridge', Williams reflects on his experience as an undergraduate and subsequently:

> It was not my Cambridge. That was clear from the beginning. I have now spent eighteen years in the university, in three distinct periods. In each of them I started by being surprised to be there, and then, in time, made some kind of settlement. But this has always, even in the longest period, felt temporary.
>
> (Williams, 1989b:3)

When he returned to Cambridge in 1961 to take up a post as a lecturer, he arrived with a growing reputation derived particularly from *Culture and Society* and *The*

Long Revolution. He took the business of the Faculty of English seriously and contributed carefully to the discussions about course syllabi and related matters. In spite of his ambivalence about universities, Cambridge became a secure base, not only for his work in literature and drama, but also for his social and political criticism and activity. As noted earlier, it was in his rooms at Cambridge for example that the bulk of *The May Day Manifesto* was written with Edward Thompson and Stuart Hall.

Among a number of critical disputes in which he became involved at Cambridge, two stand out and demonstrate his deep commitment to the university as a centre for independent and critical thought. In his biography of Williams, Fred Inglis (1995) recounts how, in 1970, a former radical student leader from Germany, Rudi Dutschke, had applied to Williams to undertake a study of the work of Georg Lukacs. Though Dutschke had been shot and wounded in a neo-Fascist assassination attempt and suffered some brain injury as a result, he was still seen as a threat by the German authorities. With Williams's support the university decided to admit him. It was then the British Home Office which put conditions on his entry into the country including a requirement that he not consort with any 'political adults' (this is the phrase Inglis uses). He was put under surveillance and not surprisingly found to have made contact with some political activists and duly issued with a deportation order. There was considerable outrage in the academic community at this attack on academic freedom, and Inglis reports on a protest meeting organized by the National Council for Civil Liberties in January 1971. He says:

Over a thousand academics petitioned on behalf of Dutschke and academic freedom, and Williams spoke ringingly for them all when he invoked the essential internationalism of university research:

> For me as for others this is an intrinsic value of the university, and the effects of this case have very deeply shaken it. Very crude definitions of national security and very alarming prejudices about people stereotyped as foreign nationals, have shaken that value, and have alarmed many respected and welcome members of the university, at very different stages of their lives.
>
> (Williams, 1995:228–9)

Dutschke moved to Denmark, but sadly died not long afterwards.

Inglis also gives a detailed account of the internal row which erupted around the appointment of a young lecturer to the Faculty of English in 1976. Colin MacCabe was to take up a new post in 'English language in relation to literature since 1500', the creation of which post Williams strongly supported. MacCabe was seen as too theoretical in his structural approach to literature, at least by some members of the Cambridge establishment. Inglis recalls with typical dry wit that some members of the appointments committee resigned over the issue of the appointment being made permanent:

> The MacCabe Affair broke noisily into the culture columns of the press. It bears heavily in this biography for two reasons. First, Williams himself played a key role in the battle to redefine the academic subject to and for which he gave his life. Second, the quarrel bespeaks much about the high-principled vindictiveness in which much intellectual life is lived, dedicated as it is to discovering the great sources of sweetness and light.
>
> (Inglis, 1995:279)

Williams himself studiously avoided adopting the latter tendencies ('high-principled vindictiveness') and always used carefully chosen moderate language to present his case, even when passionately involved. In due course, after a number of formal procedures and much spleen vented (not by Williams), MacCabe was confirmed in his post.

These two cases demonstrate the strength of Williams's commitment to internationalism and academic freedom. During his lifetime he several times expressed concerns that education at all levels, including the university, was becoming increasingly functional, that the industrial trainers had the upper hand and that courses and programmes were becoming increasingly employment-related. To some extent this could be seen in the prioritization of science and engineering subjects and more generally in the constraining effects of the introduction of measures of effectiveness in education. Such measures were one element in the Plan X outlined by Williams in *Towards 2000*, which would slow down – we might now say reverse – the long revolution.

There can be little argument that the nature of the university has changed dramatically since Williams's day with the encroachment of managerialism and performativity (Deem, Hillyard and Reed, 2008). Indeed such tendencies were signalled as early as 1970 with the unrest at the University of Warwick, including sit-ins by students in protest at the university's decision not to build a new students' union. During the occupation, evidence of political surveillance of students and staff by the university was discovered and the campaign developed into a broader one in response to corruption and the commercialization of the institution. Williams's fellow traveller E. P. Thompson, then employed as a history lecturer at Warwick, edited a Penguin Special called *Warwick University*

Limited which revealed this to the wider world. A reissue of this book in 2014 includes reflections by some of those involved at the time, suggesting that the trends being opposed then have taken an even stronger hold in academia since (Thompson, 1970/2014). The pursuit of funding has, it is suggested, led to elements of corruption and to tight controls on the freedom of staff and students across higher education.

As these tendencies continue, there are still voices being raised which seek to reinvigorate effectively the critical independence of higher education. In the UK we might suggest that extended essays such as those by Stefan Collini (2012) and Jon Nixon (2011) are good examples of this kind of opposition. Nixon actually cites Williams's claim that 'education is ordinary' in support of his argument that there is a need to articulate:

> a sense of possibility for higher education: the possibility of bringing the public back into higher education and bringing higher education back to its rightful place within the public.
>
> (Nixon, 2011:118)

Collini questions the dominance of economic thinking in universities in the twenty-first century and calls for a reinstatement of 'non-economic values'. Williams might well have had some difficulty with a term such as this (as he might suggest that all values have some kind of economic connection) and, although Collini does not cite Williams's work, he concludes with words that are at least partly consistent with his views:

> Universities are not just good places in which to undertake ... fundamental questioning; they also embody an alternative set of values in their very rationale. Attending to these values may help us remember, amid difficult and distracting circumstances, that we are merely custodians of the present generation of a complex intellectual inheritance which we did not create – and which is not ours to destroy.
>
> (Collini, 2012:199)

Where Williams might well part company with Collini is in the assertion that universities have an 'alternative' set of values. Williams always insisted, as Nixon noted, that education is ordinary. There is a danger in the kind of call made by Collini of universities becoming elitist again. It is certainly not a working-class voice that emerges from this essay and it has a flavour of the old humanists. Collini may well be an example of a public intellectual but could not be described as an organic intellectual.

Nor, we might suggest, on the other side of the Atlantic, could the prominent philosopher Martha Nussbaum be so described. She calls for a re-emergence of the humanities as an important social force and writes, again in terms that may seem familiar to readers of Williams's work:

> Democracies have great rational and imaginative powers. They are also prone to some serious flaws in reasoning, to parochialism, haste, sloppiness, selfishness, narrowness of the spirit. Education based mainly on profitability in the global market magnifies these deficiencies, producing a greedy obtuseness and a technically trained docility that threaten the very life of democracy itself, and certainly impede the creation of a decent world culture. … If we do not insist on the crucial importance of the humanities and the arts, they will drop away, because they do not make money.
>
> (Nussbaum, 2010:142–3)

Nussbaum's writing is deeply imbued with a humanism that is similar to Williams's, if not by a commitment to socialism.

Williams was first and foremost a public educator, who became recognized widely as a public intellectual and, as has been suggested in this chapter, an organic intellectual. Other organic intellectuals have followed and some of them have been mentioned here. We can also think of geographers such as David Harvey, whose work from *Social Justice and the City* (Harvey, 1973) onwards has consistently argued from a Marxist position about the degradation caused by capitalist systems. Similarly, of a later generation, Danny Dorling, whilst less explicitly Marxist, nevertheless has used geographical analysis to expose some of the deeply harmful effects of global capitalism (Dorling, 2015). In education studies we have seen a tradition of critical socialist scholarship on both sides of the Atlantic, some of which have been referred to earlier in this book, such as Michael Apple. However, if we seek to identify intellectuals who have consistently argued that education in England should be liberated from the constraints of social class we can identify a tradition – partly inspired by Williams – that might include Brian Simon, Clyde Chitty, Sally Tomlinson, Geoff Whitty, Ken Jones and Diane Reay (to name just a few).[9]

Cultural Studies and the Educational Role of the Arts and Media

Introduction

There was an old, mainly agricultural England, with a traditional culture of great value. This has been replaced by a modern, organized, industrial state, whose characteristic institutions deliberately cheapen our natural human responses, making art and literature into desperate survivors and witnesses, while a new mechanized vulgarity sweeps into the centres of power. The only defence is in education, which will at least keep certain things alive, and which will also, at least in a minority, develop ways of thinking and feeling which are competent to understand what is happening and to maintain the finest individual values. I need not add how widespread this diagnosis has become, though little enough acknowledgement is made to Leavis himself. For my own part, I was deeply impressed by it; deeply enough for my ultimate rejection of it to be a personal crisis lasting several years.

(Williams, 1958, 'Culture is ordinary',
reprinted in Williams, 1989:9 and in McGuigan, 2014:8)

The essay from which this excerpt is taken was written early in Williams's working life and reflects the deep tensions and anxieties he was experiencing about the nature of culture, class and opportunity. In wanting to acknowledge his debt to F. R. Leavis he set out the exclusive and dismissive view of the popularization of culture – of 'what is wrong with English culture' – (not dissimilar to the views expressed in T. S. Eliot's 1948 essay *Notes Towards a Definition of Culture*) but then confirms that he seeks to explore an alternative view, one that is inclusive and democratic. In this chapter we explore some dimensions of the ways in which he developed these ideas in relation to a range of media forms. We also see in the extract above how education was being positioned within this conservative view as a bastion, a last resort for the few, enabling them to retain cultural superiority. Williams's view of education was, of course, completely the opposite of this, believing as he did, that, in and through the arts and literature, it could become a force for creativity and community development.

Having previously established the importance of the analysis of culture in Raymond Williams's work, in this chapter we explore selected aspects of its significance in greater depth. We start by discussing Williams's commitment to the 'democratization' of culture, and what it meant in the second half of the twentieth century. His analyses reshaped how culture was understood and broadened access to many cultural forms and expressions to an extent that 'popular' culture was frequently distinguished from 'high' culture and interesting divisions were created. It was tensions such as these, in part at least, which gave rise to the emergence of 'cultural studies' as a subject for research and teaching. But the growing diversity of media forms as vehicles for cultural transmission also led to the creation of 'media studies', which became a subject for study – and examination – in secondary schools in England. This development was not without controversy. We turn to look at Williams's distinctive critical contribution in cultural forms other than fiction (which was discussed in earlier chapters, especially Chapter 2) to consider his approach to film, drama and television. We also consider how his analyses might be applied to the rapid development of electronic forms of communication, including 'social media', only just emerging at the time of his death. The chapter concludes by considering the implications of the foregoing discussions for our understanding of the arts in education today, including a consideration of the ways in which Williams's understanding of 'creativity' might be interpreted in contemporary education in schools and in universities.

6.1 The Democratization of Culture

As Williams frequently pointed out, words can be difficult and complex. We have established that 'culture', with its particular complexities, was at the centre of his work. He argued, as we noted, that 'culture is ordinary'. We have also seen how, in many ways, Williams saw all culture as closely aligned with educational processes, and indeed that education itself is 'ordinary'. What then were his aspirations and intentions for seeking the 'democratization' of culture, for the development of a 'common culture', culture as 'a whole way of life', as inclusive rather than exclusive? His own literary criticism derived almost entirely from within the exclusive (some would say elitist) culture of fiction, drama and poetry, yet he sought, on the one hand, to create openings which would enable much wider appreciation of these traditions while, on the other hand, he wanted to acknowledge and pay due recognition to aspects of culture already widely available, i.e. newspaper, magazines, paperback books or film, and increasingly radio and TV. For Williams too, as his cultural criticism and political thinking became more intertwined, so he was increasingly pointing out the importance of the economics of these cultural processes, for example considering who owned the means of their production and how they were controlled. We saw how these kinds of questions began to appear in *Communications* and also in *The Long Revolution*.

Culture is a site of social and political struggle, historically and contemporaneously, and this is what Williams explores in the sociological text *Culture* (Williams, 1981). It is also why it is vital that culture continues to be the focus of serious study.[1] We saw earlier on (Chapter 5) how Williams recognized that 'culture' is one of the most complex words in the English language and how he suggested a threefold definition in *Keywords*. The third of these is:

> the independent and abstract noun which describes the works and practices of intellectual and especially artistic activity.
>
> (Williams, 1976:80)

This is 'often now the most widespread use: **culture**[2] is music, literature, painting and sculpture, theatre and film' (Williams, 1976:80).

'Art', Williams suggests, has taken on a new, more particular, more limited meaning in the modern world. He notes:

> The **artist** is ... distinct ... not only from *scientist* and *technologist* – each of whom in earlier periods would have been called **artist** – but from *artisan* and *craftsman* and skilled worker, who are now operatives in terms of specific definition and organisation of WORK.
>
> (Williams, 1976:34)

'Science' became increasingly distinct from other forms of activity and practice, during the nineteenth century, to the extent that:

> **Scientific, scientific method** and **scientific truth** became specialized to the successful methods of the **natural** sciences, primarily physics, chemistry and biology. Other studies might be theoretical and methodical, but this was not now the main point: it was the hard *objective* character of the material and the method, which in these areas went together, which was taken as defining.
>
> (Williams, 1976:234)

Williams also connects culture to civilization:

> [Civilisation] has come to be a relatively neutral term for any achieved social order or way of life, and in this sense has a complicated and much disputed relation with the modern social sense of *culture*.
>
> (Williams, 1976:50)

From each discussion of these key words Williams alerts us to the ways in which language carries deeply symbolic and social significance, demonstrated through the changing meanings of particular words and their interrelationships. This sensitivity to the power of words underlies much of what we now understand as 'cultural studies'. It is one of Williams's major educational legacies – indeed it might be seen as a pedagogical tool – to have shown this so clearly and precisely, not just in *Keywords* but in all of his writing.

The connections between culture and education were restated by Williams when in the 1960s he revisited Matthew Arnold's *Culture and Anarchy* (Arnold, 1867). He notes that 'the spirit of Arnold', typified by a narrow view of 'learning from all the best that has been thought and said in the world', had been invoked in the (now) notorious *Black Papers*, the series of publications emanating from a cluster of conservative ideologues in the 1960s which attacked the progressivism (as they saw it) of much contemporary public education. As Williams put it:

> It ... matters very much whether those who believe in reason and in informed argument are able, within the noise of confrontation, to go on making the necessary distinctions. It matters also whether, in the inevitable tensions of new kinds of argument and new kinds of claim, the defenders of reason and education become open to new and unfamiliar relationships, or instead relapse to their existing habits and privileges and then – as is now happening, just as significantly didn't happen in Arnold – manoeuvre and combine to restrict, to purge, to impoverish education itself. For the culture which is then being defended is not excellence but familiarity, not the knowable but only the known values.
>
> (Williams, 1970, reprinted in Williams, 1980:8)

Perhaps one of the most concise and cogent outlines of Williams's commitment to the connection between culture and education comes in the essay 'The Idea of a Common Culture'[3] which, like much of his work, starts autobiographically:

> Culture was the way in which the process of education, the experience of literature, and – for someone moving out of a working-class family to a higher education – inequality came through ... [E]verywhere, but very specifically in

England, culture is one way in which class, the fact of major division between men, shows itself.

(Williams, 1968d, reprinted in Williams, 1989a:32)

His conclusion is the idea of a common culture which equates to 'the idea of an *educated and participating democracy*' (emphasis in the original), as he explains:

> Participating for the reasons which we have said; educated because it must be the case that the whole tradition of what has been thought and valued, a tradition which has been abstracted as a minority possession, is in fact a common human inheritance without which any man's participation would be crippled and disadvantaged. In this meaning of education, a man would not see himself simply as continuing a particular tradition, educated into a particular way of thought, as so much of an education is viewed at present; the point, simply, is that one would not be fully qualified to participate in this active process unless the education which provides its immediate means – developed speaking, writing, and reading – and which allows access to the terms of the argument so far, were made commonly available. So a common culture is an educated and participating democracy, and the idea of a socialist democracy is based, very firmly, on those values.
>
> (Williams, 1989a:37)

Here we begin to appreciate the connections between culture, education and democracy. In Williams's view of the world these connections could not be more fundamental. But in the 1960s, as now: social inequalities still meant that access to this aspirational common culture is far from universal and culture continues to be highly differentiated, even while the development of the 'mass media' has created many more channels of communication throughout society.[4]

6.2 Popular Culture, 'High' Culture and Cultural Studies

In his analysis of *The Emergence of Cultural Studies 1945–65*, Tom Steele strongly asserts that the subject was born out of adult education, not universities. As he puts it:

> A popular misconception about British cultural studies as an academic subject is that it sprang fully-armed from the side of a university department of English. While such a department may have been a midwife, the project of cultural studies more properly beings to the experimentation, interdisciplinarity and

political commitment of adult education immediately before and after the Second World War.

(Steele, 1997:9)

Raymond Williams agreed. In 1983, at a speech in memory of adult educator Tony McLean, he said:

> we are beginning I am afraid, to see encyclopedia articles dating the birth of Cultural Studies from this or that book in the late 'fifties. Don't believe a word of it. That shift of perspective about the teaching of arts and literature and their relation to history and to contemporary society began in Adult Education, it didn't happen anywhere else.
>
> (Williams, 1989b:162)

Both Steele, in his 'archaeology' of cultural studies, and Williams himself, in his reflections on the subject, agree that the major inspirations for the emergence of cultural studies within adult education were, first, the study of English literature in universities, notably led by F. R. Leavis, and second, the growing awareness of the 'hidden history' of the British working class, its culture and institutions.[5] There is also agreement that there were three important voices in its emergence and three particular publications which provided a key foundation: Williams's *Culture and Society* (1958/2013), Richard Hoggart's *The Uses of Literacy* (1957) and Edward Thompson's *The Making of the English Working Class* (1963/1970).[6] Neither Steele nor Williams would suggest that these three authors or their respective books were alone responsible for carving out the field of study. There were many fellow travellers, and, like the three above, the majority were working in adult education in different parts of the country. Steele also draws attention to the significance of the arrival of Jewish emigres from Europe, most notably Karl Mannheim, whose Germanic sociology proved very influential, not least in education.

While maintaining the position that cultural studies emerged out of adult education, the subject did begin to influence what was happening in the university sector. Steele notes the continuing uneasy relationship between English studies and cultural studies in higher education. English itself had emerged as a legitimate subject of study in universities only towards the end of the nineteenth century and in referring to what he calls 'the English question', Steele suggests the subject played an important part in establishing national identity within Britain. It also acted as force to sustain British colonialism around the world. There was indeed a hegemonic element to the development of the subject which can still be detected, not least when debates rage around the content of the school curriculum for English, for example when 'core texts' are being identified. So the arrival of a radical adjunct to English in the form of cultural studies caused some consternation and strong reactions within the university establishment. It was certainly some time before it was accepted as a legitimate subject of study within higher education and, most notably, it was in the then polytechnics (now 'post-92 universities') where it was taken up most actively. The main exception to this was in the civic university of Birmingham. Here, as noted in Chapter 5, Richard Hoggart succeeded in establishing the Centre for Contemporary Cultural Studies (CCCS) in 1962. This became the most fertile site for the exploration of cultural studies, with an enormous range of studies covering youth cultures, policing, deviance, gender, race and other matters. A key appointment made to the CCCS was that of Stuart Hall, who went on to succeed Hoggart as Director and stimulated a new wave of productivity, not least in his work exploring the connections between the politics of the New Right and culture. Hall's was a key voice in the coining of the concept of 'Thatcherism'. As mentioned earlier, subsequently Hall moved to The Open University, the second major institutional site for the development of the subject, introducing thousands of adult learners to aspects of cultural studies. Although Raymond Williams was closely associated with Hall (see for example the references to *The May Day Manifesto* in Chapter 5), he himself was by now working at Cambridge in the English Faculty and did not play a particularly active role in CCCS, although he did contribute significantly to some of the courses provided by the OU and he did see the creation of the OU as a major step in the democratization of adult education. Several of his books also became core set texts on OU courses.

How then might we define 'cultural studies'? While it is certainly interdisciplinary, in its early formation it drew largely on studies in English and sociology with a strong historical awareness. It sought to build on a broad definition of culture – as 'a way of life' – thus alluding to an anthropological perspective. In particular it attempted to identify and analyse aspects of culture that were not 'mainstream' or elitist, although of course, by implication, the relationships between this less visible culture and the establishment were of central interest. Terms abounding at the time included 'high culture', 'mass culture' and 'popular culture', each carrying considerable symbolic significance and particular values. 'High' was used (and still is) to refer to the traditional English/Western canon of literature, opera, classical music, poetry and suchlike. 'Mass' was often related to the influence of new media forms, notably television, the tabloid press (as it would now be called) and was often associated with Americanization. 'Popular', while often recognizing distinctive cultural elements among the interests of younger people, was also more broadly related to film and to music, most notably 'pop music'. It was a recognition that all these cultural influences were shaping the experience and lives of 'ordinary' people; a growing interest in class divisions within society was a key building block of the subject. There was an underlying politics which was certainly radical and, in its origins at least, certainly of a socialist disposition. Since those early days, however, we have seen the ways in which cultural studies has also attracted the interest of right-wing commentators who have expressed condemnation of the 'dilution' of culture through such developments. In the United States one might cite Alan Bloom or, in the United Kingdom, Melanie Phillips. Bloom's *The Closing of the American Mind* (Bloom, 1987) was subtitled 'How higher education has failed democracy and impoverished the souls of today's students'. Melanie Phillips's *All Must Have Prizes* (Phillips, 1996) is an attack on the liberal establishment which she argues, in the vein of Matthew Arnold, has so influenced contemporary schooling in England and led, in her view, to 'low education standards and expectations'. She was vehement in her attack on 'cultural relativism' in education:

> Education and culture have passed into the hands of philistines. From the failure to teach infants to read, through the repudiation of grammar, punctuation and spelling, all the way to teaching Oxford English undergraduates about gangster movies, the new illiteracy was blessed by a cowed and enfeebled establishment that no longer believed it had the right to engage its critical faculties except to support the notion that anything goes.
>
> (Phillips, 1996:121)

Phillips was also associated with the late Chief Inspector of Schools, Chris Woodhead, who explicitly attacked media studies in 2000, describing it as 'a doss' (see http://news.bbc.co.uk/1/hi/uk/665308.stm). These 'culture wars' have recurred time and again in debates about school and university education in England – and elsewhere – and no doubt Williams would have seen them as being based on continuing class tensions in contemporary society.

While all three of the leading voices in the emergence of cultural studies were deeply concerned with the working class, each had a somewhat different take on the connections between culture and class. For Williams, working towards an inclusive common culture was a question of developing a consensus, demonstrated clearly by the concept of the long revolution. For Thompson, on the other hand, progress towards equality would only result from actual class struggle; indeed, the critique he offered of *The Long Revolution* was that

Williams saw culture as 'a way of life', whereas in his own work he saw working-class culture as 'a way of struggle'. The making of the English working class was for him a process of self-determination. Of the three, Hoggart may be seen as the most reformist or gradualist, with his preferred term to describe his interests being 'popular culture', exemplified in *The Uses of Literacy*. Thompson's profile developed more as an historian and as a social theorist, which did overlap with the profiles of Williams and Hoggart, but the latter two would come to be more strongly identified with the cultural element of cultural studies.

Early on in his work, Williams demonstrated his interest in popular forms of media through the publication of *Communications* (Williams, 1962/1966), the book which grew out of his address to a teachers' conference in the early 1960s. The conference, organized by the National Union of Teachers, was called 'Popular culture and personal responsibility'. In the book, Williams demonstrates ways of analysing newspapers,[7] magazines, radio and television programmes, including discussing the economics of such media, and their reliance on advertising revenue. This also leads him towards offering policy proposals about the regulation and governance of these media. As we have seen Williams was very concerned about questions of ownership, power and influence in the media. He was always seeking to promote more democratic forms of governance and management. By comparison with Hoggart's *Uses of Literacy*, Williams's approach may be seen as more 'technical', suggesting quantitative approaches to analysing media and it was also more policy oriented. Hoggart's work is certainly analytical but in general terms more qualitative and arguably more sociological than *Communications*.

In his contribution to a collection dedicated to consideration of Raymond Williams and cultural politics, Dworkin suggests that some elements of Williams's cultural analysis are now less useful, not least because of the major social and political transformations we have seen since his time. However, he does suggest:

> Williams's negotiation between Leavisite criticism and Marxism helped to create a new intellectual space, one in which culture was the essential link between social organization and experience. From this perspective, culture included 'high' and 'popular' expressions but was reducible to neither – culture as 'the whole way of life'.
>
> (Dworkin, 1993:38)

In a lecture given in London in 1986 on 'The future of cultural studies', Williams inevitably reflected on the past. He saw the 'central theoretical point of Cultural Studies' as that:

you cannot understand an intellectual or artistic project without also understanding its formation; that the relation between a project and its formation is always decisive; and that the emphasis of Cultural Studies is precisely that it engages with *both*, rather than specializing itself to one or the other.

(Williams, 1989c:151)

This is in essence a description of what came to be called cultural materialism, a term we will focus on in Chapter 7.

6.3 Film, Drama, Television

I was concerned with a major cultural shift of our own period, in which the relations between writing and speech, between writing and dramatic action, and then, in quite new ways, between writing and the composition of images, were changed or were newly developed in radio, television and film (Williams, 1983/1991:6).

Film

So Williams writes in introducing his collection of essays called *Writing in Society*. In his undergraduate days at Cambridge he had been deeply interested in film, frequently attending cinema showings and becoming a member of a film society. He wrote about and reviewed films in the student newspapers he was involved with and went on to collaborate with fellow student Michael Orram in one of his first book-length publications, *A Preface to Film* (Williams and Orrom, 1954). It was in this publication that we see the emergence of what was to become a key concept in Williams's work: 'structure of feeling'. His mode of analysis for all cultural forms was to rely heavily on this concept, which draws attention to the ways in which particular cultural outputs relate to their time and to the subjectivity of the culture from which they emerge, thus revealing insights to the nature of social relations in a specific context. McGuigan, in an introduction to a selection of Williams's writing, suggests that structure of feeling 'is Williams's alternative to the idealist notion of zeitgeist, the spirit of the times' (McGuigan, 2014:27). This is a helpful pointer to the significance of the materialist element in Williams's thinking (as well as to the weaknesses of 'zeitgeist'). In the selection from *The Long Revolution*, which McGuigan is introducing, he considers how Williams expands his thinking on this concept. Structure of feeling, Williams suggests:

is as firm and definite as 'structure' suggests, yet it operates in the most delicate and least tangible parts of our activity. In one sense, this structure of feeling is the culture of a period: it is the particular living result of all elements in the general organisation. And it is in this respect that the arts of a period, taking these to include the characteristic approaches and tones in argument, are of major importance. For here, if anywhere, this characteristic is likely to be expressed; often, not consciously, but by the fact that here, in the only examples we have of recorded communication that outlives its bearers, the actual living sense, the deep community that makes the communication possible, is naturally drawn upon.

(Williams, 1961/2011:69)[8]

In acknowledging the importance of documents in this analysis, he then moves on to outline what he means by 'the selective tradition', the process through which, over time, some aspects of the former culture remain in focus while others may disappear. This selective tradition is one of the motivations towards his calling for the democratization of culture, as discussed in the previous section. Indeed, here Williams suggests that within any given time or context, structure of feeling:

does not seem to be, in any formal sense, learned. One generation may train its successor, with reasonable success, in the social character or the general cultural pattern, but the new generation will have its own structure of feeling, which will not appear to have come 'from' anywhere. For here, most distinctly, the changing organisation is enacted in the organism: the new generation responds in its own ways to the unique world it is inheriting, taking up many continuities, that can be traced, and reproducing many aspects of the organisation, which can be separately described, yet feeling its whole life in certain ways differently, and shaping its creative response into a new structure of feeling.

(Williams, 1961/2011:69/70)

Here we have the core of Williams's perspective, not only on the importance of the arts within society but also on the processes of cultural change and their temporal and spatial influences. In Chapter 2, we saw how fictional writing about education and schooling can lead us into perceiving the structure of feeling of a particular time and place, but the same is also true when we analyse other cultural forms such as film, drama and television. Williams himself planned to produce a film with Michael Orrom, but funding could not easily be found and other matters intervened.[9]

Williams's positioning of film within contemporary culture is well summarized in a chapter called 'Film History' in the collection of articles entitled *What I*

Came to Say, introduced by Francis Mulhern (Williams, 1989b). Developed more fully by the end of his life, his cultural materialist view on the origin of film as a popular medium is succinctly stated:

> Modern popular culture ... is not only a response to predominantly urban and industrial living. It is also in its central processes, (1) largely urban-based, (2) an application of new industrial processes to a broad range of old and new cultural processes and forms, and thus (3) predominantly mobile and innovative, but with very complex relations to older and still persistent conditions and forms. Film arrived at the end of a century of such developments.
>
> (Williams, 1989b:137)

In his analysis of connections between Williams's cultural materialism and 'the break-up of Britain', Hywel Dix (2013) offers an account of the ways in which Williams's approach to film and particularly how the concept of 'flow', developed in his analysis of television programmes, can reveal insights into the ideological messages on national identity being conveyed in much mainstream metropolitan cinema. He takes as examples films starring Hugh Grant portrayed as an 'English buffoon' (as Dix calls it) and contrasts these with more regionally based or national films from Wales, Scotland and Northern Ireland. The latter, Dix implies, offer a more serious and realistic portrayal of the culture and politics of the smaller nations than do the Hugh Grant films of England.

Alan O'Connor, also a key contributor to the analysis of Williams's work, suggests that Williams shifted his use of the 'structure of feeling' over time. On some occasions he would tend to associate it with a particular writer or even a particular work. At other times he used it to represent a wider view of society. Writing in 1989, O'Connor suggests that:

> Williams no longer uses the term in the general sense of the structure of experience of a whole generation. In *Marxism and Literature* the term is given the specialized meaning of a pre-emergent cultural phenomena: a trend that is developing but is not yet clearly emergent. We may have a sense of something new that is developing but as not yet fully formed: it is very difficult to describe it at this stage. This is a particularly interesting phenomenon and it is useful to have a term which refers to it.
>
> (O'Connor, 1989:84)

O'Connor goes on to suggest that the concept may best be used as 'a kind of hermeneutic'. With reference to Williams's writings on drama, O'Connor points out:

dramatic scripts have a deep dependence on conventions shared with the audience. To read drama is to read parts, to read for a cultural history – including the material conditions of the performance of the drama. Williams's hermeneutic is to read a general history into particular scripts.

(O'Connor, 1989:85)

One might also suggest, within the context of educational discourse, that 'structure of feeling' may be seen as a kind of pedagogical device, a term that helps us to understand the links between particular cultural artefacts, novels, works of art or films and the social and economic conditions of their creation.

Drama

Williams's work on drama was crucial to the development of his thinking; indeed for several years, his post at Cambridge was as Professor of Drama. As O'Connor points out, drama, at least in its main conventions, is more obviously social than poetry or the novel (O'Connor, 1989:84). There are three major works in drama criticism produced by Williams during his life: *Drama from Ibsen to Brecht*, 1968 (a revision of *Drama from Ibsen to Eliot*, published in 1952); *Drama in Performance* (originally published in 1954, but then revised in 1968 and reprinted with a new introduction by Graham Holderness in 1991); and *Modern Tragedy*, 1966. It is apparent from the ways in which Williams revisited, augmented and revised these works to the way in which they were taken up by others, including The Open University, what a major contribution he made to the critical study of drama. In his foreword to the 1968 edition of *Drama from Ibsen to Brecht*, Williams himself describes the three books respectively as a critical study, a study of the relations between the written and acted play, and an analysis of ideas (Williams, 1968/1987:no page number).

'The problems of drama,' said Williams in his inaugural lecture of 1974, 'are now serious enough to be genuinely interesting and indeed to provoke new kinds of question' (Williams, 1983:11).

> New kinds of text, new kinds of notation, new media and new conventions press actively alongside the texts and conventions we think we know, but that I find problematic just because these others are there. Dramatic time and sequence in a play of Shakespeare, the intricate rhythms and relationships of chorus and three actors in a Greek tragedy: these I believe, become active in new ways as we look at a cutting bench or an editing machine, in a film or television studio, or as we

see new relations between actor and audience in the improvised theatre of the streets and basements.

(Williams, 1983:11)

We see again how changes in the means of production of different artistic forms so fascinated Williams. He had a deep interest in the influence, for example, of traditional theatre on film and television. The development of this thinking is fully described in Part 3 of *Politics and Letters*, where he discusses what he believes to be important in *Drama from Ibsen to Brecht*, but says much less about the other two books on drama. His interlocutors point out that *Modern Tragedy* is not limited to a discussion of drama, but also considers novels, philosophy and political history (see Williams, 1979/2015:210). In his response Williams describes how *Modern Tragedy* emerged from a course he gave at Cambridge on that topic, how he went into these lectures expecting to recount a chapter from *Drama from Ibsen to Eliot* 'and came out with the text of a chapter from *Modern Tragedy*' (Williams, 1979/2015:211). He points out:

> The same authors are discussed in the two books, the same themes developed, the same quotations used – which is the key point of continuity. But the discussion was now in a different mode. Where much of the earlier work had been rather technical, concentrating on dramatic conventions and the relationship to theatrical staging and individual playwrights, the new work was closer to ideological criticism.
>
> (Williams, 1979/2015:211)

Drama in Performance, as Holderness remarks in his introduction to the version published by Open University Press in 1991, was originally an early product of Williams's work in adult education. The early version from 1954 was highly original in its approach to the analysis of drama.

> The methods Williams developed here, that of situating for analysis plays or scenes within their original conditions of production, has become almost universal in theatrical and dramatic criticism. Yet, it was in its time, as the author himself proposed in the 1954 edition, 'original', and quite strikingly so.
>
> (Holderness,1991:9)

Holderness suggests that *Drama in Performance* proposes:

> a method of understanding drama as a material process of cultural production. There is virtually no focus on the dramatist, and no projected vision of a culture's ideological totality: the dramatic performance itself, conceived as the physical

realization of an enacted relationship with social convention, belief and ideology, mediates between them.

(Holderness, 1991:4–5)

This view was to provide the foundation for Williams's approach to understanding all forms of performance, whether in theatre, film or television.

As with his commitment to writing fiction alongside his critical study of literature (as we saw in Chapter 2) so with drama, Williams was not only a reviewer, commentator and critic, he was also a producer, a playwright. He wrote a number of plays for television (which are not available now for viewing, but see O'Connor, 1989:131 for details) and also a drama called *Koba*, the script of which appears in the 1966 edition of *Modern Tragedy*. The play is set in a country going through a bloody revolution. It appears to be based on events in Russia and in *Politics and Letters*, Williams's interviewers suggest it is a fundamentally pessimistic account, suggesting that revolution and totalitarianism go hand in hand. Williams acknowledges this as a possible reading but goes on to suggest that the ending actually offers a much more hopeful future – in contrast to what is happening in the actual Soviet Union where 'a denouement is still to be awaited' (Williams, 1979/2015:394). Williams was not alive to see the emergence of glasnost and perestroika or the fall of the Berlin Wall. In his highly critical discussion of the play in his book *The Alien Mind of Raymond Williams*, Jan Gorak suggests that:

> Williams lacks the theatrical means to communicate the horror and the violence of a revolution whose leadership has withdrawn from humanity ... Williams can neither recreate this terror convincingly in the minds of his characters nor display it in a spectacle across the stage.
>
> (Gorak, 1988:33–4)

The play has never been produced on the stage, whereas at least two of Williams's TV plays were produced and broadcast in 1966 and 1967 respectively. These plays were set in contemporary Britain and offer respectively a critique of government (Harold Wilson's Labour Government was in power at the time) and an examination of the experiences of railway workers in Wales. Gorak concludes, 'Working on the same lines as Brecht in *Galileo* or *Mother Courage*, Williams's television plays mount an inquiry into the alienating consequences of public service.' Gorak suggests all three plays are about forms of human alienation in the contemporary world, but that sadly Williams lacks 'some of the equipment of a successful playwright. He is more fond of words than of action and more fond of discussion than of argument' (Gorak, 1988:38). Parallel criticisms have been made by other commentators on Williams's fiction, but when these creative works are placed alongside the non-fictional opus, we may perhaps appreciate their relevance, significance and contribution to our understanding of the relationship between individuals and society.

Television

As we turn to consider his engagement with the medium of television, we may note that the kind of TV drama he was writing certainly complemented work by others who would become well known for their work such as Tony Garnett, Ken Loach and, later, Dennis Potter.

As noted in Chapter 5, Williams reviewed television for a number of years in the now-defunct *Listener* magazine. Writing in 1973, in the foreword to his volume called *Television: Technology and Cultural Form* (Williams, 1974), he says:

> This book is an attempt to explore and describe some of the relationships between television as a technology and television as a cultural form. In the contemporary debate about the general relations between technology, social institutions and culture, television is obviously an outstanding case. Indeed its present importance, as an element in each of these areas, and as a point of interaction between them, is in effect unparalleled.
>
> (Williams, 1974:7)

If that was true in the early 1970s, it is perhaps even more pertinent in the 2020s with the massive expansion of televisual provision, the proliferation of channels, of different commercial interests at play and the increasing role of this medium in political and social life. Williams goes on to note that in writing this book he does indeed draw heavily on his experience as a TV critic but also refers to the fact that much of the book was written during a stay in California, 'in a very different television situation' (Williams, 1974) – one, perhaps more familiar now in other Western countries.

The book analyses ways in which, through the development of a technology facilitating transmission from a central point to scattered households where individual viewers could receive broadcasts, new relationships were being established between producers and consumers. Writing in the days before the development of 'reality shows' (and one does wonder what he would have made of these) Williams outlines a number of 'forms' of television, listing: news; argument and discussion; education; drama; films; variety; sport; and, pastimes.

He then goes on to suggest a number of mixed and new forms, including drama-documentary and features. It is surprising that he does not list children's programmes as a distinctive form, although he does refer to *Sesame Street*. He moves on to discuss the key elements in programming, namely the static concept of 'distribution' and the dynamic concept of 'flow'[10] (the latter was also mentioned above in relation to film). This he does through a detailed analysis of what was offered on five channels in a week during March 1973. Three of the five channels are in the United Kingdom and two in the United States. By distribution he is essentially referring to the balance of different forms of programme shown over a period of time, for example, the proportion of news to drama to sport. With regard to flow, he suggests that broadcasting is different from other cultural forms in that the recipient/consumer/viewer may (or may not) watch a sequence of programmes or may switch from one channel to another. This is very different from the experience of watching the performance of a play or from reading a single novel, and it is this sequential aspect to which Williams gives the name 'flow'. He also points out that questions of flow *within* a programme are just as important as questions of flow *between* programmes.

In the final two chapters of the book, Williams turns to wider questions of ownership, control and alternative approaches that might be possible. In typical Williams's language he suggests:

> How the technology develops from now on is then not only a matter of some autonomous process directed by remote engineers. It is a matter of social and cultural definition, according to the ends sought ... Most technical development is in the hands of corporations which express the contemporary interlock of military, political and commercial institutions. Most policy development is in the hands of established broadcasting corporations and the political bureaucracies of a few powerful states.
>
> (Williams, 1974:134)

With the development of satellite technology, the rise of on demand viewing and 'pay as you view', the relationships between producers and viewers have become more complex and commercially liberated. Corporations still have a dominant role and the vast majority of them are now commercial organizations such as Sky or Fox News, while the public service corporations are frequently fighting for survival and struggling to remain solvent. Some of these developments are predicted by Williams in the closing chapter of the book but, as we would expect, what he calls for is greater community control of what is broadcast, greater local determination of programming, an increase in interaction through the medium and other similar democratizing developments. We may reflect that we can indeed see evidence of some such innovations (such as 'phone-ins', 'meet the public' shows, local radio and TV stations), but overall there can be little argument that the dominant forces and most watched programmes are those provided by a relatively small number of large and powerful commercial organizations.

Indeed electronic media have developed so dramatically since the 1970s that TV itself is no longer necessarily a key technology. The so-called convergence of media has led to much contemporary communication being undertaken on handheld devices – mobile phones and tablets – and many households now possess quite enormous TV screens. It is evident that these developments have changed the face of audiovisual communication without even mentioning the changes that have come about in listening to and viewing recorded material. The vinyl record replaced shellac, compact discs replaced vinyl and audio cassette tapes; most young and many older people now stream music through their own devices, perhaps through a subscription to a 'provider'. Video tapes of films and TV programmes were replaced by DVDs, but again these are approaching obsolescence as downloads and streaming take over. The deep paradox is that while these developments have increased personal choice and freedom over what to watch and listen to, they have simultaneously increased the influence and power of major corporations.[11] We can only wonder what Raymond Williams would have made of it all. Manuel Castells is one of the sociologists who have continued to analyse and discuss the impact of these and related changes, for example in developing the concept of 'The Network Society' (Castells, 1996/2000). The speed of technological developments, the rate of media 'convergence', the new ethical issues raised and the ways in which new forms of media can be exploited for abusive purposes all remind us of the crucial importance of a continuing analysis of all cultural forms, indeed the importance of a materialist understanding of culture and media.

6.4 Conclusion: Where Is Creativity in Contemporary Education?

> At the very centre of Marxism is an extraordinary emphasis on human creativity and self-creation.
>
> (Williams, 1977:207)

This is the opening sentence of the last chapter of *Marxism and Literature*; the chapter is called simply 'Creative Practice'. It would be true to say that it is not only Marxism that has this 'extraordinary emphasis', Williams himself in his cultural materialism also shared this emphasis.

If cultural studies and media studies have now become recognized subjects in the curricula of higher education and school education – even if sometimes they are still sneered at – what is the wider situation of the arts in contemporary education? Williams was passionate about defending creative activity as a key aspect of human endeavour. In this final section of the chapter we turn to consider the ways in which the arts and related areas are positioned within education and indeed how 'creativity' is framed, both by Williams himself and by others more recently. Once again *Keywords* is a starting point. We have already seen how art was examined by Williams, but 'creativity' is a closely related word which he also examined. He suggests that 'creativity emerged only as recently as the twentieth century' as 'a general name for the faculty of human action related to art and thought'. He suggests that the term creative

> has become steadily more important. But there is one obvious difficulty. The word puts a necessary stress on originality and innovation, and when we remember the history [of the word] we can see that these are not trivial claims.
> (Williams, 1976:73)

Williams goes on to suggest that:

> any imitative or stereotyped literary work can be called, by convention, **creative writing**, and advertising copywriters officially describe themselves as **creative**.
> (Williams, 1976:74)

> The difficulty is especially apparent when **creative** is extended, rightly in terms of the historical development, to activities in thought, language and social practice in which the specialized sense of *imagination* is not a necessary term. Yet such difficulties are inevitable when we realize the necessary magnitude and complexity of interpretation of human activity which **creative** now so indispensably embodies.
> (Williams, 1976)

If we take the term 'creative writing', which we see Williams use, and consider how it is deployed within education, the range of difficulties become apparent. Children in primary and secondary schools have long been required to engage in learning how to be 'creative writers' (and many university programmes are now dedicated to the subject). In schools it has become an established part of the (English) language curriculum, usually used to describe the writing processes where the pupil or student is expected to apply imagination, even though it could be argued that imagination is a crucial element in almost all acts of writing. In one sense all original writing is creative in that the writer has to select words to be used in a particular construction and shape the phrase, sentence and paragraph whether the material being recorded is fictional or not. Perhaps creative is being used as a synonym for imaginative. We could suggest that all original writing is creative but that it is not all imaginative. For usually, at least in school settings, the term 'creative writing' is associated with fictional or poetical work. When the adjective 'creative' is attached to other forms of human activity, say, music, painting or sculpture, it is often associated with 'originality' but yet some of the 'best' work may actually be derivative of the work of others. 'Creative' and its associated noun 'creativity' are thus problematic terms in an educational context. If the point of education – or at least one point – is to equip the learner with skills and knowledge that others already possess, then what is the meaning of creativity, at least in the sense of originality?

Perhaps these paradoxes are best captured by the phrase which became popular during the 1980s and 1990s in Britain, 'the creative industries'. If 'industry' had come to be related to production on a large scale and 'creative' was related to originality, the phrase 'creative industries' might be seen as something of an oxymoron. The ways in which these debates have been played out in the school curriculum, at least since the 1980s, are deeply indicative of these contradictions as we have seen numerous assaults on the arts – including music and drama – within the scope of the national curriculum in England. Indeed even within the English curriculum, the encouragement of original writing, whether poetry or prose, has also suffered considerably as increased emphasis has been given to matters of grammar, spelling and punctuation (Davison and Daly, 2020).

In one of his fullest discussions of creativity, in *Marxism and Literature*, Williams, whilst not referring in particular to education, nevertheless exposes the paradox considered here.

> Creative practice is thus of many kinds. It is already, and actively, our practical consciousness. When it becomes struggle – the active struggle for new consciousness through new relationships that is the ineradicable emphasis of the Marxist sense of self-creation – it can take many forms. It can be the long and difficult remaking of an inherited (determined) practical consciousness: a process often described as development but in practice a struggle at the roots of the mind – not casting off an ideology, or learning phrases about it, but confronting a hegemony in the fibres of the self and in the hard practical substance of effective and continuing relationships.
>
> (Williams, 1977:212)

As we saw earlier, there are tensions between the development of inherited cultural forms, human individuality and collective social progress. Williams's commitment to creativity as a driving force for overcoming these tensions is always apparent but can lead to apparent contradictions in his thinking. Gorak (mentioned in the previous section) alleges that *The Long Revolution* demonstrates just such contradictory elements. He argues that:

> Williams presents two aims that seem both separately and mutually inconsistent. First, he wants to make a gradual transition toward a radical change in consciousness, a hope that drives him back to the Labour party whose slow parliamentary reformism he had earlier condemned. And second, he wants to saturate culture as a whole way of life with the creative potential he criticizes 'high culture' for adopting as its own, a scheme that tacitly recognizes a social ladder he claims to have outgrown.
>
> (Gorak, 1988:61)

There was a resurgence of government interest in the arts and culture when 'New Labour' came to power in the UK in 1997. The Tony Blair-led government established a Department for Culture, Media and Sport. Chris Smith was appointed secretary of state at this department and argued enthusiastically for better support for people working in the arts and what he came to refer to as 'the creative industries'. His views are well expressed in the book *Creative Britain*, a collection of his speeches and articles (Smith, 1998). These developments reflected a growing recognition that the creative industries were a major success story in Britain's economy which, in other sectors, had been declining for many years.

These developments were also to have some impact in the field of state education. In 1998 Chris Smith together with David Blunkett, the secretary of state for education and employment, established 'The National Advisory Committee on Creative and Cultural Education'. The terms of reference for this committee were:

> To make recommendations to the Secretaries of State on the creative and cultural development of young people through formal and informal education: to take stock of current provision and to make proposals for principles, policies and practice.
>
> (NACCCE, 1999:4)

The Committee was chaired by Ken Robinson, the leading arts educator then at the University of Warwick. Its membership included cultural 'superstars' such as Dawn French, Lenny Henry and Simon Rattle, as well as headteachers and other arts educators. A report of more than 200 pages was published the year after the committee was established, entitled *All Our Futures: Creativity, Culture and Education*. At the beginning of the report it is noted that the work has coincided with a review of the National Curriculum (for England). We can see the interest in economic matters in the soundbite attributed to Prime Minister Tony Blair:

> Our aim must be to create a nation where the creative talent of all the people are used to build a true enterprise economy for the twenty-first century – where we compete on brains, not brawn.
>
> (NACCCE, 1999:6)

And David Blunkett is also quoted:

> we cannot rely on a small elite, no matter how highly educated or highly paid. Instead we need the creativity and enterprise and scholarship of all our people.
>
> (NACCCE, 1999)

Chris Smith echoes this:

> We must change the concept of creativity from being something that is 'added on' to education, skills and training and management and make sure it becomes intrinsic to all of these.
>
> (NACCCE, 1999)

More than ten years after Williams's death, we may deduce from a reading of the report that his influence is clear, notwithstanding the unproblematic view of the economic aspect espoused by Blair. Indeed, it is no surprise to see among the list of references at the end of report, the inclusion of *The Long Revolution*.[12]

In his introduction to the report, Ken Robinson writes:

> The key message of this report is the need for a new balance in education: in setting national priorities; in the structure and organisation of the school curriculum; in methods of teaching and assessment; in relationships between schools and other agencies. Over a number of years, the balance of education has been lost. There has been a tendency for the national debate on education to be expressed as a series of exclusive alternatives, even dichotomies: for example, as a choice between the arts or the sciences; the core curriculum or the broad curriculum; between academic standards or creativity; freedom or authority in teaching methods. We argue that these dichotomies are misleading and unhelpful. Realising the potential of young people, and raising standards of achievement and motivation includes all of these elements. Creating the right

synergy and achieving the right balance in education is an urgent task, from national policy making to classroom teaching.

(NACCCE, 1999:9)

This was a cogent articulation of the challenges facing the arts in education. The report certainly led to some interesting developments, including the establishment of a new agency: Creativity, Culture and Education, which supported a number of research and development projects in arts education. However, at the same time, the New Labour Government was introducing 'National Strategies' for literacy and numeracy. These strategies put increasing pressure on schools to 'deliver' in these aspects of learning and threatened schools with closure or conversion to academy status if they did not perform well in league tables, based on exam and test results. In reviewing curriculum policy during the Blair years, Wrigley concludes that:

> there has been a decisive shift ... towards a conception of curriculum as basic skills (literacy, numeracy, ICT) leading (for a large proportion of young people) to an early preparation for particular fields of work. Even those who are allowed a broader curriculum are expected to study it at such intensity and pace that the opportunity for critical thinking is squeezed out.
>
> (Wrigley, 2010:139)

Such pressures led once again to the sidelining of cultural matters in schooling. Certainly some schools maintained their commitment to creativity within their provision, but the majority were risk-averse and tended to limit their attention to what they had been informed was 'really important'. There were some education policies under New Labour which sought to address social inequality, such as 'Sure Start' and 'Education Action Zones', but the sheer number of initiatives as well as the emphasis on increasing diversity in secondary school provision tended to undermine the progressive policies and indeed to create a sense of incoherence (see Walford, 2006, or for a more positive account of creativity in the primary school curriculum, see Chapter 9 in Wyse et al., 2013).

The pressure on creativity and cultural matters in education was only one element in the contradictions in education policy emerging under the Labour Government from 1997 to 2010.

The impact of global neoliberalism on education in Britain has been enormous and the effects have been most pronounced in England. As one secretary of state after another read OECD reports based on PISA or the outcomes of other international league tables such as TIMSS and PiRLS,[13] we continue to see forms of retrenchment in the curriculum that appear to take us back to the early days of the twentieth century when rote learning and 'object lessons' – fact-based transmission of knowledge – were the order of the day. It is not only the scope for and encouragement of creativity, culture and the arts of the learners that are being stifled, the same is happening for teachers, whose work has become increasingly prescribed and for whom experimentation, innovation, indeed creativity are simultaneously increasingly proscribed. As Jones and colleagues put it:

> Neo-liberalism negates the past and repudiates the idea that education can be shaped by collective action, either popular or reactionary. Neither traditional conservatism, nor bureaucratically controlled selective systems nor social democratic egalitarianism are spared. Thus, rather than celebrating the achievements of its social democratic predecessors, the Blair government offers unrelenting criticism.
>
> (Jones et al., 2008:136)

The implication of this depressing analysis might well be that the Williams's triumvirate of old humanists, public educators and industrial trainers had now been reduced to the domination, the hegemony, of the industrial trainers in their new form. While Raymond Williams, had he lived to see it published, might well have been deeply critical of many elements of the report *All Our Futures*, not least in its simplistic coupling of the economy and creativity, he might have welcomed the kinds of aspirations for curriculum development and imaginative teaching that it conveys. The report overall should certainly have been a major contribution to the democratization of culture. Its almost total disappearance under the forces of performativity and standards in education in England, assiduously pursued under successive governments after Labour lost power in 2010, constitutes a considerable tragedy for education and for future citizens.

7

The Theoretical Legacy – Structures of Feeling; Cultural Materialism; Base and Superstructure

> *Theory* has an interesting development and range of meanings, and a significant distinction from (later an opposition to) practice.
>
> (*Keywords*, Williams, 1976:266)

Introduction

In *Keywords*, Williams identifies 'theory' as having had a range of meanings as early as the seventeenth century. The meaning most relevant to the discussion in this chapter is 'a scheme of ideas which explains practice' (Williams, 1976:267). 'But,' he continues, '**theory** in this important sense is always in active relation to *practice*: an interaction between things done, things observed and (systematic) explanation of these. This allows the necessary distinction between theory and practice, but does not require their opposition' (Williams, 1976). In education studies, especially in the context of professional learning, the distinction between theory and practice is frequently drawn (and has become part of the cultural debate on teacher education), but, as Williams argues, there is no need for this opposition. For example, we can consider the important idea of 'practical theorizing' as a key element in professional learning (Burn et al., forthcoming).

As we have seen in the earlier chapters of this book, Raymond Williams was highly original in the theoretical tools he deployed in his analysis of social and cultural matters. In this chapter I seek to draw out some of the key elements in his theoretical thinking and consider their application in the study of education. One of the earliest of his important ideas was that of 'structures of feeling'. Earlier we saw how this emerged not only from his study of classic English literature but also from his interest in film studies. The idea has subsequently been taken up by many scholars and developed – as well as critiqued. The full blossoming of an explicitly cultural materialist perspective perhaps developed more gradually, but this is now seen as the most important overall paradigm of thinking within which Williams's work lies. We will examine how such a paradigm offers an important perspective in the study of education. Cultural materialism is very much an outcome of a blending of literary criticism with elements of Marxist theory. We have seen how Williams's relationship with Marxism was a complex and changing one, yet, never one to avoid difficult discussions, he increasingly addressed his own (and others') engagement with this crucial element of twentieth-century social theory, not least in his 1977 work *Marxism and Literature*. One particularly interesting idea from an educational point of view is that of 'base and superstructure' and it is to this idea that we subsequently turn. The conclusion to the chapter offers a review of the ways in which the deployment of Williams's theoretical ideas has informed the study of education and offers some directions for further work in this area.

7.1 Structures of Feeling

Williams concedes that structures of feeling is a difficult term. In *Marxism and Literature* he writes:

> 'feeling' is chosen to emphasize a distinction from more formal concepts of 'world-view' or 'ideology'. It is not only that we must go beyond formally held and systematic beliefs, though of course we have always to include them. It is that we are concerned with meanings and values as they are actually lived and felt, and the relations between these and formal or systematic beliefs are in practice variable (including historically variable), over a range from formal assent with private dissent to the more nuanced interaction between selected and interpreted beliefs and acted and justified experiences.
>
> (Williams, 1977:132)

In some sense Williams is seeking a term which can straddle the objective and subjective domains of human experience. It is a term which has the solidity of 'structure' and the fluidity of 'feeling'. It is perhaps surprising that more explicit use has not been made of this notion within education studies, where these two elements are so clearly present. We have, for example, the *structure* of a curriculum and of assessment procedures but simultaneously the *feeling* of the individual learner as he or she goes through the processes of developing understanding and skills. Some insights in relation to this were provided in Chapter 2, where we considered fictional depictions of learning and teaching and could begin to see how the conditions for learning and the lived experience of teachers and learners relate to each other. This, it must be emphasized, is not a process of determination; rather, it is a dialectical relationship between what we might call the educational environment and the experiences of the teachers and learners who are living and working therein.

In their work on the globalization of education policy, Rizvi and Lingard (2010:34) have suggested that Williams's 'structure of feeling' is 'akin' to 'the social imaginary', a term which has become popular in sociological discourse over recent years; they suggest that both of these terms are in some sense equivalent to Bourdieu's development of 'habitus'. Certainly all these terms represent an attempt to capture something which in some ways is intangible, yet which the materialist urge in the sociologist – an element of the 'sociological imagination', to use Wright Mill's term (Mills, 1959) – seeks to make tangible.

In one of the earliest discussions of Williams's concept of structures of feeling in the context of education, Rex Gibson, in *Structuralism and Education* (Gibson, 1984), devoted a chapter to the topic. Gibson readily acknowledges that it is a complex term to deploy and actually equates it with 'feeling structure', a term Williams himself did not use and may actually be seen as more akin to 'mood' or even, in an educational context, 'ethos'. Gibson writes about the classroom where structures of feeling:

> identify the particular modes and tones of relationship, perception and valuing which characterise any classroom, school or community (indeed all forms of social grouping). They are the ethos or climate within which individuals have their being, and they are the values and assumptions which colour, influence, inform or dominate each individual's response.
>
> (Gibson, 1984:62)

While being an interesting and potentially productive deployment of the term, this seems somewhat weaker than Williams's use. Williams always emphasized the historical and wider social and cultural elements of the term. The difficulty with Gibson's attempts to link structures of feeling with education is that he has a tendency to reify the term, to attach it to particular relatively narrow concepts which fail to capture the wider implications. For example he takes 'achievement', 'social welfare' and 'spontaneity' each as exemplars of structures of feeling within schooling. These are terms that have some relevance in education but seem too limited to demonstrate the power of Williams's concept.

Gibson then takes a number of research studies from the 1970s and 1980s and explores them for further instances of educational structures of feeling. Including work by David Hargreaves, Stephen Ball, Paul Willis and Ronald King, he identifies the following as examples of structures of feeling revealed in these studies: professionalism; individualism; community; democracy; academic; disciplinary; idealist; instrumental rationality. Each of the terms included in this rather disparate list signifies something interesting which has emerged from the study concerned, but to equate any one of them to a structure of feeling seems to diminish the power of that term, as Williams himself deploys it, in failing to signify again the broader social, historical and cultural connections.

In order to explain this further, let us consider what we might argue to be the most tangible recent example of how structures of feeling may help in explaining educational change. This example is the case of public education in England in the 1980s. The wider social changes, often collected under the term coined by Stuart Hall, as 'Thatcherism' (Hall, 1988; see also Jessop, Bonnett, Bromley and Ling, 1988), were captured in novels, films and TV, for example in David Lodge's novel, *Nice Work* (1985) or Hanif Kureshi's film *My Beautiful Laundrette* (1985). The characteristics most commonly associated with this dramatic shift in culture and society include the privatization of public utilities and services, the attacks on trade unions, the promotion of 'fast capitalism' (Agger, 2004) and the legitimation of selfish individualism. Prime Minister Margaret Thatcher (in)famously suggested in 1987 that 'there is no such thing as society, there are individual men and women and there are families' (https://www.theguardian.com/politics/2013/apr/08/margaret-thatcher-quotes).

In education at this time, we saw an increasing domination of the 'industrial trainer' forces in education and the promotion of measurement, competition and a prescribed curriculum in state schools, if not in the private school sector. The introduction of 'market forces' into state education provision, the emphases on parental choice and diversity in school selection began to emerge strongly during this period (LeGrand and Bartlett, 1993; Ball, 2003). The history of the 'economization' of English education has been well documented. Most frequently, the Labour prime minister James Callaghan's speech at Ruskin College, Oxford, in 1976, is suggested to have been the beginning of the process (as was mentioned in Chapter 3). He expressed anxiety about the quality of education provision in England and, in particular, its alleged failure to provide the kind of workforce which could make significant contributions to national prosperity in the context of an increasingly competitive global economy. By the time the Conservative Government led by Thatcher came to power in 1979, attacks on the quality of state education had proliferated in many parts of the public media and through publication of a range of pamphlets published by right-wing think tanks (see Jones, 1989). One of Thatcher's leading monetarist colleagues, Keith Joseph, became education secretary in the mid-1980s and published a White Paper on *Teaching Quality* (DES, 1983). This paper was significant in initiating the processes of 'shaking up' the educational establishment but turned out to be a precursor to even more dramatic changes to come. The 'Great Education Reform Bill' of 1987 led to the Education Reform Act in 1988, which brought in a prescribed National Curriculum as well as new national assessment procedures with testing of children at the ages of 7, 11 and 13, in addition to the existing public examinations at 16 and 18 (see Simon, 1988). Significant changes were also brought about in the management and governance of schools and in the introduction of new types of schools, including 'City Technology Colleges'. These changes were overseen by Kenneth Baker, who had previously been at the Department of Trade and Industry and was indubitably, in Williams's term, an industrial trainer of the most committed kind.

A range of studies of education in England undertaken in the 1990s reveal how the nature of experience within the system was changing. While Stephen Ball and colleagues were tracking the changing nature of policy processes in education (Bowe and Ball with Gold, 1992) and ways in which the market – or at least a 'quasi-market' (LeGrand and Bartlett, 1993) – was being introduced (Ball, 1990; 1994; 2003), other researchers were exploring the ways in which these policies were reshaping teaching and learning in schools, so creating a new structure of feeling in English education. A major study led by Andrew Pollard used a mixed-methods approach to ascertain what was happening in primary schools (Pollard et al., 1994). English primary education had developed a tradition of placing the relationship between children and their class teachers as central, as depicted, for example, in Nias's study of *Primary Teachers Talking* (Nias, 1989). However, the study by Pollard and colleagues showed that the enormous magnitude of policy changes introduced in the wake of the 1988 Education Reform Act was having a dramatic effect on these relationships. Emphasizing teachers' attempts to minimize the negative impact of these changes they suggested that primary school teachers in England tended to be:

> concerned about the children in their class in social, emotional and physical terms, as well as intellectually. They were concerned about parents, the school, its role in the community and the nature of education policy.
>
> (Pollard et al., 1994:237)

Pollard and colleagues went on to say, however, that:

> Some teachers feared that pupils' values, especially their level of commitment to school, might also become more instrumental because of the fragmentation and overload of the National Curriculum, the necessary changes in classroom routines and the categoric labelling of national assessment procedures.
>
> (Pollard et al., 1994)

In a subsequent study of the experiences of primary pupils through examining their 'strategic biographies', Pollard, working with Ann Filer, suggested that:

> the subject-based National Curriculum introduced to England and Wales in the early 1990s was traditional in structure, conservative in content and may unwittingly undermine forms of education which are necessary preparations for the future ...
>
> ... Systemic curricular specification, assessment, inspection and accountability systems, combined with professional training and support, should certainly increase the quality and consistency of teaching across schools. However, this reflects a partial and ultimately invalid model of learning itself.
>
> (Pollard and Filer, 1999:309)

Pollard and Filer go on to express concern about the risk of increasing the differential impact of the reforms:

> Despite considerable knowledge of inequalities associated with social class, ethnicity, gender and disability, systemic education reforms of the 1990s were not designed responsively.
>
> (Pollard and Filer, 1999)

These extracts demonstrate how dramatically the structure of feeling in English primary education was changing during the 1990s. A rather different kind of study of primary education carried out at much the same time explicitly connected the changing nature of teachers' work to the creation of 'post-Fordist' working practices. Drawing on labour process theory, the study found many teachers were experiencing a deep psychic conflict brought about both by the volume of policy change and by the nature of these reforms, undermining their established professional identities (Menter, Muschamp, Nicholls and Ozga with Pollard, 1997). This study more directly links the experiences of these educational reforms to the wider changes in the structure of feeling at this time. This is a rather different way of making use of the concept from that used by

Gibson, more complex and abstract perhaps, but more closely aligned with Williams's theoretical orientation in his use of the term.

7.2 Cultural Materialism

Structure of feeling is an excellent example of a concept that captures the significance of cultural materialism. 'Cultural materialism is surely the key to the understanding and assessment of Williams's intellectual legacy.' So wrote John Higgins in his important assessment of Williams as a literary critic (Higgins, 1999:171).

'Cultural materialism' is the term which is most frequently used to describe Williams's perspective or overall theoretical orientation. Jim McGuigan, a leading exponent of Williams's ideas, explains cultural materialism in this way:

> Critical analysis, for [Williams] was always historical, including interrogation of the balance of power in present-day culture and society. And, most importantly, the changing meaning of words in public circulation over time and both 'traditional' and 'modern' cultural forms and media. And most importantly, Williams contested accounts of social and cultural change that privileged technological innovation in isolation from economic, ideological and political factors. He stressed the importance of human agency and its capacity to change the world, albeit within determinate conditions inherited from the past and held in place by dominant structures and institutions.
>
> (McGuigan, 2019:2)

McGuigan compares Williams with Pierre Bourdieu and Jurgen Habermas, suggesting in relation to the former that:

> Williams's cultural materialism and Bourdieu's sociology of culture have much in common, particularly with their mutual concern for class and inequality. Bourdieu was much more empirically inclined than Williams, however, but certainly shared similar inclinations such as critical alarm at the implications of neo-liberalism for social democracy.
>
> (McGuigan, 2019:8)

McGuigan compares Habermas's work on the public sphere with Williams's on common culture and suggests that Williams had 'much greater appreciation of culture, especially popular culture' (McGuigan, 2019). Habermas is often seen as a founding parent of 'critical theory'. It is therefore fascinating to read that in a book linking critical theory and education, following his earlier work on structuralism and education, Gibson suggests:

> The British version of critical theory can be called 'cultural materialism', a term stemming from the work of Raymond Williams. Based on the notion that meaning is always produced, never simply expressed, cultural materialism sets itself a wide aim. It seeks:
>
> ... the analysis of all forms of signification, including quite centrally writing, within the actual means and conditions of production.
>
> Its attitude to 'culture' is expansive and analytic: television, pop music, skinheads comprise its objects of study as well as the works of Shakespeare. Its 'materialism' is marked its insistence on the necessary interdependence of culture and the economic effects of life. Shakespeare cannot be understood without reference to the economic and political system of his age – and ours.
>
> (Gibson, 1986:99; the Williams quotation is from *Writing in Society*)

Williams himself offers an extended discussion of materialism in *Keywords*, recognizing a range of meanings and again identifying it as a complex word. In his elaboration he refers to Marxian theory and discusses both historical and dialectical materialism. He does not mention cultural materialism as such, perhaps indicating that he had not yet fully formulated his ideas about this concept when compiling the famous lexicon. Even in *Marxism and Literature* (Williams, 1977), in one sense a book which is a full exposition of this very term, Williams only makes explicit use of it in the introduction, where he writes of his own stance:

> It is a position which can be briefly described as cultural materialism: a theory of the specificities of material culture and literary production within historical materialism ... it is, in my view, a Marxist theory, and indeed that in its specific fields it is, in spite of and even because of the relative unfamiliarity of some of its elements, part of what I at least see as the central thinking of Marxism.
>
> (Williams, 1977:5–6)

Similarly in his contribution to the Fontana 'New Sociology' series, *Culture* (Williams, 1981), published four years after *Marxism and Literature*, the term 'cultural materialism' is not explicitly used, although the whole text might again be seen as an exposition on this subject. He perhaps comes closest to using the term in the chapter entitled 'Means of Production', at the start of which he discusses the words 'material' and 'culture':

whatever purposes cultural practice may serve, its means of production are unarguably material. Indeed, instead of starting from the misleading contrast between 'material' and 'cultural', we have to define two areas for analysis: first, the relations between these material means and the social forms within which they are used ... and, second, the relations between these material means and social forms and the specific (artistic) forms which are a manifest cultural production.

(Williams, 1981:87–8)

In his discussion of the term, Higgins suggests:

Cultural materialism ... challenged the commitment to the singular, absolute and unicausal priority of the economy and refused its equally firm relegation of cultural activity to a secondary role in the reproduction of the social order. The means and relations of communication belong alongside the means and forces of production as one of the constituents of any explanations of the functioning of the social totality.

(Higgins, 1999:125)

Here, Higgins is suggesting that, while Williams developed this perspective largely through his work in literary criticism, it is also an invaluable resource in analysing any social processes and formations. We may productively consider what distinctive insights we hope to gain by deploying a cultural materialist analysis of educational policy and practice. For if educational processes are not fundamentally cultural – and in the broadest sense – literary, then little else is. As McGuigan points out, the emphasis placed by Williams on writing within this definition led to:

understating the scope of cultural materialism as a *sociological* methodology. It has had unfortunate consequences in artificially delimiting the potential applications of cultural materialism in the Social Sciences.

(McGuigan, 2014:xxi)

This is perhaps another partial explanation of why Williams's theoretical ideas have not been adopted more extensively in education studies. But from the chapter on education in *The Long Revolution* onwards, it is apparent that the material conditions for the production of educational experiences for both teachers and learners are highly significant. If there is truth in Bernstein's famous dictum that 'education cannot compensate for society' (Bernstein, 1970), it is equally true that educational systems and processes cannot be understood if they are analysed in isolation from the wider society in which they take place.

Elsewhere, Bernstein (1971) also suggested three particular 'message systems' apparent when studying education. He defined these as curriculum, pedagogy and evaluation. If we take each of these in turn we can consider how a cultural materialist perspective provides a distinctive set of insights. Indeed the notion of message systems is remarkably close to Williams's own preferred term of 'signification'. Higgins suggests:

> The task of a cultural materialism was to attend to that constitutive role of signification within cultural process, and so to seek to integrate the three usually separated dimensions of textual, theoretical and historical analysis ...
>
> ... Cultural materialism is the analysis of the constitutive grounds and force of all forms of signification at work in human society.
>
> (Higgins, 1999:135)

Let us here consider the three signifiers identified by Bernstein as being distinctively educational and seek to integrate the textual, the theoretical and the historical.

Curriculum

The term 'curriculum' is taken to represent what is taught and learned in the educational process, in crude terms the 'content' of education. As we saw in earlier chapters, any curriculum is by definition a selection from the wider culture. What we are alerted to when taking a cultural materialist approach is the significance of determining who makes these selections and why they make them in the way they do. Williams addressed this directly in Chapter 7 of *Culture*, on the topic of reproduction. He discusses first education and then tradition as two vehicles of cultural reproduction.

> It is characteristic of educational systems to claim that they are transmitting 'knowledge' or 'culture' in an absolute, universally derived sense, though it is obvious that different systems, at different times and in different countries, transmit radically different selective versions of both.
>
> (Williams, 1981:186)

Referring to Bourdieu's and Passeron's book on *Reproduction in Education, Society and Culture* (1977) Williams suggests that there are 'fundamental and necessary relations between this selective version and the existing social relations'. These:

> can be seen in the disposition of a curriculum, in the modes of selection of those who are to be educated and in what ways, and in definitions of educational (pedagogic) authority. It is then reasonable, at one level, to speak of the general educational process as a key form of cultural reproduction, which can be linked with that more general reproduction of existing social relations which is assured by existing and self-prolonging property and other economic relations, institutions of state and other political power, religious and family forms. To ignore these links is to submit to the arbitrary authority of a self-proclaimed 'autonomous' system.
>
> (Williams, 1981)

'Tradition' too is a social construct which selects what are considered to be desirable elements from the past and uses those to posit 'our cultural heritage'.[1] Williams writes: 'In this it [tradition] resembles education, which is a comparable selection of desired knowledge and of modes of learning and authority' (Williams, 1981:187).

If we turn again to consider the impact of what happened to state education in England in the 1980s (as discussed above), for teachers who trained at some point from the 1990s onwards, it may have been less than apparent that there was any curriculum at all before 'The National Curriculum'. The central determination of much of what is now taught in the state sector of schools is historically a relatively recent development – although there were precedents early in the twentieth century. In the period from the 1944 Education Act, through to the 1988 Education Reform Act, teachers and schools had considerable autonomy in deciding what it was that their pupils should learn. The most powerful constraint on this was the syllabi of public examinations taken in secondary schools at 16 and 18. This is not to say that there were not significant differences of educational experience for pupils during this period. The 'tripartite system' of secondary schooling which developed after the Second World War was one in which – as we saw in Chapter 3 – purportedly different kinds of children were given different types of education. The grammar schools provided educational experiences designed to prepare students eventually to move on to higher education. The secondary modern schools, on the other hand, were for children who were not expected to move on to university but enter the economy as skilled workers of some sort. The technical schools (there were actually not many of these established) were very much for those expected to enter manual labouring jobs; the curriculum here was 'practical' and strongly skills-based: what would now commonly be called a vocational curriculum.

The critiques of this differential provision grew stronger during the 1960s and 1970s and there were moves towards 'comprehensivization', the provision of a common school for all students in the state sector. This created considerable curriculum challenges for teachers and saw the differential provision becoming increasingly internalized *within* schools, in the forms of streaming and/or banding. Nevertheless at this time it was largely teachers themselves shaping decisions about what particular classes would study, albeit with support and guidance from subject associations and professional agencies such as The Schools Council. There was considerable experimentation with cross-curricular approaches and within primary schools some commitment to integrated learning. These approaches were based on the study of a particular topic with far less emphasis on discrete subjects, even though the subjects were still present. Curriculum autonomy of this kind came to a rapid end following the 1988 Act, when within two or three years, a curriculum was introduced distinguishing between 'core' and 'foundation' subjects and setting 'attainment targets' for children of different ages as they moved through the 'Key Stages'. A radically different framework was here imposed on schools in England, transforming both the curriculum experienced by pupils and the ways in which teachers were managed and controlled. In Bernstein's terms the 'classification' of the curriculum was stronger than ever, with clear demarcations between different subjects and, although there were initially some efforts to continue the development of 'cross-curricular themes' (see Whitty, Rowe and Aggleton, 1994), it was not long before these became virtually invisible.

Pedagogy

If the National Curriculum was strongly *classified* through the implementation of the 1988 Act, then approaches to teaching and learning, what Bernstein referred to as pedagogy, were, in his terms, increasingly strongly *framed* (Bernstein, 1971). We saw earlier how the central government began to take control of teachers and teaching from the mid-1980s onwards and the 'reforms' of teacher education which commenced in 1984 took stronger and stronger hold (the 'tightening grip'; see Childs and Menter 2013). The 1988 Act, however, required teachers to 'deliver' the National Curriculum and they had little choice. Massive programmes of in-service training were organized by the government under the auspices of the National Curriculum Council (see Graham, 1993) to ensure that teachers understood the framework and could enact their new responsibilities. In due course a series of 'standards' by which teachers could be judged were introduced. These applied in initial teacher education (Mahony and Hextall, 2000) and beyond and were also used when the subsequent 'New Labour' government introduced, in the late 1990s, forms of performance-related pay. Standards were deemed to be observable skills and qualities which teachers were required to demonstrate if they were to be deemed successful in the classroom. The New Labour government went even further in 1997 when, in pursuit of improved standards in literacy and numeracy, they introduced 'National Strategies' into primary education. These strategies stipulated not only what should be taught but very specifically how it should be done. Primary teachers were now required to provide a 'literacy hour' and a 'numeracy hour' each day, with a very particular plan over that hour for particular activities. In literacy the only acceptable way of teaching reading was through what was called 'synthetic phonics', an approach that has been seriously contested by many experts in early literacy around the world. Considerably more in-service training ('death by overheads' as some teachers referred to it at the time) was required to ensure that teachers could implement these policies.

Overall, teachers were being directly managed and controlled in their work in a way which became characterized by the term 'performativity'. Their work was controlled, measured, judged and, depending on these judgements, led to promotion and reward or to demotion and dejection. The processes of cultural production in the profession of teaching had completely altered the nature of teachers' work and also their professional identities. As Ball wrote, when he reviewed these changes (as did others in similar vein):

> Over time, as the effect of the concatenation of policy moves, *teachers have been remade within policy,* and the work and meaning of teaching has been discursively rearticulated. This has been brought on by the introduction of new forms of preparation, new work practices and new workers into the classroom, and the use of a new language through which teachers talk about what they do and are talked about, think about themselves and judge themselves and one another and are measured and appraised, and paid, in relation to their performance.
> (Ball, 2013:171, *emphasis in original*)

Evaluation

The third message system, referred to by Bernstein as evaluation, is more readily understood today as assessment. The ways in which radical reforms in this aspect of schooling in England have affected experiences of teachers and learners are clear. Although public examinations in the form of GCSEs at 16 and A Levels at 18 were well established in the 1980s, the policymakers in Whitehall decided much more rigour was required in tracking pupil achievement throughout their schooling. Thus, it was proposed to carry out 'Standard Assessment Tasks' (SATs) at the end of each of Key Stages 1, 2 and 3. These would be standardized tests in the core subjects of English, mathematics and science and the results of individuals' performance would be reported to parents. The results, in collated form, would also be published in the form of 'league tables', to ascertain how 'effective' particular schools were in 'raising standards', as well as being used by the schools' inspectorate, Ofsted, to help inform their judgements about the overall performance of schools. This was another element of the performativity and accountability agenda imposed on schools.

For this scheme to be implemented, a new and elaborate technology of testing was developed. There was concern over questions of validity and reliability, of unintended outcomes such as 'teaching to the test' and also, given the high-stakes nature of the outcomes of these procedures, concerns about possible fraudulence. The overall signification (to use Williams's term) was to legitimate the idea that all learning could be meaningfully measured and that all processes of teaching and learning could be assessed by specific outcomes. This highly technologized view of education fits well with an industrial training model but far less well with notions of old humanism and/or of public education.

Summary

Having reviewed these three message systems from the perspective of cultural materialism, we can perhaps begin to understand the importance of educational provision itself as a system of cultural production. Writing some years before the eruption of the Education Reform Act, Williams could well have been foreseeing this as an example of how social institutions should be studied, when he wrote (in *Culture*):

> The social character of cultural production, which is evident in all periods and forms, is now more directly active and inescapable than in all earlier developed societies. There are then persistent and major contradictions between this central social character of cultural production and, on the one hand, the residual forms of specific cultural production and, on the other hand, the still determining forms of political and economic control.
>
> (Williams, 1981:233)

Such a description certainly evokes what was happening in English schooling from the 1980s onwards. In the next section we will consider in more detail what Williams meant by residual (and other) forms of production.

7.3 Base and Superstructure in Social Theory – Where Is Education?

In 1973, an influential paper written by Williams, called 'Base and superstructure in Marxist cultural theory', was published in *New Left Review* (and subsequently reprinted in Williams, 1980: *Problems in Materialism and Culture*). In it he reflects on the then-current debate within Marxian scholarship of the relationship between the underlying economic base and the cultural superstructure. He suggests:

> Any modern approach to a Marxist theory of culture must begin by considering the proposition of a determining base and a determined superstructure.
> (Williams, 1980:31)

This proposition, he goes on to say, may be in some tension with another fundamental Marxist tenet, that 'social being determines consciousness'. The word 'determines' in both propositions causes the difficulty. As we have seen at previous points in our discussion, Williams was resistant to any view of the social world which suggests that human beings have little or no agency. Williams constantly stressed the complexity and nuances evident in the relationships between humans and their environment. One aspect of this complexity, certainly in the study of culture, is that of the processes of change over time. To address this he identifies three cultural forms: the dominant, the residual and the emergent. To clarify what he means by the dominant culture he refers to Gramsci's notion of hegemony and suggests there is a 'central system of practices, meanings and values' which constitute the dominant culture in any particular time and place.

> It ... constitutes a sense of reality for most people in the society, a sense of absolute because experienced reality beyond which it is very difficult for most members of the society to move in most areas of their lives.[2]
> (Williams, 1980:38)

But this reality is constructed through social processes, leading to 'incorporation'. He writes:

> The modes of incorporation are of great social significance. The educational institutions are usually the main agencies of the transmission of an effective dominant culture, and this is now a major economic as well as cultural activity; indeed it is both in the same moment.
>
> (Williams, 1980:39)

This is the nub of the idea which gave rise to popular sociological theories of education in the 1970s of 'correspondence' between schooling and the economy (Bowles and Gintis, 1976) and of 'reproduction' (Bourdieu and Passeron, 1977), discussed earlier in Chapter 3.

Here Williams goes on to reiterate his views about 'the selective tradition',

> that which, within the terms of an effective dominant culture, is always passed off as '*the* tradition', '*the* significant past'. But always selectivity is the point; the way in which from a whole possible area of past and present, certain meanings and practices are chosen for emphasis, certain other meanings and practices are neglected and excluded.
>
> (Williams, 1980:39)

This idea is close to that which the much more determinist Marxist Louis Althusser called the 'Ideological State Apparatus' (ISAs) (Althusser, 1971). Schooling in Althusser's view was a key element of the ISAs within any capitalist society, along with other key institutions, such as the church and the family.

Within education, at least in advanced capitalist societies, we can frequently see how the dominant culture is strongly imbued with elements of the residual culture. Even at a time of considerable upheaval in state education policies, we can see evidence of the ways in which the traditional curriculum is defended and protected. The culture wars around the history and English curricula are the clearest manifestations of this. From the days of the Black Papers onwards (see Chapter 3) we can see how 'tradition' plays a strong and emotive role in the debates about reform.

In Williams's terms, emergent culture can take various forms. In education, emergent culture can be seen in efforts to 'modernize' the curriculum or attempts to make greater use of new technologies in educational processes. There have also been moments in education history when emergent cultural forms have been seen to pose a threat certainly to the residual elements, but also to the dominant elements. The so-called educational progressivism of the 1960s and 1970s could be seen as a period of emergent cultural forms coming into considerable tension with dominant and residual tendencies (Wright, 1977). At such times, in sociological terms, the tensions may be seen as posing a threat to the 'correspondence' between education and society, as a potential rupture in the processes of social reproduction that the education system has underpinned. The same might be said around the struggles over anti-racism and gender equality in education that arose so prominently during the 1980s (and continue to this day, albeit often less visibly) (Jones, 1989).

For Williams, education and education systems may be seen as key sites of cultural struggle where the disjunctions between base and superstructure may be perceived as opening up and causing disruption in society. These processes continue in Western societies and, whereas Williams would no doubt have seen them as reflecting continuing underlying social class struggles, this is very rarely the interpretation placed on these debates in the early twenty-first century. They are more frequently analysed in terms of ideological conflict, or as tensions between politicians or policymakers and professionals working in education. However, if we are prepared to see the struggle for popular universal and empowering education as a key element of the long revolution then we may be much more inclined to recognize and understand the undercurrents of these struggles in class terms.

7.4 Review: Making Sense of Education Policy Today

These theoretical ideas developed by Williams over his lifetime provide a powerful resource, or set of resources for helping us make sense of contemporary developments in education. Although, perhaps unsurprisingly, cultural materialism is most frequently deployed within the field of cultural studies per se, and other closely related fields, the proposal to be made here is that it has a much wider applicability. But, in keeping with Williams's own views, it is important to remind ourselves that both education and culture need to be seen as broad terms. Education does not take place only within formal institutions; it is a wider social process of being and becoming, of social experience. Culture is indeed ordinary, informal and a whole way of life, but also includes literature, films, music, drama and other formally creative activities. The formal expressions of education and culture within our society, can nevertheless be more deeply understood through the lens of cultural materialism, thanks to Williams's thinking. It is vital that we examine the history of the relevant institutions and cultural forms and explore the ways in which they have been and are produced. In particular we will need to determine who has developed them and ask what their interests are in doing so.

In the final section of this chapter my purpose is to demonstrate ways in which Williams's ideas offer distinctive insights to some contemporary features of education and culture. As examples I take in turn issues around: management, leadership and governance in education; developments in the education of teachers; the development of 'environmental education'; the framing of inequality in education, as expressed through the metaphor of 'closing the gap'; and, finally, a discussion about the impact of the coronavirus pandemic in 2020–1 on educational provision in England and elsewhere. Though the backdrop for these discussions is a distinctive structure of feeling which has shaped experience across much of the 'Western' world, the discussion will focus most particularly on England, where, it may be suggested, there is a distinctive variant of that structure of feeling.

The past fifty years, from the late 1970s until the early 2020s, has been a period during which the long revolution has in many senses stalled, if not reversed, in education and in the wider society. The political climate has shifted from one of 'social democracy' to one of consumerist populism. The industrial base has shifted from one based on manufacturing and heavy industry to one of finance and technological applications. The cultural make-up has diversified radically with the old popular and elitist forms continuing but being overlain by rapid developments in audio and screen technologies. Yet inequalities in wealth and power have not only persisted but have also been amplified (Dorling, 2015; Wilkinson and Pickett, 2009; Savage, 2015; Friedman and Laurison, 2020). Terms that commentators have used in an attempt to capture some of this structure of feeling include 'neoliberalism', 'post-truth' and 'chumocracy'. Each of these terms conveys elements of the prevalent structure of feeling, but none of them does full justice to the complex set of relationships and production characterising this period.

Before discussing these five cases, all of which are concerned primarily with education in England, it is crucial to remind ourselves of the significance of globalization. The structure of feeling just described is strongly connected to global influences involving economic as well as cultural elements (structural as well as superstructural). Education policy developments in many countries, including England, are now strongly influenced by global organizations such as the OECD, not least through the power of the 'PISA' league tables (see Sahlberg, 2010). When we consider network governance in the next section, or, in teacher education, the "Teach for All" movement with its English version "Teach First", we have good examples of how international organizations are influencing education in England (Ball, 2007, 2012; Thomas, Rauschenberger and Crawford-Garrett, 2021). Nevertheless there is a distinctively English version of educational developments. To use a term created by Appadurai and developed by Rizvi and Lingard (2010), we see here a particular manifestation of 'vernacular globalization'.

Management, leadership and governance in education

We have already noted (in Chapter 3) ways in which the nature of policymaking in education began to change in the 1970s. The break-up of a consensus approach, a 'partnership' between key stakeholders in making decisions about the future of education, took place rapidly during the 1980s. In the name of choice and diversity, schools, colleges and universities were each given greater independence. By the time of the 2010 Coalition government, in relation to compulsory schooling, there was an official rhetoric of 'a school-led system'. This transition involved a major change in the nature of school leadership, with the role of the headteacher becoming much more aligned to that of a chief executive officer of a business or company, rather than the leading pedagogical figure of an educational institution. The business orientation of public sector organizations was not limited to educational establishments of course but was visible across all sectors, including health and public amenities. However, within education, the ways in which this 'new managerialism' or New Public Management (Clarke and Newman, 1997; Newman, 2001) influenced educational establishments were as visible in the university sector as they were in schools and early years provision (Deem, Hillyard and Reed, 2008; Collini, 2012; Nixon, 2011).

If at one level, however, it appeared that the individual institution and the leadership within it were becoming all important (namely 'the heroic leader'), at the same time, new forms of wider governance were emerging. As locally accountable elected local governments declined in their powers and authority, so we experienced the emergence of forms of 'network governance', in which private sector organizations moved into positions of leadership and influence (Ball and Junemann, 2012). For example, we saw the creation of 'Multi-Academy Trusts', chains of schools sponsored and managed by private companies. Other third-sector organizations such as the Co-operative Society and a range of religious organization also took on new roles and responsibilities in the provision of publicly funded education.

Teacher education

The same period has also seen change, some would say turmoil, in the provision of teacher education, especially pre-service or initial training. During the 1970s and 1980s there was considerable derision heaped on what the critics described as 'the teacher training colleges' by a number of right-wing think tanks. Following a similar line to *The Black Papers*, pamphlets with titles such as '*Who Teaches the Teachers?*' or '*The Wayward Elite*' not only suggested that beginning teachers were 'having their heads overfilled' with spurious educational theory rather than being given experience of practice, but also that they were being taught in the colleges by subversive lecturers who sought to destabilize the educational establishment through promoting such ideas as anti-racism or progressive education. The ideological battles of the 1980s were virulent and were also reflected in struggles between Conservative governments and 'progressive' local education authorities, such as the London Borough of Brent, the Inner London Education Authority (which the Thatcher government succeeded in closing down) and Birmingham. Accounts of these events can be found in the literature (e.g. Jones, 1989), but in terms of teacher education policy, the result was a rapidly 'tightening grip' from the central government on the process, structure and content of initial teacher education provision (Childs and Menter, 2013; Menter, Mutton and Burn, 2019). The system was held accountable through a rigorous procedure of inspection led by Ofsted, which for many providers led to a 'culture of compliance' as they sought to adhere to the government 'Standards' for teaching, as well as to other prescribed stipulations. A small number of universities withdrew from the provision of initial teacher education as a result of these pressures.

At the same time as these interventions in teacher education were being made by central government, including the establishment, for a period, of 'arm's length' agencies to manage the system (the Teacher Training Agency and its successors), there was also a move towards diversification of provision. While the contribution of higher education institutions was being questioned, marginalized and undermined, we also saw the introduction of new 'employment-based' routes to teaching and then 'school-based' approaches. By the beginning of the 2020s there was an enormous variety of provision leading to Qualified Teacher Status including schemes such as Teach First, Troops into Teachers (although this has now closed), School Direct, as well as more traditional university-led versions of the one year PGCE route and degrees (Whiting, Whitty, Menter et al., 2018; Sorensen, 2018). It is also worth pointing out that these initiatives again demonstrated 'the peculiarity of the English' as developments in other parts of the United Kingdom were much more gradual and created far less turbulence. England became very much an outlier within the United Kingdom, perhaps more closely resembling the United States in its approach to teacher education (Teacher Education Group, 2016; Tatto, Burn, Menter, Mutton and Thompson, 2019).

'Environmental education'

As we saw above, one effect of the imposition of a National Curriculum in England and Wales in 1988 was to reinforce a rigid subject structure in schools. The emphasis on the 'core subjects', English, mathematics and science, was clear. The designation of other subjects as 'Foundation Subjects' – including modern foreign languages, music, art, history, design technology and physical education – generated considerable debate at the time with arguments about the content of each subject, or, in the language of the time, how the statements of attainment should be defined. But what was even more seriously under threat were any educational practices which sought to break down the barriers between subjects. In response to this concern, as mentioned above, a number of 'cross-curricular themes' were identified and guidance developed to support these.

The themes emerging from these discussions included citizenship education and environmental education. Not least, because of Raymond Williams's increasing interest in matters environmental towards the end of his life (for example, see *Towards 2000*), we will consider environmental education as a case in point here, although the other cross-curricular themes have also had similarly interesting and somewhat tortuous trajectories since the late 1980s. When the foundation subjects were defined initially, interest in environmental education seemed to lie most obviously within the geography curriculum. According to Duncan Graham, Chairperson of the National Curriculum Council, Kenneth Clarke, secretary of state at the time, was concerned about introducing ecological issues into the curriculum. Graham wrote:

> The ecological issue showed the government's dilemma. In rapid succession ministers were against the proposals because they were worried about the expense and the possibility of encouraging pressure groups, and for them because of the growing public interest in green issues and forthcoming regulations from the European Community. As regards skills, the message was constant: knowledge first and knowledge last. It was increasingly hard work to achieve a sensible balance.
>
> (Graham, 1993:74)

That growing public interest did, of course, increase, leading to the identification of environmental education as a cross-curricular theme that would draw not only on geography but also on a range of other subjects, including the sciences and art. A guidance document was published in 1990 (National Curriculum Council, 1990) and, for a few years at least, was used, especially by teachers with a commitment to that aspect of work. However, as with all the other official cross-curricular themes, it was removed during one of the many reviews of the National Curriculum as decision makers sought to 'slim down' and clarify the curriculum priorities. There was, in other words, a reversion to a narrower and less integrated form of curriculum provision.

Nevertheless, the underlying issues did not go away. During the second decade of the twenty-first century, the rise of radical environmentalism began to emerge very visibly within schools. The Extinction Rebellion movement mobilized numerous young people, including school students, all around the world and thousands of them started to follow Greta Thunberg in supporting school strikes. Their basic tenet was, 'what is the point of schools and schooling for us if there is no planet for us to inhabit in the future?' The significance of environmental education took on a vital new aspect, but its presence within the official curriculum remained obscure.

'Closing the gap'

As we have seen in previous chapters, the relationship between socio-economic background and educational achievement has been enduring, persistent and resistant to attempts to overcome it. The preoccupation of sociologists of education by these issues developed in the post-war era leading to, among other things, the growth of a so-called comprehensive approach to secondary education. However, while there were examples of children from economically poor homes succeeding in education and 'making it' into high-status occupations, they were still far fewer in number than their peers from wealthier homes. Raymond Williams was profoundly committed to a common school system and to ensuring that all children had access to the best quality educational provision. The sociological work just referred to increasingly suggested that such matters as teacher expectations, children's differing cultural capital and language codes were playing a significant part in maintaining the patterns of inequality. The arguments ranged from Keddie's 'myth of cultural deprivation' (Keddie, 1973) to Bernstein's 'education cannot compensate for society' (Bernstein, 1970).

During recent times, we have seen continuing calls for creating 'genuine equality of opportunity' in education with a meritocratic rhetoric being a central element of all main political parties' electioneering. During the first part of this century a new metaphor arose in this discourse: 'closing the gap'. A major project led from the National College for Teaching and Leadership took that phrase as its title and involved hundreds of schools around the country (Childs and Menter, 2018). We may note (somewhat sardonically) that this closing of the gap is always apparently to be achieved by raising the achievement of the lower-attaining pupils, rather than lowering that of the higher achieving, which might be an alternative – if politically unacceptable – means of reducing the differences in attainment! Governments have invested considerable sums in interventions designed to bring about a closing of the gap. A charitable foundation, the Sutton Trust, headed by Sir Peter Lampl, a 'philanthropist' with a background in investment management, has received funds to invest in the Education Endowment Foundation (EEF) which has supported numerous trials of new approaches in schooling which are designed to improve the attainments of the poorest – and poorest performing – pupils. Most of these initiatives are undertaken on the basis of a randomized controlled trial (RCT) and the outcomes are reported in terms of an 'effect size' reflecting the project's apparent success or otherwise, as well as the cost of the intervention. The EEF publishes a 'toolkit' to summarize the outcomes of its work. The educational ideology supporting this kind of approach has been dubbed a 'what works' approach, but both this and the heavy reliance on RCTs have been heavily criticized as being inappropriate and/or misleading (Biesta, 2007, 2010; Gale, 2018; Menter, 2021). Nor have the initiatives led to a sustained reduction in the attainment gap.

The impact of the coronavirus pandemic in 2020

In March 2020, the coronavirus pandemic caused by Covid-19 led to a first 'lockdown' in Britain, not long after the election of a new prime minister, Boris Johnson, who had appointed a former disgraced defence minister, Gavin Williamson, as secretary of state for education. Public health policy rapidly came to dominate all policy and all media coverage as the seriousness of the pandemic became clear. On the advice of the government's main scientific advisory group, schools were closed down shortly before the traditional Easter break and remained closed throughout this first national 'lockdown' which lasted about four months. It soon became apparent that the public examinations that were an 'essential' element of the school calendar would not be able to go ahead in the normal way in the summer period. A time of considerable chaos and alarm for school students and their families ensued, as various steps were taken to attempt to find an alternative to the traditional assessment which relied heavily on students sitting in school taking written examinations. Initially, it was proposed that exam boards would seek to estimate the grades that students would have achieved, through combining their results in 'mock' exams (trials taken several months before the actual exam) with a factor based on the previous records of exam results of each school. The proposed reliance on the latter factor immediately created considerable concern – and some outrage – not least among those who feared that difficulties of the association between schools' achievements and pupils' social background could exacerbate the kinds of inequalities discussed in the previous section, so leading to a significant further widening of 'the gap'. What eventually emerged was a system which took into account both the results of previous assessments undertaken by students and a teacher judgement about the trajectory of each student. In many ways this was a more subjective process than the usual practice, and students and their families were given a right to appeal against the outcomes. Many students did appeal and a significant proportion achieved an upward regrading (see Breslin, 2021). The great irony of the whole experience was that overall, it appeared that an alternative to the 'essential' process of public examinations had been found and children were enabled to proceed into their next stage of schooling or employment – if there were jobs available. Whether these alternatives to traditional assessment will have any lasting impact on practices is doubtful. The examination boards are a major education industry in themselves and are unlikely willingly to accept the replacement of traditional exams by a more formative approach of this kind.

The higher education sector was also significantly affected by the pandemic. Again the traditional methods were most seriously hit, in both teaching and assessment. There was a huge switch from 'face-to-face' teaching to the use of virtual forms of communication. These developments did not start from scratch, however. There had already been significant investments in online learning, including the use of 'virtual learning environments' (VLEs), massive open online courses and 'blended learning'. Though the pandemic created huge demands on the available systems, there was rapid and largely successful development of the technologies, including the use of Microsoft's 'TEAMS', and 'Zoom', and VLEs such as 'Blackboard', to facilitate communication between teaching staff and students. Assessment, again largely carried out during the summer months, was undertaken through a combination of coursework submitted electronically and exams sat on the VLEs. The universities themselves were deeply concerned about the financial impact of the pandemic. Since the introduction of student fees as a major income stream, initiated under the New Labour government of the late 1990s and early noughties, the element of student satisfaction had become much more commercially sensitive, When students were not receiving face-to-face tuition many of them began to question whether they were getting 'value for money' from their provider. There were also many empty rooms in halls of residence which, in many cases, students were still being charged for. When students were encouraged to return physically to attend in September/October 2020, there were many tense 'standoffs' (and worse) between the university authorities and their 'customers', the students.

Conclusion

In selecting these five examples drawn from recent educational developments in England – and plenty of other cases could have been chosen – we can see how ways in which they have been understood have been influenced by cultural materialism of the kind Raymond Williams did so much to develop. Each of the cases is a snapshot of a particular education topic or event where the wider structure of feeling has been powerfully influential on people's actions and experiences. In each case there has been a sense of struggle or contest in pursuit of education, this struggle which was a key element in the long revolution. Such struggles are also a reflection of the continuing tensions between respective elements of the social base and the social superstructure. We have also seen ways in which the achievements witnessed by Williams in the 1960s through to the early 1980s have not only failed to continue flourishing but have in some sense reversed. This has been a period of 'counter-revolution'. Education in England remains deeply divided and yet highly significant symbolically, in the way it demonstrates the reality of social and cultural development – or lack of it. Furthermore, in this discussion we have concentrated on considering education in the public sector – state schooling and higher education. Once the continuing existence of a privileged private sector in education is taken into account the picture is even more uneven and unequal than the foregoing discussion suggests.

In allowing the ideas of Raymond Williams to shape our analysis of educational provision in this society we are led to two simple questions. First, who is education for? Second, how can it be provided justly and equitably? These are among the concerns we will reflect upon in the final chapter.

8

Conclusion – Language and Culture; Tradition and Revolution

What I have said about growth can be related to the idea of permanent education ... This idea seems to me to repeat, in new and important idiom, the concepts of learning and of popular democratic culture ... What it valuably stresses is the educational force ... of our whole social and cultural experience. It is therefore concerned, not only with continuing education, of a formal or informal kind, but with what the whole environment, its institutions and relationships actively and profoundly teaches.

(*Communications*, Williams, 1962/1966:14)

Introduction

In drawing this book to a conclusion we review some of the main ideas discussed in earlier chapters and draw attention to the three words which supplement the book's title: history, culture and democracy. The first section revisits Williams's concern with language, not least with words and how they communicate meaning in and through culture. The educational significance of these connections is considered. Then, in considering ways in which the processes and institutions of education change over time, we revisit the historical element in Williams's thinking. In the third section Williams's growing interest in and concern about the environment are taken forward to consider their implications for educational policy and practice. The concluding section seeks to draw together the themes of the book and summarize the significance of Williams's thinking and writing for the study of education now and into the future. Inevitably there is a speculative element to this final chapter. It is impossible not to be asking ourselves what sense Raymond Williams would have made of social and educational developments that have taken place since the time of his death. What would he have made of the burgeoning of social media, of the new forms of populism, of the global pandemic, of the shifts in global power or the threat of climate change?

8.1 Language and Culture in Education

The works which first demonstrated Williams's deep interest in words and in language were *Culture and Society* (Williams, 1958/2013) and then, rather later, *Keywords* (Williams, 1976). While the first of these explored the relationship between works of literature and social context, the second was essentially an etymological study, a glossary of words which, for Williams, were significant in capturing the dynamics of social change in England historically: words which could help define structures of feeling at particular times. Each of these key words carried meaning and reflected tensions and social struggle as England, and Britain, went through the processes he later captured in the title of his important book about social institutions and cultural and political change: *The Long Revolution*.

The relationship between culture and human experience captured in the concept of 'structures of feeling', encapsulates the central tenet of Williams's cultural materialism: that there is an important link between the material world of production and the subjective experience of human existence. This insight demonstrated the importance of the study of culture in making sense of the world – the relationship of cultural expressions with the forces and means of their production helps us understand social relations and ways in which societies develop and change. These were profoundly original insights early in the second half of the twentieth century, even if we may take them for granted now. The emergence of cultural studies as a field reflected the importance of these insights and also has affected education much more widely. The influence is not limited to particular locations of cultural studies in universities in the UK and around the world. The very media for communication, also at the heart of Williams's interest in the ways in which contemporary societies operate, began demonstrating keener awareness of the significance of culture defined in this broader way: culture as ordinary, culture as a way of life. Newspapers, magazines, film and television all transformed into great industries within our economies. More recently, and largely since Williams's death, the burgeoning digital technologies, with their attendant 'social media', have become key means of communication for people around the globe, facilitating an unprecedented level of 'connectedness'.

Digital technologies have also been powerful in reshaping educational practices. The ease with which enormous data sets can be analysed, sorted and converted into tables, including 'league tables', has enabled new forms of accountability to be introduced into education systems, with exam results, school inspection results, higher education 'quality indicators', for example, all facilitating ready comparisons between both institutions and individuals. In terms of teaching and learning, search engines have meant that both teachers and learners can find information and knowledge speedily and without the necessity of referring to books or other printed materials. As was discussed at the end of Chapter 7, the development of virtual learning environments and concepts such as 'blended learning' have all been facilitated through digital technologies.

The wider educational implications of these developments are still perhaps not fully recognized. Educational institutions for children and older students continue to operate largely along the lines of their nineteenth-century predecessors within classrooms and lecture theatres, laboratories and workshops, gymnasia and playing fields. The greatest challenge to these patterns of provision arrived suddenly and largely unexpectedly in 2020 as the coronavirus pandemic swept most parts of the world and threw educational provision into turmoil. Across the UK, as in many other countries, the sudden fear of putting learners and teachers in close physical proximity led to school closures and the abandonment of traditional assessment procedures, most notably public examinations (Breslin, 2021). This bedrock of the social functioning of education as a system of sorting and differentiating the population into different employment paths was abruptly halted, creating considerable anxiety and uncertainty for students but also raising major questions about whether 'modern' education systems are fit for purpose in the twenty-first century.

8.2 Continuity and Change in Education

In Chapter 3 we examined the analysis of education in Britain (mainly England) offered by Williams in *The Long Revolution*. This analysis clearly demonstrates how a full understanding of contemporary education must be based on tracing developments through history. The ways in which Williams connects wider social developments with the emergence of those public institutions providing education are extraordinarily rich and subtle. Throughout this and discussions elsewhere in his work, we see a great tension arising between his view of education, as coming from the wider social environment, that is part of 'becoming', and the necessarily selective curriculum offered within formal schooling and higher education. Of course there will be tensions within the processes of selection leading to what is frequently a curriculum differentiated in alignment with social divisions. As we have seen, the very provision of schooling may be socially differentiated, even within the public sector. The tripartite secondary schooling of state education in England in the post-war era was something to which Williams was strongly opposed, joining calls for a unified or 'common' approach to schooling as well as the development of a common 'core' curriculum. It was his deep awareness of historical social divisions that enabled him to identify the three key ideologies that represented these struggles in England: the old humanists, the industrial trainers and the public educators. We have seen ways in which tensions between these three forces continue to be played out to this day. Furthermore, while Williams developed this framework from his analysis of education in Britain, the same forces can be seen to have been active in the United States and in all Western democracies, although the balance between them is often different, for example, with the 'old humanists' being more visible in European contexts than in North American. These struggles are sometimes labelled as 'culture wars' and can be detected in higher education as well as in schooling. Two interesting examples of the defence of old humanism within higher education, on either side of the Atlantic, may be found respectively in Stefan Collini's *What Are Universities For?* (2012) and Martha Nussbaum's *Not for Profit* (2010), the latter having the subtitle 'Why democracy needs the humanities'.

For Williams, though, overarching these policy debates and contestation about the structures and content of formal education, whether in schools or in universities, is the concern to stimulate and develop what was referred to as popular education through both formal and informal approaches. From his immersion in, and very significant contribution to, adult education during the first part of his own formal career, we saw (in Chapter 4) how significant for Williams was the provision of educational opportunities for older people. In a society where so many young people had not had opportunities to fulfil their educational potential while at school, it was crucial to the development of a democratic society and culture that there should be opportunities for them in later life – and that these should be of the highest quality and offer access to the full range of culture, including the literary canon in which Williams's own higher education was steeped. In England (and also more broadly in Britain), the range of provision of adult education has been severely curtailed over recent years. While The Open University has created an important location for higher education for adults which has been significant in furthering the learning and the careers of many people, the more local community-based provision historically provided by university extramural departments has been severely cut back. It is now a minority of universities that offer any extensive programme. The Workers' Educational Association continues to make provision both in community locations and online (especially since the pandemic).

But for Williams, while all these forms of educational provision – schooling, higher education, adult education – were important, his insights also crucially drew attention to the wider aspects of the processes of education through popular media, indeed popular culture. The influence of printed newspapers may have diminished since his time, but is still there, not least as these organizations have developed their online platforms. The commercial base of much of the news and media sectors persists; advertising is an integral part not just of television and news platforms but also of communication networks such as those provided by Google, Twitter and Facebook. For Williams, peoples' knowledge and understanding of the world in which they live – their education in the broadest sense – are profoundly shaped by these forms of communication. As suggested in Chapter 6, it might well be argued that power and influence in the publicly available media have become even more centralized and that popular culture is in some ways less democratic in Western societies than it has ever been. The growth of political populism has been a key factor in these developments (Eatwell and Goodwin, 2018). However, as Williams pointed out, even with the wider general social movement of the long revolution being turned in a 'reverse' direction, we can still identify 'resources of hope' arising from his underlying optimism. Recent examples of progressive forces countering the repressive and freedom limiting elements of our culture might include the *Me Too* movement, challenging sexual exploitation in the media industry; *Black Lives Matter*, challenging police brutality against Black people; and *Extinction Rebellion*, offering opposition to governments and industries whose activities are accelerating climate change. Social movements such as these have a powerful educational impact, in a way Williams would have recognized.

Another element developed significantly since Williams's time is what has been labelled as 'globalization', the term primarily used to refer to the increasing flow of international trade and communication. This too has been greatly accelerated through the development of digital media as well as (relatively) cheap air travel. The 'mobile privatization' that Williams identified in Britain as a phenomenon in the second half of the twentieth century has in some ways become a worldwide phenomenon in the twenty-first century. Or at least that was the case prior to the coronavirus pandemic which struck in 2020, its rapid spread itself a feature of contemporary globalization. The 'internationalization' of many forms of popular culture, including film, television and music, has drastically changed worldwide awareness of cultural diversity but also paradoxically has simultaneously led to increasing cultural convergence, even a kind of homogenization (Klein, 2000).

These developments in culture and in international communication provide yet more powerful reasons for emphasizing the significance of well-designed, open and inclusive educational provision in order to promote the kinds of freedoms to which societies around the world aspire. The provision needs to be designed according to the currently appropriate balance between the cultural, economic and democratizing purposes that Williams identified in his historical analysis. Education needs to be concerned with helping the learner to understand society and his/her own place within it, and with providing the intellectual tools and political skills to exercise meaningful agency – individually and collectively – within that society.

8.3 Sustainability in Education

Towards the end of his life Williams showed growing interest in ecosocialism and environmental matters. As we saw in Chapter 7, environmental awareness is a key current concern in education. In the final part of 'The Welsh Trilogy' of novels, *The Fight for Manod*, Williams (1979/88) returns to the border country of the first volume bringing a somewhat older Matthew Price back onto the scene, along with Peter Owen, the younger sociological researcher from Oxford, a central character in *Second Generation*. The two protagonists had been taken on as consultants to advise the government on a major development proposal to establish a new estate, including residential and industrial provision, at the site of 'Manod'. The novel explores the potential environmental impact of a major development in a predominantly rural location, though one element of the plan is the use of new technologies for power generation and communication. It also explores the complexity and contradictions inherent in the management, government and finance of such a scheme, including significant involvement of European oil companies in the background. Matthew Price finds himself deeply conflicted by simultaneous commitment to improvement of the local economy and the creation of job opportunities in this declining community, while, at the same time, witnessing apparent exploitation and likely corruption involving some of the local people and the dubious activities of the corporate main players. It is a fascinating insight into Williams's own gradualist but nevertheless revolutionary socialism. We also see him exploring again the tensions between residual, emergent and dominant cultural forces, as discussed in Chapter 7, and what these tensions mean in the lived experience of people.

In 1982, three years after that novel was published, the Socialist Environment and Resources Association published a pamphlet by Williams, entitled *Socialism and Ecology* (reprinted in *Resources of Hope*, Williams, 1989). In this he examines the word 'ecology' and discusses the links between the industrial revolution, ecology and socialism. He invokes William Morris in seeking to explore how these apparently disparate themes can be productively connected to form 'an ecologically conscious socialism' (Williams, 1989:225).

The following year, 1983, the 'sequel' to *The Long Revolution*, *Towards 2000*, was published and offered another extended discussion on ecology. In this, he suggests that:

> The hard issues come together on two grounds: the ecological argument, and changes in the international economic order. There are times when all that seems to flow from these decisive issues is a series of evident and visible disadvantages, losses of position, to the employed majorities in the old industrial economies.
> (Williams, 1983:255)

Williams goes on to discuss how a sustainable alternative might be developed that would involve both new working practices and also new educational approaches:

> through the linked development of shorter working time and new schemes of education and retraining, and through the new processes of locally audited decisions on the kinds of work undertaken, there is every chance of making, even in very diverse and sometimes unfavourable circumstances, stable and equitable economies in which all necessary work is reasonably shared ... What could be a major opportunity for easing the strains of work without discarding large numbers of people will be seized only if this kind of commitment to a directly determined social order, rather than to either corporate capitalism or a centralised socialist common economy, begins to grow from a popular base.
> (Williams, 1983:259)

Again we see the way in which Williams places himself as a socialist reformer, proposing that new forms of political organization and governance are crucial to the development of democracy, with education – both formal and informal – playing a central part.

8.4 Conclusion: Education for Democracy in the Twenty-First Century

In the final section of *Towards 2000*, subtitled 'Resources for a journey of hope', Williams again emphasizes the importance of human action and agency. On the down side he says:

> First, ... the objective changes which are now so rapidly developing are not only confusing and bewildering; they are also profoundly unsettling. The ways now being offered to live with these unprecedented dangers and these increasingly harsh dislocations are having many short-term successes and effects, but they are also in the long term, forms of further danger and dislocation.
>
> (Williams, 1983:268)

But Williams goes on to say:

> Secondly, there are very strong reasons why we should challenge what now most controls and constrains us: the idea of such a world as an inevitable future. It is not some unavoidable real world, with its laws of economy and laws of war, that is now blocking this. It is a set of identifiable processes of *realpolitik* and *force majeure*, of nameable agencies of power and capital, distraction and disinformation, and all these interlocking with the embedded short-term pressures and the inter-woven subordinations of an adaptive commonsense.
>
> (Williams, 1983:268)

This was a far-seeing vision, realized now through the creation of our post-truth, mediatized culture of the twenty-first century. As cited earlier, he concludes *Towards 2000* with this call for a positive change:

> If there are no easy answers there are still available and discoverable hard answers, and it is these that we can now learn to make and share. This has been, from the beginning, the sense and impulse of the long revolution.
>
> (Williams, 1983:269)

Through our analysis over these eight chapters, written 100 years after he was born, I have sought to explore and amplify Williams's demonstration of the crucial relationships between education policy and practices on the one hand, and the study and creation of culture and democracy on the other. Williams himself was always a teacher, what you might call a relentless and tireless pedagogue. As Stanley Aronowitz and Henry Giroux, leading US critical theorists of education, put it in their book *Education under Siege*:

> Williams, ever the pedagogue in writing as much as teaching, became the most important figure in 'English' cultural studies precisely because he made the explicit connection between cultural study and educational policy. But for Williams 'education' was not identical with formal schooling. Instead, his was a broad political notion of education that led him to what might be termed cultural 'policy', the most important aspect of which, in the postwar era, was the study of communications media in virtually all of its crucial manifestations.
> (Aronowitz and Giroux, 1995:326)

Aronowitz and Giroux go on to discuss *Communications*, and use the quotation that opened this chapter to demonstrate the way in which Williams relates culture and education.

The three words used as the underpinning of this book on Raymond Williams and education – history, culture, democracy – have been demonstrated to be fundamental to our deployment of Williams's ideas in the study of education. History reminds us of the importance of considering the antecedents of contemporary cultural forms. We can only understand the significance of current social processes and institutions if we consider their origins and development. For Williams, of course, this was particularly important in terms of examining social relationships of power and the distribution of wealth. 'Culture' was the word which became almost uniquely identified with Williams's work; his whole oeuvre constitutes a lifelong exploration of what this word actually means and how it can signify so much about social experience and consciousness. Democracy reminds us of the ways in which Williams's politics was a profound commitment to open communication and the sustenance of what we might now call inclusive communities. The perspective of cultural materialism, as developed by Williams, provides a powerful insight into these matters.

I wish to conclude by reminding us (and echoing Aronowitz and Giroux, cited above) that it was not only Williams's ideas that were and are important, it was also his teaching. While for many people this teaching comes through his writing, there can be little argument that his whole career and life's work may be seen as a pedagogical mission. In politics and in letters he was on a ceaseless, passionate quest to enquire, to learn and to teach. In that sense, for everyone who sees themselves in any way as an educator (for Williams, as we have seen, that is all of us), his efforts and achievements provide a lasting inspiration. For those of us living, teaching and learning in the twenty-first century we need to take into account much that has changed. Most notably these features would be the wider realization of environmental threat to the planet, the continuation, indeed escalation, of inequalities and injustice and the threats of new forms of populism in democratic politics. But it would be Raymond Williams's contention – and this is the message I hope has been conveyed in this volume – that education, in his words, permanent education, is an essential part of addressing the future and securing safety, stability, security, justice and equity for the citizens of the globe.

Notes

Preface

1. See, for example, Michael W. Apple, *Ideology and Curriculum* (4th edition). New York: Routledge, 2018 and Michael W. Apple, *Education and Power* (Routledge Classic Edition). New York: Routledge, 2012.
2. *The Year 2000* is the title given to *Towards 2000* (Williams, 1983/1985) in its US imprint.
3. Antonio Gramsci, *Prison Notebooks, Volume III*. New York: Columbia University Press, 2007, p. 378.
4. Stuart Hall, *Familiar Stranger: A Life between Two Islands*. Durham, NC: Duke University Press, 2017, p. 265. For more on Hall's relationship with and influence by Williams, see Stuart Hall, *Cultural Studies 1983: A Theoretical History*. Durham, NC: Duke University Press, 2016, pp. 25–53.
5. Raymond Williams, *Resources of Hope*. New York: Verso, 1989, p. 322.
6. Raymond Williams, *The Year 2000*. New York: Pantheon, 1983, p. 269. For what the implications of this position are specifically in education, see Michael W. Apple, *Can Education Change Society?* New York: Routledge, 2013.

Introduction

1. Where relevant, the original date of publication is given as well as the date of republication, either as a new edition or as an item included in a collection.
2. Williams had planned three volumes but the third was not written.

Chapter 2

1. The contemporary writer Geoff Dyer, in his introduction to the 2015 edition of *Politics and Letters*, writes that before reading of Williams's life and *Culture and Society*: 'I had no understanding of the social process I'd lived through even though it was, by then, a well-documented one: the working-class boy who keeps passing exams – exams that take him first to grammar school, then to an Oxbridge college – and discovers only in retrospect that there was more to all this than exams, or

even education. It's entirely appropriate that *Culture and Society* – a new way of considering authors with whom I was already familiar – played a crucial part in this discovery' (Dyer, 2015:ix–x).

2   See Williams, M. (1972). Father and daughter, Raymond and Merryn, also collaborated on an edition of poems by John Clare (Williams and Williams, 1986).
3   Cobbett had also featured in *Culture and Society* and was later the sole subject of a short monograph by Williams (1983c); see Chapter 5.
4   Indeed such insights are all too rarely captured in non-fiction (whether formal sociology or not) – powerful exceptions to this that do capture something of the structure of feeling are two musicological works on Black American music, *Blues People* by Leroi Jones (Amiri Baraka) (1963) and *Black Nationalism and the Revolution in Music* by Frank Kofsky (1970).
5   These phrases connect directly to the dedication Williams placed at the beginning of the book: 'For the country workers who were my grandparents James Bird, Mary Ann Lewis, Joseph Williams, Margaret Williams.'

Chapter 3

1   It is interesting to note that the editorship of this book series was later taken over by Lionel Elvin, then Director of the London Institute of Education, who, as we noted in Chapter 1, was one of Williams's tutors at Cambridge.
2   The free schools of the 1960s and 1970s were of a very different nature from the free schools set up by the English Government in the second decade of the twenty-first century.
3   Bernstein's work is discussed later, in Chapter 5.
4   This is a reference to an edition of *The Long Revolution* (Williams, 1961/2011).
5   Apple has been an important voice in making Williams better known in the world of education studies and what he said in 1979 is still the case today – hence this book and hence the invitation to Michael Apple to write the foreword!
6   A leading British scholar in curriculum studies, Ivor Goodson draws on Williams's later book *Keywords*, in making the suggestion, early in a book entitled *The Making of Curriculum*:

> In our studies of schooling curriculum is a 'keyword' in the full sense of Raymond Williams' definition. The use of such a word and its place in our discourse on schooling needs to be fully examined because like any other social reproduction it is the arena of all sorts of shifts and interests and relations of dominance. (Goodson, 1988/1995:12)

7   Daniel Williams has drawn together a wide range of Raymond Williams's writing about Wales and Welshness in *Who Speaks for Wales? Nation, Culture, Identity*

(D. Williams, 2003). The invaluable introductory essay by Daniel Williams stresses the complexities that Williams drew attention to in his discussions of these matters.

8. Dix, taking his main inspiration from Raymond Williams, also draws heavily on the work of Tom Nairn (*The Break-up of Britain*, 1981; *After Britain*, 2001) and of Benedict Anderson (*Imagined Communities*, 1991).

Chapter 4

1. On this final point, the relationship between philosophy and pedagogy, see Philip Stevens's doctoral thesis (Stevens, n.d.).
2. These books were published in Britain as 'Penguin Education Specials' in similar vein to the other Penguin Specials referred to elsewhere below and also in Chapter 3.
3. The concept of cultural materialism will be more fully discussed in Chapter 7.
4. The word 'ordinary' again! Culture is ordinary, education is ordinary and now communication is ordinary …
5. We refer to Giroux again later, in Chapter 8.
6. See *The Dangerous Rise of Therapeutic Education* by Ecclestone and Hayes (2019).

Chapter 5

1. In *Keywords*, Williams uses 'eC19' to mean early nineteenth century. In this book, I have copied Williams's own formatting and conventions in all quotations from *Keywords*.
2. And this superior notion of culture is also pursued by T. S. Eliot in his *Notes towards a Definition of Culture*, originally published in 1948 (Eliot, 1948/1962). We may note that Eliot also offers 'three senses of culture', but these are different from Williams's typology and relate respectively to the whole society, the group and the individual.
3. This is a reference to the volume by Bourdieu and Passeron (1977), *Reproduction in Education, Society and Culture*.
4. As well as the references to Bourdieu in *Culture*, Williams also refers to him in *Politics and Letters* (Williams, 1979:327). Derek Robbins, who had been a student of Williams's at Cambridge, offers a fascinating critical account that suggests that Bourdieu's approach to culture is ultimately more constructive than Williams's (Robbins, 1997).
5. Themes such as these are actually explored by Williams in his novel *Loyalties* (Williams, 1985/1989).
6. See Hanley (2020) for an interesting discussion of Orwell's significance for education and education studies.

7   See also Williams's review of Rudolf Bahro's book, *Socialism and Survival*, reprinted as 'Red and green' in *What I Came to Say* (Williams, 1989b).
8   This interest in social movements has echoes of Castells's interest in 'urban social movements' (Castells, 1977).
9   See for example: Simon (1992), Chitty (1989), Tomlinson (2001), Whitty (1985), Jones (2003) and Reay (2017).

Chapter 6

1   As I write this, reference in the press is being made to 'culture wars', in relation to debates about whether the words of jingoistic patriotic songs should be sung at the 'Last Night of the Proms', the annual celebration of music organized by the BBC in London.
2   I have retained the typographical elements used in *Keywords* in all of these quotations.
3   The source for this is the collection of Williams's essays called *Resources of Hope*, where the first three chapters are grouped under the heading of 'Defining a democratic culture', all of which are very relevant to this discussion (Williams, 1989a).
4   Williams's influence on, and responses to, national policy on cultural matters are discussed by McGuigan (1997) in his chapter 'A Slow Reach Again for Control: Raymond Williams and the Vicissitudes of Cultural Policy'.
5   See also Williams's lecture on his retirement from Cambridge, 'Beyond Cambridge English', which also reaffirms this relationship (Williams, 1983:212–26).
6   Another fascinating historical account which focuses more on the politics of the proponents than Steele does is Stephen Woodhams's *History in the Making: Raymond Williams, Edward Thompson and Radical Intellectuals 1936–1956*. (Woodhams, 2001). This 'collective biography' traces the influence of the University of Cambridge and the experience of the Second World War on the emergence of these radical intellectuals as key members of the New Left in Britain.
7   See also his very interesting historical analysis of newspapers in a chapter called 'The Press and Popular Culture: An Historical Perspective', reprinted in Williams (1989b:120–31).
8   Williams also offers an extended discussion of 'structure of feeling' in the introduction to *Drama from Ibsen to Brecht* (Williams, 1952/1968:16–20).
9   Although Williams did not produce a feature film, he did collaborate with filmmaker Michael Dibbs in making a TV documentary film based on *The Country and the City*.
10 For a much fuller and very interesting discussion of 'televisual flow', see the chapter by Stuart Allan (1997) called 'Raymond Williams and the Culture of Televisual Flow'.

11 This paradox is explored by Williams himself in two chapters in *What I Came to Say* (Williams, 1989b): 'Isn't the News Terrible?' (originally published in 1980) and 'Communications, Technologies and Social Institutions', from 1981.
12 The only actual reference to Williams in the text of the report appears as a strange little box at the side of page 70, alongside a paragraph about physical education: 'To communicate through the arts is to convey an experience to others in such a form that the experience is actively recreated actively lived through by those to whom it is offered.' No page number is given for this rather strange sentence, but it would appear to derive from Chapter 1 of *The Long Revolution*, 'The creative mind'. The closest I was able to find to this was the following on p. 44: 'When art communicates, a human experience is actively offered and actively received.' This is thus a tokenistic gesture towards Williams and to *The Long Revolution*, given that a reading of the report reveals many ideas that are directly derived from this and other writing by him. The whole report is a masterpiece of nuanced political positioning, and it may be that any greater identification with Williams might have been regarded as tendentious by the government officials who were no doubt responsible for editing it. The report, excellent though it is in many ways, provides a prime case study for an extended exercise in discourse analysis.
13 OECD: Organisation for Economic Cooperation and Development; PISA: Programme for International Student Assessment; TIMSS: Trends in International Mathematics and Science Study; PiRLS: Progress in International Reading Literacy Study.

Chapter 7

1 See Patrick Wright's *On Living in an Old Country* for an analysis of 'cultural heritage', much influenced by Williams's work (Wright, 2009).
2 This is very close to what John Berger, in *A Fortunate Man*, refers to as the construction of 'common sense' (Berger and Mohr, 1967/2016).

References

1 See the note at the beginning of the reference list for explanation of multiple dates of publication.

References

Note: Many of Raymond Williams's publications have been issued in more than one edition. In most cases, the original date of publication is given, followed by subsequent dates of revisions, and the publisher cited is that of the version that has been used in writing the present book.

Agger, B. (2004) *Speeding Up Fast Capitalism Boulder*. Colorado: Paradigm.
Allan, S. (1997) 'Raymond Williams and the culture of televisual flow' in Wallace, J., Jones, R. and Nield, S. (Eds.) *Raymond Williams Now – Knowledge, Limits and the Future*. New York: St. Martin's Press. 115–43.
Althusser, L. (1971) 'Ideology and ideological state apparatuses' in Cosin, B. (Ed.) (1972) *Education: Structure and Society*. Harmondsworth: Penguin. 242–80.
Anderson, B. (1991) *Imagined Communities*. London: Verso.
Apple, M. (1979) *Ideology and Curriculum*. London: Routledge & Kegan Paul.
Apple, M. (1982) *Education and Power*. Boston, MA: Ark.
Apple, M. (1993) 'Rebuilding hegemony: Education, equality and the New Right' in Dworkin, D. and Roman, L. (Eds.) *Views Beyond the Border Country: Raymond Williams and Cultural Politics*. New York: Routledge. 91–114.
Apple, M. (2013) *Can Education Change Society?* New York: Routledge.
Arnold, M. (1867) *Culture and Anarchy* (1971 edn). Cambridge: University Press.
Aronowitz, S. and Giroux, H. (1995) *Education under Siege – the Conservative, Liberal and Radical Debate over Schooling*. London: Routledge & Kegan Paul.
Baldwin, J. (1963) *The Fire Next Time*. Harmondsworth: Penguin.
Ball, S. (1990) *Politics and Policy Making in Education*. London: Routledge.
Ball, S. (1994) *Education Reform*. Buckingham: Open University Press.
Ball, S. (2003) *Class Strategies and the Education Market*. London: Routledge.
Ball, S. (2007) *Education plc*. London: Routledge.
Ball, S. (2012) *Global Education Inc*. London: Routledge.
Ball, S. (2013) *The Education Debate* (2nd edn). Bristol: Policy Press.
Ball, S. and Junemann, C. (2012) *Networks, New Governance and Education*. Bristol: Policy Press.
Barnett, A. (1988) 'The keywords of a key thinker'. *The Listener*, 4 February, 15.
Barnett, A. (2011) 'Foreword' in Williams, R. (Ed.) *The Long Revolution*. Cardigan: Parthian. vii–xxv.
Baron, S., Field, J. and Schuller, T. (2000) *Social Capital*. Oxford: University Press.
Barrett, M. (1980) *Women's Oppression Today*. London: Verso.

Barrett-Maitland, N. and Lynch, J. (2020) Social Media, Ethics and the Privacy Paradox. DOI: 10.5772/intechopen.90906 Downloaded 16.02.2021 from: https://www.intechopen.com/books/security-and-privacy-from-a-legal-ethical-and-technical-perspective/social-media-ethics-and-the-privacy-paradox

Bennett, A. (2004) *The History Boys*. London: Faber & Faber.

Berger, J. and Mohr, J. (1967/2016) *A Fortunate Man*. Edinburgh: Canongate.

Bernstein, B. (1970) 'Education cannot compensate for society' in Rubenstein, D. and Stoneman, C. (Eds.) *Education for Democracy* (2nd edn., 1972). Harmondsworth: Penguin. 104–16.

Bernstein, B. (1971a) 'On the classification and framing of educational knowledge' in Young, M. (Ed.) *Knowledge and Control – New Directions for the Sociology of Education*. London: Collier-Macmillan. 47–69.

Bernstein, B. (1971b) *Class, Codes and Control. Vol. 1*. London: Routledge & Kegan Paul.

Bernstein, B. (1977) *Class, Codes and Control. Vol.3, towards a Theory of Educational Transmissions* (2nd edn). London: Routledge & Kegan Paul.

Biesta, G. (2007) 'Why "what works" won't work: Evidence-based practice and the democratic deficit in educational research'. *Educational Theory*, 57 (1), 1–22.

Biesta, G. (2010) 'Why "what works" still won't work: From evidence-based education to value-based education'. *Studies in Philosophy and Education*, 29 (5), 491–503.

Blackburn, R. (1989) 'Introduction' in Williams, R. (Ed.) *Resources of Hope*. London: Verso. ix–xxiii.

Bloom, A. (1987) *The Closing of the American Mind*. London: Penguin.

Bourdieu, P. and Passeron, J.-C. (1977) *Reproduction in Education, Society and Culture* (1990 edn). London: Sage.

Bowe, R. and Ball, S. with Gold, A. (1992) *Reforming Education and Changing Schools*. London: Routledge.

Bowles, S. and Gintis, H. (1976) *Schooling in Capitalist America*. London: Routledge & Kegan Paul.

Braithwaite, E. (2005) *To Sir, with Love*. London: Vintage.

Breslin, T. (2021) *Lessons from Lockdown*. London: Routledge.

Brown, P. and Lauder, H. (Eds.) (1992) *Education for Economic Survival*. London: Routledge.

Burn, K., Mutton, T. and Thompson, I. (Eds.) (forthcoming, 2021) *Practical Theorising in Teacher Education: Holding Theory and Practice Together*. London: Routledge.

Carmichael, S. and Hamilton, C. (1967) *Black Power – The Politics of Liberation in America*. Harmondsworth: Penguin.

Castells, M. (1977) *The Urban Question*. London: Arnold.

Castells, M. (1996/2000) *The Rise of the Network Society* (2nd edn). Oxford: Blackwell.

Centenary Commission on Adult Education (2019) *A Permanent National Necessity ....* (downloaded from: https://www.centenarycommission.org/,20/01/21)

Centre for Contemporary Cultural Studies (CCCS) (1981) *Unpopular Education – Schooling and Social Democracy since 1944*. London: Hutchinson.

Chennault, R. (2006) *Hollywood Films about Schools – Where Race, Politics, and Education Intersect*. New York: Palgrave Macmillan.

Childs, A. and Menter, I. (2013) 'Teacher education in the 21st Century in England: a case study in neo-liberal policy'. *Revista Espanola de Educacion Camparada (Spanish Journal of Comparative Education)*, 22, 93–116. ISSN 1137-8654.

Childs, A. and Menter, I. (Eds.) (2018) *Mobilising Teacher Researchers: Challenging Educational Inequality*. London: Routledge.

Chitty, C. (1989) *Towards a New Education System – the Victory of the New Right*. London: Falmer Press.

Clarke, J. and Newman, J. (1997) *The Managerial State*. London: Sage.

Collini, S. (2012) *What Are Universities For?* London: Penguin.

Committee on Higher Education (1963) *Higher Education* (The Robbins Report). London: HMSO.

Cook, C. (1984) 'Teachers for the inner city: Change and continuity' in Grace, G. (Ed.) *Education and the City*. London: Routledge & Kegan Paul.

Dale, R. (1989) *The State and Education Policy*. Milton Keynes: Open University Press.

Dale, R., Esland, G. and MacDonald, M. (1976) *Schooling and Capitalism – a Sociological Reader*. London: Routledge & Kegan Paul.

Davison, J. and Daly, C. (Eds.) (2020) *Debates in English Teaching*. (2nd edn). London: Routledge.

Deem, R., Hillyard, S. and Reed, M. (2008) *Knowledge, Higher Education, and the New Managerialism: The Changing Management of UK Universities*. Oxford: Oxford University Press.

Dennison, G. (1969) *The Lives of Children*. Harmondsworth: Penguin.

Department of Education and Science (DES) (1983) *Teaching Quality*. London: HMSO.

Dickens, C. (1854) *Hard Times*. London: Penguin.

Dix, H. (2010) 'The pedagogy of cultural materialism: Paulo Freire and Raymond Williams' in Seidel, M., Horak, R. and Grossberg, L. (Eds.) *About Raymond Williams*. London: Routledge. 81–93.

Dix, H. (2013) *After Raymond Williams – Cultural Materialism and the Break-up of Britain* (2nd edn). Cardiff: University of Wales Press.

Donnelly, C., McKeown, P. and Osborne, R. (Eds.) (2006) *Devolution and Pluralism in Education in Northern Ireland*. Manchester: Manchester University Press.

Dorling, D. (2015) *Injustice – Why Social Inequality Still Persists*. Bristol: Policy Press.

Dworkin, D. (1993) 'Cultural studies and the crisis in British radical thought' in Dworkin, D. and Roman, L. (Eds.) *Views Beyond the Border Country*. New York: Routledge. 38–54.

Dyer, G. (2015) 'Introduction' in Williams, R. (Ed.) *Politics and Letters* (new edn). London: Verso. vii–xiv.

Eagleton, T. (Ed.) (1989) *Raymond Williams: Critical Perspectives*. Cambridge: Polity Press.

Eagleton, T. (2000) *The Idea of Culture*. Oxford: Blackwell.

Eatwell, R. and Goodwin, M. (2018) *National Populism: The Revolt Against Liberal Democracy*. London: Penguin.

Ecclestone, K. and Hayes, D. (2019) *The Dangerous Rise of Therapeutic Education* (2nd edn). London: Routledge.

Eldridge, J. and Eldridge, L. (1994) *Raymond Williams – Making Connections*. London: Routledge.

Eliot, T. S. (1948/1962) *Notes towards a Definition of Culture*. London: Faber& Faber.

Ellsmore, S. (2005) *Carry On Teachers! Representations of the Teaching Profession in Screen Culture*. Stoke-on-Trent: Trentham.

Elvin, H. L. (1968) *Education and Contemporary Society*. London: Watts.

Fanon, F. (1967) *The Wretched of the Earth*. Harmondsworth: Penguin.

Fieldhouse, R. (1993) 'Oxford and adult education' in Morgan, J. and Preston, P. (Eds.) *Raymond Williams: Politics, Education, Letters*. Basingstoke: Macmillan.

Floud, J., Halsey, A.H. and Martin, F. (1956) *Social Class and Educational Opportunity*. London: Heinemann.

Forsyth, B. (1981) *Gregory's Girl*. Lake Films.

Freire, P. (1972a) *Cultural Action for Freedom*. Harmondsworth: Penguin.

Freire, P. (1972b) *Pedagogy of the Oppressed*. Harmondsworth: Penguin.

Friedman, S. and Laurison, D. (2020) *The Class Ceiling*. Bristol: Policy Press.

Gale, T. (2018) 'What's not to like about RCTs in education?' in Childs, A. and Menter, I. (Eds.) *Mobilising Teacher Researchers*. London: Routledge. 207–23.

Gibbon, L. G. (1946/1986) *A Scots Quair*. London: Penguin.

Gibson, R. (1984) *Structuralism and Education*. London: Hodder & Stoughton.

Gibson, R. (1986) *Critical Theory and Education*. London: Hodder & Stoughton.

Gilroy, B. (1976) *Black Teacher*. London: Cassell.

Gilroy, P. (1987) *There Ain't No Black in the Union Jack*. London: Hutchinson.

Giroux, H. (1983) *Theory and Resistance in Education – A Pedagogy for the Opposition*. London: Heinemann.

Goldman, L. (1995) *Dons and Workers: Oxford and Adult Education since 1850*. Oxford: Clarendon Press.

Goodman, P. (1971) *Compulsory Miseducation*. Harmondsworth: Penguin.

Goodson, I. (1995) *The Making of Curriculum* (2nd edn). London: Falmer.

Gorak, J. (1988) *The Alien Mind of Raymond Williams*. Columbia, Missouri: University of Columbia Press.

Grace, G. (1978) *Teachers, Ideology and Control*. London: Routledge & Kegan Paul.

Graham, D. (with Tytler, D.) (1993) *A Lesson for Us All*. London: Routledge.

Green, A. (1990) *Education and State Formation: The Rise of Education Systems in England, France and the USA*. London: Macmillan.

Green, A. (1997) *Education, Globalization and the Nation State*. Basingstoke: Macmillan.

Hall, S. (1988) *The Hard Road to Renewal*. London: Verso.

Hall, S. (2017) *Familiar Stranger*. London: Penguin.

Hall, S. and Jacques, M. (Eds.) (1983) *The Politics of Thatcherism*. London: Lawrence & Wishart.

Hall, S. and Jacques, M. (Eds.) (1989) *New Times*. London: Lawrence & Wishart.

Halsey, A.H., Heath, A. and Ridge, J. (1980) *Origins and Destinations: Family, Class and Education in Modern Britain*. Oxford: Clarendon Press.

Hanley, C. (2020) *George Orwell and Education. Learning, Commitment and Human Dependency*. London: Routledge.

Harvey, D. (1973) *Social Justice and the City*. London: Arnold.

Heller, Z. (2003) *Notes on a Scandal*. London: Penguin.

Hennessy, P. (1992) *Never Again – Britain 1945–1951*. London: Jonathan Cape.

Higgins, J. (1999) *Raymond Williams – Literature, Marxism and Cultural Materialism*. London: Routledge.

Hilton, A. (2019) *Academies and Free Schools in England*. London: Routledge.

Hoare, Q. and Nowell-Smith, G. (1971) 'Introduction' in Gramsci, A. (Ed.) *Selections from The Prison Notebooks*. London: Lawrence & Wishart. xvii–xcvi.

Hoggart, R. (1957) *The Uses of Literacy*. Harmondsworth: Penguin.

Hoggart, R. (1989) *A Local Habitation, Life and Times 1918–1940*. Oxford: University Press.

Holderness, G. (1991) 'Introduction to this edition' in Williams, R. (Ed.), *Drama in Performance*. Buckingham: Open University Press. 1–14.

Huberman, M. (1993) *The Lives of Teachers*. London: Cassell.

Illich, I. (1970) *Deschooling Society*. London: Calder and Boyars.

Inglis, F. (1995) *Raymond Williams*. London: Routledge.

Jackson, B. (1966) *Streaming: An Education System in Miniature*. London: Routledge & Kegan Paul.

Jackson, B. and Marsden, D. (1962/1966) *Education and the Working Class*. London: Ark.

Jackson, P. W. (1968/1991) *Life in Classrooms*. New York: Teachers' College Press.

Jessop, B., Bonnett, K., Bromley, S. and Ling, T. (1988) *Thatcherism*. Cambridge: Polity.

Jones, G. and Roderick, W. (2003) *A History of Education in Wales*. Cardiff: University of Wales Press.

Jones, K. (1983) *Beyond Progressive Education*. London: Macmillan.

Jones, K. (1989) *Right Turn – The Conservative Revolution in Education*. London: Hutchinson Radius.

Jones, K. (2003) *Education in Britain – 1944 to the Present*. Cambridge: Polity.

Jones, K., Cunchillos, C., Hatcher, R., Hirtt, N., Innes, R., Johsua, S. and Klausenitzer, J. (2008) *Schooling in Western Europe – The New Order and Its Adversaries*. Basingstoke: Palgrave Macmillan.

Jones, L. (1963) *Blues People*. New York: William Morrow.

Keddie, N. (Ed.) (1973) *Tinker, Tailor …. The Myth of Cultural Deprivation*. Harmondsworth: Penguin.

Kelman, J. (1989) *A Disaffection*. London: Secker & Warburg.

Kelman, J. (1990) *A Disaffection*. London: Pan Macmillan.
Klein, N. (2000) *No Logo*. California: Random House.
Kofsky, F. (1997) *Black Nationalism and the Revolution in Music*. New York: Pathfinder.
Kogan, M. (1975) *Educational Policy-Making. A Study of Interest Groups and Parliament*. London: Allen & Unwin.
Kureshi, H. (1983) *My Beautiful Laundrette*. Faber & Faber.
Labov, W. (1973) 'The logic of nonstandard English' in Keddie, N. (Ed.) *Tinker, Tailor …. The Myth of Cultural Deprivation*. Harmondsworth: Penguin. 21–66.
Lawrence, D. H. (1915/2001 edn.) *The Rainbow*. Ware: Wordsworth Editions.
Lawrence, D. H. (1921/1999 edn.) *Women in Love*. Ware: Wordsworth Editions.
Lawton, D. (1968) *Social Class, Language and Education*. London: Routledge & Kegan Paul.
Lawton, D. (1975) *Class, Culture and the Curriculum*. London: Routledge & Kegan Paul.
LeGrand, J. and Bartlett, W. (Eds.) (1993) *Quasi-Markets and Social Policy*. Basingstoke: Macmillan.
Loach, K. (1969) *Kes* (Film) Distributed by United Artists.
Loach, K. (2004) *Ae Fond Kiss* (Film) Distributed by Icon Film Distribution.
Lodge, D. (1985) *Nice Work*. London: Penguin.
Mahony, P. and Hextall, I. (2000) *Reconstructing Teaching*. London: Routledge/Falmer.
Marshall, S. (1963) *An Experiment in Education*. Cambridge: Cambridge University Press.
McGuigan, J. (1997) '"A slow reach again for control": Raymond Williams and the vicissitudes of cultural policy' in Wallace, J., Jones, R. and Nield, S. (Eds.) *Raymond Williams Now – Knowledge, Limits and the Future*. New York: St. Martin's Press. 56–70.
McGuigan, J. (2014) 'Introduction – Raymond Williams on culture and society' in McGuigan, R. (Ed.) *Raymond Williams on Culture and Society: Essential writings*. London: Sage. xv–xxvi.
McGuigan, J. (2019) *Raymond Williams Cultural Analyst*. Bristol: Intellect.
McIlroy, J. (1993a) 'Raymond Williams in adult education' in McIlroy, J. and Westwood, S. (Eds.) *Border Country – Raymond Williams in Adult Education*. Leicester: National Institute of Adult Continuing Education. 269–323.
McIlroy, J. (1993b) 'Teacher, critic, explorer' in Morgan, J. and Preston, P. (Eds.) *Raymond Williams: Politics, Education, Letters*. Basingstoke: Macmillan.
McIlroy, J. (1993c) 'The unknown Raymond Williams' in McIlroy, J. and Westwood, S. (Eds.) *Border Country – Raymond Williams in Adult Education*. Leicester: National Institute of Adult Continuing Education. 3–25.
McIlroy, J. and Westwood, S. (Eds.) (1993) *Border Country – Raymond Williams in Adult Education*. Leicester: National Institute of Adult Continuing Education.
McKenzie, R. F. (1970) *State School*. Harmondsworth: Penguin.
McPherson, A. and Raab, C. (1988) *Governing Education*. Edinburgh: Edinburgh University Press.

Meadows, D., Randers, D. and Behrens, J. (1972) *The Limits to Growth.* London: Earth Island.

Menter, I. (2008) 'Tradition, culture and identity in the reform of teachers' work in Scotland and England: Some methodological considerations'. *Pedagogy, Culture and Society*, 16 (1), 57–69.

Menter, I. (2013) 'Teachers and "structures of feeling": A sociocultural approach to identity and representation' in McCluskey, R. and McKinney, S. (Eds.) *How 'The Teacher' Is Presented in Literature, History, Religion, and the Arts.* New York: Edwin Mellen Press. 21–32.

Menter, I. (2016) 'Teacher education: Generator of change or a mechanism for conformity?' in Lees, H. and Noddings, N. (Eds.) *The Palgrave International Handbook of Alternative Education.* London: Palgrave. 257–72.

Menter, I. (2021) 'Snake oil or hard science?' in Ross, A. (Ed.) *Educational Research for Social Justice – Evidence and Practice from the UK.* Singapore: Springer.

Menter, I., Gallagher, C., Hayward, L. and Wyse, D. (2015) 'Compulsory education in the United Kingdom' in Matheson, D. (Ed.) *An Introduction to the Study of Education* (4th edn). London: Routledge. 216–43.

Menter, I., Muschamp, Y., Nicholls, P. and Ozga, J. with Pollard, A. (1997) *Work and Identity in the Primary School: A Post-Fordist Analysis.* Buckingham: Open University Press.

Menter, I., Mutton, T. and Burn, K. (2019) 'Learning to teach in England: Reviewing policy and research trends' in Tatto, M. T. and Menter, I. (Eds.) *Knowledge, Policy and Practice in Teacher Education – A Cross-National Study.* London: Bloomsbury. 60–80.

Mills, C. W. (1959) *The Sociological Imagination.* London: Oxford University Press.

Mitchell, J. (1984) *Women: The Longest Revolution.* London: Virago.

Nairn, T. (1981) *The Break-Up of Britain* (2nd edn). London: Verso.

Nairn, T. (2001) *After Britain.* London: Granta.

National Advisory Committee on Creative and Cultural Education (1999) *All Our Future: Creativity, Culture and Education.* London: Department for Education and Employment.

National Curriculum Council (1990) *Environmental Education (Curriculum Guidance 7).* London: HMSO.

Newman, J. (2001) *Modernising Governance.* London: Sage.

Nias, J. (1989) *Primary Teachers Talking.* London: Routledge.

Nisbet, S. (1957) *Purpose in the Curriculum.* London: University of London Press.

Nixon, J. (2011) *Higher Education and the Public Good.* London: Continuum.

Nussbaum, M. (2010) *Not for Profit.* Princeton: Princeton University Press.

O'Connor, A. (1989) *Raymond Williams: Writing, Culture, Politics.* Oxford: Blackwell.

Orwell, G. (1933/1940) *Down and Out in Paris and London.* Harmondsworth: Penguin.

Orwell, G. (1937/1989) *The Road to Wigan Pier.* London: Penguin.

Orwell, G. (1938/1989) *Homage to Catalonia.* London: Penguin.

Orwell, G. (1945/2000) *Animal Farm* (Penguin Classics edn). London: Penguin.
Orwell, G. (1949/1989) *Nineteen Eighty-Four*. London: Penguin.
Ozga, J. and Lawn, M. (1981) *Teachers, Professionalism and Class*. London: Falmer Press.
Paterson, L. (2003) *Scottish Education in the Twentieth Century*. Edinburgh: Edinburgh University Press.
Phillips, M. (1996) *All Must Have Prizes*. London: Little, Brown & Co.
Pinkney, T. (1991) *Raymond Williams*. Bridgend: Seren Books.
Pollard, A., Broadfoot, P., Croll, P., Osborn, M. and Abbott, D. (1994) *Changing English Primary Schools?* London: Cassell.
Pollard, A. and Filer, A. (1999) *The Social World of Pupil Career*. London: Cassell.
Reay, D. (2017) *Miseducation – Inequality, Education and the Working Classes*. Bristol: Policy Press.
Richards, I. A. (1929) *Practical Criticism*. London: Kegan Paul, Trench, Trubner.
Rizvi, F. (1993) 'Williams on democracy and the governance of education' in Dworkin, D. and Roman, L. (Eds.) *Views Beyond the Border Country*. New York: Routledge. 133–57.
Rizvi, F. and Lingard, B. (2010) *Globalizing Education Policy*. London: Routledge.
Robbins, D. (1997) 'Ways of knowing cultures: Williams and Bourdieu'. in Wallace, J., Jones, R. and Nield, S. (Eds.) *Raymond Williams Now. Knowledge, Limits and the Future*. New York: St Martin's Press. 40–55.
Roberts, S. (Ed.) (2003) *A Ministry of Enthusiasm*. London: Pluto.
Rosen, H. (1972) *Language and Class: A Critical Look at the Theories of Basil Bernstein*. Bristol: Falling Wall Press.
Sahlberg, P. (2010) *Finnish Lesson*. New York: Teachers' College Press.
Salter, B. and Tapper, T. (1981) *Education, Politics and the State: The Theory and Practice of Educational Change*. London: Grant McIntyre.
Savage, M. (2015) *Social Class in the 21st Century*. London: Penguin.
Sharp, R. and Green, A. (1975) *Education and Social Control – a Study in Progressive Primary Education*. London: Routledge & Kegan Paul.
Silver, H. (1980) *Education and the Social Condition*. London: Methuen.
Simon, B. (1971) *Intelligence, Psychology and Education*. London: Lawrence & Wishart.
Simon, B. (1988) *Bending the Rules - The Baker 'Reform' of Education*. London: Lawrence & Wishart.
Simon, B. (1991) *Education and the Social Order – British Education since 1944*. London: Lawrence & Wishart.
Simon, B. (1992) *What Future for Education?* London: Lawrence & Wishart.
Simon, B. (1994) *The State and Educational Change*. London: Lawrence & Wishart.
Simon, B. (1998) *A Life in Education*. London: Lawrence & Wishart.
Smith, C. (1998) *Creative Britain*. London: Faber & Faber.
Smith, D. (2008) *Raymond Williams – A Warrior's Tale*. Cardigan: Parthian Press.
Smyth, J. and Wrigley, T. (Eds.) (2013) *Living on the Edge: Rethinking Poverty, Class and Schooling*. New York: Peter Lang.

Sorensen, N. (Ed.) (2019) *Diversity in Teacher Education*. London: UCL Institute of Education Press.

Spark, M. (1961/2000) *The Prime of Miss Jean Brodie* (Penguin Modern Classics edn). London: Penguin.

Steele, T. (1997) *The Emergence of Cultural Studies 1945–65*. London: Lawrence & Wishart.

Stevens, P. (n.d.) *Education, Culture and Politics: The Philosophy of Education of Raymond Williams* (Doctoral thesis) Institute of Education, University of London.

Stevens, P. (2015) *Rita and Gerald – Adult Learning in Britain Today*. London: IoE Press.

Tatto, M. T., Burn, K., Menter, I., Mutton, T. and Thompson, I. (2018) *Learning to Teach in England and the USA: The Evolution of Policy and Practice*. London: Routledge.

Teacher Education Group, The (2016) *Teacher Education in Times of Change*. Bristol: Policy Press.

Thomas, M., Rauschenberger, E. and Crawford-Garrett, K. (Eds.) (2021) *Examining Teach for All*. London: Routledge.

Thompson, E. P. (1963/1970) *The Making of the English Working Class*. Harmondsworth: Penguin.

Thompson, E. P. (Ed.) (1970/2014) *Warwick University Ltd* (New edn). Nottingham: Spokesman.

Tibble, J. (Ed.) (1966) *The Study of Education*. London: Routledge & Kegan Paul.

Tomlinson, S. (2001) *Education in a Post-Welfare Society*. Buckingham: Open University Press.

Vaizey, J. (1958) *The Costs of Education*. London: Allen & Unwin.

Wainwright, H. (1994) *Arguments for a New Left*. Oxford: Blackwell.

Walford, G. (Ed.) (2006) *Education and the Labour Government*. London: Routledge.

Wallace, J., Jones, R. and Nield, S. (Eds.) (1997) *Raymond Williams Now – Knowledge, Limits and the Future*. New York: St. Martin's Press.

Ward, J. (1981) *Raymond Williams*. Cardiff: University of Wales Press and Welsh Arts Council.

Weinbren, D. (2010) 'Allegations of Marxist bias in the 1970s and 1980s' Downloaded on 16.02.2021 from: http://www.open.ac.uk/blogs/History-of-the-OU/?p=46

Westgate, C. (2010) 'Fellow-travellers at the conjunction: Williams and educational communicators', in Seidel, M., Horak, R. and Grossberg, L. (Eds.) *About Raymond Williams*. London: Routledge. 68–80.

Whiting, C., Whitty, G., Menter, I., Black, P., Hordern, J., Parfitt, A., Reynolds, K. and Sorenson, N. (2018) 'Diversity and complexity: Becoming a teacher in England in 2015–16'. *Review of Education*, 6 (1), 69–96.

Whitty, G. (1985) *Sociology and School Knowledge*. London: Methuen.

Whitty, G., Rowe, G. and Aggleton, P. (1994) 'Discourse in cross-curricular contexts: Limits to empowerment'. *International Studies in Sociology of Education*, 4 (1), 25–42.

Widdowson, F. (1983) *Going Up into the Next Class: Women and Elementary Teacher Training, 1840–1914*. London: Harper Collins.

Widgery, D. (Ed.) (1976) *The Left in Britain 1956-1968*. Harmondsworth: Penguin.
Wilkinson, R. and Pickett, K. (2009) *The Spirit Level*. London: Penguin.
Williams, D. (Ed.) (2003) *Who Speaks for Wales? Nation, Culture, Identity. Raymond Williams*. Cardiff: University of Wales Press.
Williams, J. and Williams, R. (Eds.) (1973) *D. H. Lawrence on Education*. Harmondsworth: Penguin.
Williams, M. (1972) *Thomas Hardy and Rural England*. London: Macmillan.
Williams, M. and Williams, R. (Eds.) (1986) *John Clare – Selected Poetry and Prose*. London: Methuen.
Williams, R. (1950) *Reading and Criticism*. London: Muller.
Williams, R. (1952) *Drama from Ibsen to Eliot*. London: Chatto & Windus.
Williams, R. (1952/1968/1987) [1] *Drama from Ibsen to Brecht*. London: Hogarth Press.
Williams, R. (1954/1968/1991) *Drama in Performance*. Buckingham: Open University Press.
Williams, R. (1958/2013) *Culture and Society*. Nottingham: Spokesman.
Williams, R. (1958) 'Culture is ordinary', reprinted in Williams (1989a) and in McGuigan, J. (Ed.) (2014) *Raymond Williams on Culture and Society: Essential Writings*. London: Sage.
Williams, R. (1959a) 'The teaching of public expression'. Reprinted in McIlroy, J. and Westwood, S. (Eds.) (1993) 181-4.
Williams, R. (1959b) 'The press and popular education' *The Highway, April*. Reprinted in McIlroy, J. and Westwood, S. (Eds.) (1993). 121-6.
Williams, R. (1960/1988) *Border Country*. London: Hogarth Press.
Williams, R. (1961/2011) *The Long Revolution*. Cardigan: Parthian.
Williams, R. (1962/1966) *Communications*. Harmondsworth: Penguin.
Williams, R. (1964/1988) *Second Generation*. London: Hogarth Press.
Williams, R. (1966/1992) *Modern Tragedy*. London: Hogarth Press.
Williams, R. (1968a) *Drama from Ibsen to Brecht*. Harmondsworth: Penguin.
Williams, R. (Ed.) (1968b) *The May Day Manifesto*. Harmondsworth: Penguin.
Williams, R. (1968c) 'Different sides of the wall', *The Guardian*. 26 September. Reprinted in McIlroy and Westwood (Eds.), 1993. 242-6.
Williams, R. (1968d) 'The idea of a common culture'. Reprinted in Williams (1989a). 32-8.
Williams, R. (1970/1984) *The English Novel from Dickens to Lawrence*. London: Hogarth Press.
Williams, R. (1970) 'A hundred years of culture and anarchy', reprinted in Williams (1980) 3-10.
Williams, R. (1971) *Orwell*. London: Fontana.
Williams, R. (1973/2011) *The Country and the City*. Nottingham: Spokesman.
Williams, R. (1974) *Television: Technology and Cultural Form*. London: Fontana.
Williams, R. (1976) *Keywords*. London: Fontana.
Williams, R. (1977) *Marxism and Literature*. Oxford: Oxford University Press.
Williams, R. (1978/1985/2011) *The Volunteers*. Cardigan: Parthian Press.

Williams, R. (1979/1988) *The Fight for Manod*. London: Hogarth Press.
Williams, R. (1979/2015) *Politics and Letters*. London: Verso.
Williams, R. (1980) *Problems in Materialism and Culture*. London: Verso.
Williams, R. (1981) *Culture*. London: Fontana.
Williams, R. (1983/1985) *Towards 2000*. Harmondsworth: Penguin.
Williams, R. (1983/1991) *Writing in Society*. London: Verso.
Williams, R. (1983a) 'Drama in a dramatized society' (Inaugural lecture) In Williams (1983/1991). 11–21.
Williams, R. (1983b) 'Beyond Cambridge English' (Retirement lecture) In Williams (1983/1991). 212–26.
Williams, R. (1983c) *Cobbett*. Oxford: Oxford University Press.
Williams, R. (1985/1989) *Loyalties*. London: Hogarth Press.
Williams, R. (1989a) *Resources of Hope*. London: Verso.
Williams, R. (1989b) *What I Came to Say*. London: Hutchinson Radius.
Williams, R. (1989c) *The Politics of Modernism*. London: Verso.
Williams, R. (1989d) *People of the Black Mountains I. The Beginning*. London: Chatto & Windus.
Williams, R. (1990) *People of the Black Mountains II. The Eggs of the Eagle*. London: Chatto & Windus.
Williams, R. and Orrom, M. (1954) *Preface to Film*. London: Film Drama.
Woodhams, S. (2001) *History in the Making: Raymond Williams, Edward Thompson and Radical Intellectuals 1936–1956*. London: Merlin Press.
Wright, N. (1977) *Progress in Education*. London: Croom Helm.
Wright, P. (2009) *On Living in an Old Country*. Oxford: Oxford University Press.
Wrigley, T. (2010) 'Curriculum change and the Blair years' in Green, A. (Ed.) *Blair's Educational Legacy – Thirteen Years of New Labour*. New York: Palgrave Macmillan. 121–44.
Wyse, D., Baumfield, V., Egan, D., Gallagher, C., Hayward, L., Hulme, M., Leitch, R., Livingston, K. and Menter, I. with Lingard, B. (2013) *Creating the Curriculum*. London: Routledge.
Young, M. F. D. (Ed.) (1971) *Knowledge and Control: New Directions for the Sociology of Education*. London: Collier-Macmillan.

Index

adult education 4–6, 8, 19–21, 24–6, 41, 79–80, 91–6
   cause of 81
   curriculum and pedagogy 83–7
   defence of 87–91
   for democracy 80–3, 90, 129
   history of 82
   language of 92
   significance of 85–6
   television and radio 95
   tension in 84
After Raymond Williams – Cultural Materialism and the Break-up of Britain (Dix) 77
Alien Mind of Raymond Williams, The (Gorak) 137
All Must Have Prizes (Phillips) 130
Althusser, L. 162
Animal Farm (Orwell) 108
Apple, M. 68–9, 72–3, 110, 122, 184 n.5
Arnold, M. 76, 99, 126, 130
Aronowitz, S. 180–1
Arts Council, The 105–6

Ball, S. 70–2, 151, 159
Bantock, G. H. 67
Barnett, A. 9, 57–8
Bennett, A. 52–3
Bernstein, B. 7, 66, 102–4, 155, 156, 158, 159, 168
Bevan, A. 18
Blackburn, R. 97, 117–18
Black Power (Carmichael and Hamilton) 114
Blair, T. 73, 90, 143–5
Border Country (Williams) 4, 11–12, 20, 21, 55, 75
   schooling and the teachers 28–34
Bourdieu, P. 7, 66, 67, 101, 103, 104, 149, 153, 156
bourgeois hegemony 109
Braithwaite, E. 52

Callaghan, J. 101, 150
Cambridge English 15
Cambridge University 4, 13–20, 29, 33, 47, 84, 118–20
Cambridge University Socialist Club (CUSS) 14, 15
Centenary Commission on Adult Education, The (CCAE) 92–3
Centre for Contemporary Cultural Studies (CCCS) 102, 111, 114, 129
Class, Culture and the Curriculum (Lawton) 67
'closing the gap' 164, 168–9
Coalition government 73, 165
Cobbett, W. 106–7, 184 n.3
Collini, S. 26, 121, 176
Communications (Williams) 87–9, 125, 131, 181
comprehensive approach 168
Conservative government 70, 90, 112, 150, 166
coronavirus pandemic (Covid-19) 94, 164, 169–71, 175, 178
counter-revolution 171
Country and the City, The (Williams) 4, 10, 15, 22, 23, 44, 45, 47, 50, 51, 75
Creative Britain (Smith) 143
creative/creativity 2, 7, 48, 124, 140–6
   industries 142, 143
   practice 140–2
   process 9
   writing 141–2
critical
   assumptions 111
   education 72, 73
   independence 121
   pedagogy 89
   theory 154
Critic, The 18
cultural
   capital 98–104, 168
   hegemony 110

relativism 130
reproduction 100, 101, 156, 157
restorationists 72, 76
revolution 56, 57
studies 3, 7, 24, 40, 42, 87, 98–100, 102, 124, 126–32, 141, 163, 174, 181
superstructure 109, 161
Cultural Action for Freedom (Freire) 86
cultural materialism 3, 4, 7, 22, 45, 47, 132, 134, 141, 148, 153–6, 163, 171, 174, 181
  curriculum 156–8
  evaluation 159–60
  pedagogy 158–9
culture 41, 87, 97–101, 124–7, 154, 156, 181
  and class 130
  common 43, 63, 67, 78, 87, 113, 124, 126, 127, 130, 153
  of compliance 166
  democratization of 124–7
  dominant 161, 162, 179
  education and 104, 109, 126, 130, 163–4, 181
  high 124, 129, 143
  and human experience 174
  industries 89
  language and 174–5
  mass 129–30
  material and 154–5
  popular 124, 127–31, 134, 153, 177, 178
  and teacher identity 54
Culture and Anarchy (Arnold) 99, 126
Culture and Society (Williams) 4, 20–2, 35, 41–3, 47, 55, 82, 83, 101, 106, 107
curriculum
  common 24, 61, 67
  construction 69
  core 63, 64
  cultural materialism 156–8
  in England 74–5
  English 13
  grammar school 62
  Latin 59
  and pedagogy 83–7, 112
  school 5, 13, 24, 29, 55, 63–9, 129, 142, 144

D-Day landings 4, 16
democracy 2, 122, 180–2
  adult education for 80–3
  cultural institutions and 4
  internal 94
  parliamentary 112
  participatory 109, 127
  self-governing 73
  social 153, 164
  threat to 88
Department of Education and Science (DES) 70
D.H. Lawrence on Education (Williams and Williams) 35
Dibb, M. 23
digital technology 40, 174, 175
Disaffection, A (Kelman) 51–2
Dix, H. 77, 86, 91, 134, 185 n.8
drama 52, 135–40, 151, 152
Drama from Ibsen to Eliot (Williams) 17, 135, 136
Drama in Performance (Holderness) 136–7
Dworkin, D. 131

Eagleton, T. 8, 99
economic base 109, 161
education. *See also* adult education; education policy
  banking 86, 91
  Black Papers on 68
  and British society 56–64
  continuity and change 175–8
  critical 72, 73
  and culture 104, 109, 126, 130, 163–4, 181
  for democracy 180–2
  and economy 76
  environmental 164, 167–8
  formal 10, 12, 18, 45, 50, 59, 143, 176
  general 58, 101, 157
  higher 3, 6, 23, 24, 26, 60, 80, 90–1, 118–22, 128–30, 141, 157, 166, 170, 171, 175–7
  informal 10, 96, 143, 176, 179
  language and culture 174–5
  Lawrence on 35–9
  liberal 59–62, 110–11
  post-school 89–90
  primary 60, 74, 151, 152, 159
  process of 66
  purpose of 65

secondary 60-2, 74, 168
and society 163
sociology of 65-6
standard 46
sustainability in 178-9
system 54, 58, 60, 68, 69, 72, 76, 100-2, 104, 155, 156, 163, 175
teacher 51, 64, 65, 78, 82, 94, 147, 158, 159, 164-7
Education Act of 1944 18, 61, 157
educational
  bureaucrats 71
  outcomes 55, 65, 103
  progressivism 162
  provision 2, 5-7, 74, 77, 91, 95, 160, 164, 168, 171, 175, 177, 178
Education and Power (Apple) 69
Education and State Formation (Green) 76
Education Endowment Foundation (EEF) 169
Education, Globalization and the Nation State (Green) 76
education policy 56, 77, 145, 149, 151, 162-5
  approach 168-9
  construction of 69-74
  Covid-19 169-71
  in England 70-1
  environmental education 167-8
  management, leadership and governance 165
  teacher education 165-7
Education Reform Act (ERA) 71, 73, 74, 151, 157, 160
Education under Siege (Aronowitz and Giroux) 180-1
electronic media 140
Elvin, L. 15, 184 n.1
Emergence of Cultural Studies, The (Steele) 127-8, 130, 174
emergent culture 38, 47, 162
England
  adult education 176-7
  education policy 70-1
  National Curriculum in 24, 74, 142, 144
  neoliberalism 25
  public education in 150
  schooling in 2
  state education in 176

English Novel from Dickens to Lawrence, The (Williams) 35, 43
English Novel from Hardy to Lawrence, The (Williams) 22
English primary education 151, 152
English studies 47, 128-9
Extinction Rebellion 117, 168, 177

face-to-face teaching 94, 170, 171
fast capitalism 150
feeling. *See* Williams, R., structure of feeling
feminism 114, 115
Fieldhouse, R. 82
Fight for Manod, The (Williams) 22, 178
Filer, A. 152
film 8, 16, 132-5
formal schooling 18, 176, 181
Foucault, M. 71
Freire, P. 6, 86, 105, 110

gender 7, 37, 64, 98, 114-16, 163
Gibbon, L. G. 50, 51
Gibson, R. 149-50, 153, 154
Gilroy, P. 114-15
Giroux, H. 89, 180-1
globalization 149, 164, 165, 177, 178
Goodson, I. 184 n.6
Gorak, J. 137-8, 143
Gove, M. 73
Graham, D. 167
Gramsci, A. 6, 69, 98, 100, 105, 107, 109, 110, 161
Grant, H. 134
Great Debate, The 101
Great Education Reform Bill 151
Green, A. 76

Habermas, J. 153-4
Hall, S. 79, 110-12, 114, 119, 129, 150
Halsey, A. H. 65
Harvey, D. 122
hegemonic 68, 106, 109, 110, 128
hegemony 69, 72, 109-11, 142, 146, 161
Heller, Z. 52
Higgins, J. 153, 155, 156
Hilton, A. 73-4
Hirst, P. 67
History Boys, The (Bennett) 52-3
Hobsbawm, E. 16

Hoggart, R. 7, 38–9, 42, 101–2, 111, 129, 131
Holderness, G. 136–7

Idea of a Common Culture, The (Williams) 126–7
Idea of Culture, The (Eagleton) 99
identity
　adult 34
　biography and 10
　learner's 50
　national 51, 54, 76, 115, 128, 134
Ideological State Apparatus (ISAs) 162
ideology 100
industrial
　capitalism 60, 117
　revolution 41, 56–7, 60, 106, 179
　trainers 61, 62, 68, 71, 76, 91, 111, 120, 146, 150, 151, 176
inequality 2, 74, 93, 114, 126, 145, 153, 164, 168
Inglis, F. 7, 15, 23, 119–20
intellectual 80, 97–8
　deracinating 13, 29
　Marxist 47
　middle-class 38
　organic 6, 74, 98, 104–12, 118, 121, 122
　public 6, 98, 107, 109, 121, 122, 167–8
intelligence 62, 63, 93

Jones, K. 146

Keddie, N. 66, 103, 168
Kelman, J. 51–2
Keywords (Williams) 4, 8, 21, 49, 83, 98–9, 104, 109, 125–6, 141, 147, 154, 174, 184 n.6, 185 n.1
King Henry VIII Grammar School 12, 32
knowable community 43, 45, 81
Knowledge and Control 66
Kogan, M. 70

labour movement 11, 68, 94, 114
labour process theory 152
language
　acerbic 76–7
　of adult education 92
　and culture 174–5
　English 119–20, 125, 141
　of intelligence 62
　literature and society 41
　and social class 94, 102
　working-class 103
Lawrence, D. H. 5, 28, 35–9, 42, 45, 51–3
Lawton, D. 67–8
leadership 15, 18, 94, 111, 137, 164, 165
Leavis, F. R. 15, 17, 19, 42, 80, 83, 105, 123, 128
Lingard, B. 149, 165
Listener, The 22, 105
Local Education Authorities 60
London School of Economics (LSE) 15
Long Revolution, The (Williams) 4, 5, 10, 18–25, 29, 42, 74, 75, 87, 110, 113, 119, 130–1, 143, 144, 155, 179, 187 n.12
　Education and British society 56–64
Loyalties (Williams) 22, 185 n.5

MacCabe, C. 119–20
McCarthyism 82, 94
McGuigan, J. 8, 132, 153–5
McIlroy, J. 80–1, 84, 85, 87, 95, 96
Macmillan, H. 90
McPherson, A. 70
Man and Society Series (Muller) 39
Mannheim, K. 128
Marxism and Literature (Williams) 4, 22, 39, 46–7, 49, 103, 134, 140–2, 148, 154
Marxist theory 148, 154, 161
mass communication 87, 102
mass media 50, 88, 127
May Day Manifesto, The (Williams) 6, 23, 46, 74, 87, 112–19, 129
media 6, 7, 40, 54, 76, 88, 89, 131, 140, 141, 169, 174, 177
message systems 156, 159, 160
Mills, C. W. 50, 149
Modern Tragedy (Williams) 136, 137
Muller, F. 39
Multi-Academy Trusts 165

National Advisory Committee on Creative and Cultural Education 143
National Council for Civil Liberties 119
National Curriculum 24, 74, 76, 142, 144, 151, 152, 157, 158, 167, 168

National Strategies 145, 159
neoliberalism 25, 63, 76, 112, 117, 145, 164
neo-liberalism 146, 153
network governance 164, 165
New Labour government 143, 145, 159, 170
New Left Review (Williams) 6, 7, 11, 49, 102, 112–18, 161
New Right 5, 71–3, 129
New Sociology of Education 66
Nias, J. 151
Nineteen Eighty-Four (Orwell) 108, 109
1988 Act 72, 158
Nixon, J. 26, 121
Notes on a Scandal (Heller) 52
Nussbaum, M. 26, 122, 176

O'Connor, A. 134–5
Ofsted 160, 166
old humanists 61, 62, 68, 71, 72, 75, 76, 111, 121, 146, 160, 176
online learning 170
Open University (OU) 6, 26, 80, 90, 91, 94, 96, 110, 111, 129, 135, 136, 176–7
Orrom, M. 16, 133
Orwell, G. 7, 44, 107–9
over time 27, 48, 133, 134, 153, 159, 161, 173
Oxford 19, 20, 24, 59, 79–81, 83, 92, 94

Passeron, J. -C. 156
pedagogy 80
    critical 89
    cultural materialism 158–9
    curriculum and 83–7, 112
    invisible 103
Penguin Education Specials 35, 185 n.2
Penguin Special 87, 120, 185 n.2
People of the Black Mountains (Williams) 5, 10, 12, 23, 48
performativity 6, 25, 52, 105, 120, 146, 159, 160
Phillips, M. 130
Pinkney, T. 8, 28
policymaking 69–71, 78, 165
Politics and Letters (Williams) 7–9, 11, 14, 16, 18, 49, 57, 75, 81, 85, 90, 107, 112, 113, 136, 137, 183 n.1

Politics and Policy Making in Education (Ball) 71
Pollard, A. 151, 152
populism 17, 76, 109, 110, 164, 174, 177, 182
practical criticism 15, 80, 83
Preface to Film (Williams and Orrom) 49, 132
Primary Teachers Talking (Nias) 151
Prison Notebooks (Gramsci) 105
public education 39, 55, 56, 63, 78, 86, 87, 95, 104, 117, 126, 150, 160
public educators 61, 68, 71, 76, 111, 146, 176
Public Schools Act 1868 60

Qualified Teacher Status 166

Raab, C. 70
race 7, 98, 114–16, 129
racism 114–15
radical 2, 5, 6, 25, 26, 56, 58, 65, 68, 71, 80, 86, 87, 90, 94, 101, 107, 112–14, 117, 119, 129, 143, 159, 168
Rainbow, The (Lawrence) 36–7
Ralphs, A. L. 13, 29, 32, 33, 40
randomized controlled trial (RCT) 169
Reading and Criticism (Williams) 20, 39, 42, 43, 83, 84
Reproduction in Education, Society and Culture (Bourdieu and Passeron) 156–7
Resources of Hope (Williams) 7, 22, 117, 179, 186 n.3
Richards, I. A. 15, 42
Rizvi, F. 73, 149, 165
Robbins Report 90
Robinson, K. 143, 144

Salter, B. 71
school
    curriculum 5, 13, 24, 29, 55, 63–9, 129, 142, 144
    elementary 12, 24, 29, 30, 35, 37, 60, 61
    grammar 2, 3, 13, 24, 29, 32, 33, 40, 52, 59, 61–2, 75, 157
    and inequality 74
    primary 61, 62, 64, 145, 151, 158
    private 75, 150

public 32, 60
secondary 51–3, 60–2, 64, 124, 141, 145, 157, 176
and teachers 28–34
technical 61–2, 157–8
third-grade 60, 62
schooling
in acerbic language 76–7
achievement in 104
compulsory 165
development of 2
and economy 162
grammar 29
history of 69
and inequality 74
secondary 62, 64, 157, 176
state 38, 110, 171
school-led system 165
Science 125
Scots Quair, A (Gibbon) 50, 51
Second Generation (Williams) 20, 178
Second World War 4, 14, 21, 38, 61, 81, 109, 128, 157, 186 n.6
selective tradition 68, 69, 133, 162
Silver, H. 69
Simon, B. 69
Smith, C. 143, 144
Smith, D. 7, 10, 16–20, 23, 28, 32
social
change 21, 39, 42, 45, 51, 55, 105, 108, 110, 150, 174
class 2, 24, 60, 62, 65, 75, 94, 101–3, 105, 109, 114, 122, 163
democracy 153, 164
media 40, 48, 105, 124, 174
socialism 98, 108, 113, 115, 122, 179
Sociological Imagination, The (Mills) 50, 149
Sociology and School Knowledge (Whitty) 67–8
sociology of education 65–6, 103, 109
Standard Assessment Tasks (SATs) 160
Steele, T. 127–8
Stevens, P. 82, 96
Structuralism and Education (Gibson) 149
Students Library of Education, The 65
superstructure 49, 109, 161–3, 171
sustainability 178–9
synthetic phonics 159

Tapper, T. 71
Taunton Commission of 1869 60, 62
teacher
education 51, 64, 65, 78, 82, 94, 147, 158, 159, 164–7
identity and national culture 54
school and 28–34
Teaching Quality 151
television 23, 40, 42, 88, 90, 95, 134, 138–40
Television: Technology and Cultural Form (Williams) 138
Tenses of Imagination, The 48
Thatcherism 111, 112, 129, 150
Thatcher, M. 5, 26, 70, 73, 111, 112, 129, 150, 151, 166
Thomas Hardy and Rural England (Williams) 44
Thompson, E. P. 8, 16, 23, 25–6, 112, 114, 118–20, 128, 130, 131
Tibble, J. W. 65
Tillyard, E. M. W. 15
To Sir, With Love (Braithwaite) 52
Towards 2000 (Williams) 4, 10, 22, 23, 46, 76–7, 91, 104, 115–17, 120, 179, 180
tripartite system 62, 157
TV: Technology and Cultural Form (Williams) 23

university 24–6, 120–1. *See also* Cambridge University; Open University (OU)
Aberystwyth 48
hard and soft 91
University Extra-Mural Departments 39
Uses of Literacy, The (Hoggart) 42, 101, 128, 131

Vaizey, J. 69
Vernon, P. E. 62
virtual learning environments (VLEs) 170
Volunteers, The (Williams) 22, 115

Wainwright, H. 98, 118
Ward, J. P. 8
Warwick University Limited 26, 120–1
Welfare State, The 18, 81
Welsh trilogy 4, 20, 22, 28, 48, 178

Westgate, C. 85, 89
Westwood, S. 80, 81
what works approach 169
Whitty, G. 67–8
Williams, D. 184 n.7
Williams, J. 5, 10
Williams, M. 44
Williams, R.
   to adult education 19–21, 79–80, 87
     (*See also* adult education)
   art 125
   base and superstructure 47, 161–3
   childhood and school 10–14
   classroom teaching 84
   creativity 140–6
   four-year programme of study 84
   humanity 57–8
   ideologies 61
   incorporation 161–2
   on Lawrence's writing 35–9
   Leavisite criticism and Marxism 131
   life and work 1–8, 21–3
   personal experience 44
   politics 2, 5, 18, 25–7, 80–1, 112–17, 181
   to socialism 113
   structure of feeling 5, 7, 10, 27, 31, 34, 35, 37–9, 42–4, 47–54, 83, 99, 104, 132–5, 148–53, 164, 174
   students view 85
   theory 147
   typology 71
Women in Love (Lawrence) 35–6
women's movement 115
Workers' Educational Association (WEA) 4, 6, 19, 20, 26, 39, 79, 82, 87, 88, 90, 93–4, 96, 177
Wrigley, T. 145
Writing in Society (Williams) 39, 47, 48, 132

Young, Michael F. D. 66–7

Printed in the USA
CPSIA information can be obtained
at www.ICGtesting.com
LVHW022230020224
770781LV00002B/184